The String Players' Guide
to Chamber Music

The String Players' Guide
to Chamber Music

James Christensen

OPEN COURT
Chicago and La Salle, Illinois

To order books from Open Court, call toll-free 1-800-815-2280, or visit our website at www.opencourtbooks.com.

This book, *The String Players' Guide to Chamber Music*, is an expanded and thoroughly revised edition of *Chamber Music: Notes for Players*, by James Christensen, published by Distinctive Publishing Corporation of Plantation, Florida, in 1992.

Copyright © 2008 by Carus Publishing Company

First printing 2008

Printed and bound in the United States of America.

Library of Congress Cataloging-in-Publication Data

Christensen, James, 1932-
   The string players' guide to chamber music / James Christensen.
      p. cm.
     Previously published as: Plantation, Fla. : Distinctive Pub. Corp. : Chamber Music, c1992.
     Summary: "A guide to chamber music for small string ensembles, including works by Mozart, Haydn, Beethoven, Schubert, and lesser-known composers. Describes and evaluates the works, assesses their level of difficulty, and identifies specific problems involved in performance"—Provided by publisher.
    ISBN-13: 978-0-8126-9627-1 (trade paper : alk. paper)
    ISBN-10: 0-8126-9627-1 (trade paper : alk. paper)
    1. Chamber music—Instruction and study. I. Christensen, James, 1932- Chamber music. II. Title.
    MT728.C48 2007
    785.7'143--dc22
                                     2007037673

Contents

PART II: Works for Three, Five, and More Strings 169

PART III: Strings with Piano: Piano Trios, Quartets, and Quintets

Preface

In modern general usage, the term Chamber Music (which defies exact definition, like all terms of art) implies especially works from the late eighteenth century to the present written for small groups of players with or without piano. For many, it indicates mainly works that were written for the bowed stringed instruments. That's the sort of music I wrote this little book about.

The golden age for such music, largely in the Classical and Romantic periods, from about 1750 through about 1950, produced a great mass of literature especially in central Europe. This body of chamber music never was the exclusive province of the authorities and masters. From the time of its origin, it belonged in part to an educated middle class whose tastes and thirsts for such music for performance by themselves at home provided some of the incentive for the composers to continue to write it.

The evolution of Western culture did not obliterate the eighteenth-century custom of amateur performance of this work, but actually enhanced it. The preservation and expansion of the literature came about in part because amateurs kept playing these classics and asking for more, and the activity persists. These are the players to whom I have addressed this book.

Amateur players will exist only so long as a part of the public continues to receive the right preparation. For many people, the ability to play a musical instrument remains an important, even essential, element in a liberal education. This tradition means that hundreds of skilled players of the stringed instruments and piano emerge from our colleges, universities and conservatories each year. Only a small fraction of them enter professional careers in music. Given the right circumstances, the rest may be able to follow their passion for music without depending upon it for a livelihood. They will do so best when they find opportunities. The performance of chamber music at home still provides that opportunity for countless such people all around the world.

Why do we play? At its simplest, the pleasure of listening to music is the pleasure of all art. In actually playing such works, however, we find much more. Playing enables us to see inside a unique mind, that of the composer, in a way that no mere listener can. The combination of hearing a work, seeing it on the page and feeling it in the limbs and fingers all at the same time gives the player a view of the heart of the composer that cannot be derived in any other way. Composers used this medium to express themselves without reserve and with complete dedication. In playing these classics, we communicate with another mind, nonverbally, about many abstract matters, some too deep to be named. In playing chamber music, we do this alongside other people, friends with whom we share common interests and values.

Many amateur players of the string chamber music tend to stay with the works they know and love, venturing into the unknown from time to time through the casual readings of unfamiliar works. I prepared these notes as a guidebook to serve the needs of those players who seek an expanded experience in playing. The notes treat all those works that constitute the devoted amateur string players' standard or potential repertoire. The selection represents that which most interests me and lies within the capacity of most players like me. This is the core literature as I see it. There are certainly many more works, but some seem to me to be too difficult, others too obscure, still others too opaque or just not very interesting for purposes of amateur performance.

Who am I to make such judgements? As an amateur cellist, trained in music during and just after the Second World War and a constant player since then, I selected the core literature we played in that period, the works my generation of amateurs still favors. Contemporary composers, on the whole, did not attract us. For that reason, readers will find few twentieth-century works here. Younger players probably have more modern tastes, yet they must find pleasure as well in these time-tested works.

The authoritative scholarly histories, descriptions and analyses of these classics, usually written by and for musicologists, do not exactly serve the wants or needs of amateur players as I see them. That is why I compiled these notes. The entries constitute brief biographical sketches of the composers and their times, descriptions of the works and special comments meant to serve the interests of amateur performance. I wrote the notes to put these works into context and to reveal their natures, origins and interrelationships. Such knowledge, I believe, enhances the pleasure of playing them. I drew on my own reading and playing experience and on decades of talk with like-minded friends to make these notes.

The musical descriptions are largely non-technical. I have touched on technique where that seemed useful in order to answer some of the questions that players might want answered. Is the work difficult to play? Is it difficult to understand or to interpret? Is it fun to play? What makes it pleasurable? Why is it interesting? What was its significance to the composer and to his contemporaries?

In trying to answer such questions, I cannot pretend to be either wholly objective or expert. Like everyone, I have my favorite works. In order to reduce the bias in my comments, which are really statements of personal opinion, I have tried to summarize the feelings of all those with whom I have played or discussed these works. My experience has been almost exclusively American and my opinions must reflect that fact.

I chose the works described here simply because I have observed over the decades that my friends like to play them. The works vary, of course, in the pleasure they can give and in the effort they require. I tried to summarize these qualities for each work. I devised a scoring system in which "4" is high and "1" is low. Thus, "Pleasure—4" means that a work can give the highest degree of pleasure to amateur players, while "Effort—1" means that relatively little effort is required to enjoy playing it.

These evaluations must not be taken as anything more than the crude and opinionated reckoning of one devoted player. Such a system seems necessary, even though it must fall far short of one that would meet the need. What pleases one player will not please all. What one finds difficult, another will find easier. One work may be devilishly hard for the cellist but easy for the rest to play. Newcomers to a work, however, will want to get some idea of both its difficulty and its rewards before they read it. It was for them that I provided this scoring system.

The composers provided the popular names given for a few of these works. Others arise from long tradition among players and listeners. I have given many of these names because they are an important part of the history and charm of the art. Some of these names are used in common in all countries, some are unique to one country or another, and a few are only names that I have heard used among my friends. I have also included dates that indicate the years of composition as closely as I could discover them.

My intent in assembling these notes was to prepare a guide for those who play mainly for pleasure and casual instruction. I meant it to be neither a listener's comprehensive guide nor a musicological source book. Its only purpose is to encourage a wider appreciation and performance of these works at home and in private, the place where this kind of chamber music began. I hope these notes may find a place as well with music teachers, for chamber music offers students at all levels the chance to develop the special skills of ensemble playing.

I owe a special debt of gratitude to Richard M. Caplan, one of the hundreds of players with whom I have shared a lifelong hobby. I learned to love this literature also from my exposure to many dedicated teachers, especially Emanuel Wishnow, Carol Work, Rachmael Weinstock and the members of the Manhattan String Quartet, Eric and Roy Lewis, John Dexter, Judith Glyde, Ken Freed, Chris Finckel and Cal Wiersma.

PART I

String Quartets

ARRIAGA (1806–1826)

Arriaga (Juan Crisostomo Jacobo Arriaga y Balzola) was born in Bilbao, in the Basque part of Spain. A child prodigy, he composed an opera before he was fourteen, one that was actually produced. At fifteen he went to the Paris Conservatory where he studied violin and composition with Baillot and Fetis, major teachers of the day. The three quartets, written when he was sixteen, appeared in print in Paris in 1824. Fetis commented favorably on their style and elegance. Arriaga also wrote a fine Mozartean symphony, a stabat mater, a mass, and some songs. These quartets show the influence of his immediate predecessors and contemporaries, especially Mozart and Haydn, but they bear the stamp of the Spanish idiom. Arriaga came to be called the Spanish Mozart after his rediscovery and exaltation in the middle of the twentieth century at the time of a renewal in the spirit of Spanish nationalism. The quartets were first heard in New York in 1953.

Quartet in D minor | (1824)

I *Allegro*. II *Adagio con espressione*. III *Menuetto: Allegro*.
IV *Adagio; Allegretto*.

The *first movement*, a conventional sonata allegro, has a pronounced Spanish character. The simple, charming, lyrical and melancholy movement ends with a coda, featuring the viola, in the major mode.

The *second movement* is melodious, rather simple in style and development, with a decorated line in all parts. This is the least impressive movement of the work.

The *third movement*, like the first, is Spanish in character, especially in the trio where the pizzicato of the lower voices mimics the sound of a guitar beneath the graceful theme in the first violin.

The *fourth movement* opens with a short adagio introduction that establishes the harmonic base and sets a mood of anticipation for the brisk rondo to follow. The rondo is built on a dotted-rhythm theme that appears in six major episodes, during which the opening adagio recurs. The movement possesses a melancholy grace.

Commentary. This dramatic work is the most interesting of the three quartets of the set. It is not profound music, but it is easy to play and to understand. The mood varies among the four movements. All voices have satisfying parts. Pleasure—3; Effort—1.

Quartet in A major | (1824)

I *Allegro con brio.* II *Andante.* III *Menuetto: Scherzo.*
IV *Andante ma non troppo; Allegro.*

The *first movement*, a conventional sonata allegro, has a cheerful and declamatory character. It features upbeat trills. The movement has a più allegro coda.

The *second movement* constitutes a theme with five variations and a coda. The variations show many original touches, a second violin solo in one, a viola solo in another, a pizzicato variation and extreme contrasts in dynamics throughout.

The *third movement* is a minuet, but one with the character of a scherzo, a fine example of the transitional minuet-scherzo form that was introduced by Haydn.

The *fourth movement*, as in the quartet in D minor, opens with a brief slow introduction. This is followed by a rather frisky rondo. The opening andante material returns again before the rondo resumes.

Commentary. This delightful quartet greatly resembles the quartet in D minor, differing from it in its more consistently cheerful, light-hearted and humorous character. It is easy to play and to understand. All voices have satisfying parts. Pleasure—3; Effort—1.

Quartet in E-flat major | (1824)

I *Allegro.* II *Pastorale: Andantino.* III *Menuetto: Allegro.*
IV *Presto agitato.*

The *first movement*, a sonata allegro built on rather unimaginative thematic material, exhibits a Mozartean spirit in its tidy but somewhat sparing elaboration.

The *second movement*, a ternary form, has a pastoral character because of the simplicity of the themes and the birdcall figurations. The contrasting animato of the second section represents, some would say, a thunderstorm, after which the peaceful country mood resumes.

The *third movement* is wholly unremarkable, but a fine Haydn imitation worthy of the master himself.

The *fourth movement*, the most interesting of the work, constitutes a light and transparent rondo. The presto agitato indicated by the composer seems to be not quite appropriate as a tempo marking. The movement seems to work better played rather as a scherzo.

Commentary. This quartet is just as accessible to amateurs as the quartets in D minor and A major. It is, however, the least interesting of the three, for it lacks the intense Spanish flavor that characterizes the others and the compositional technique seems a little less original. Pleasure—2; Effort—1.

BARBER (1910–1981)

Samuel Barber, born to a well-to-do family in Pennsylvania, showed his talent early, studying the piano at age six. His interest may have been prompted by the fact that his aunt was the prominent singer, Louise Homer. He entered the recently established Curtis Institute in Philadelphia where he studied composition with Rosario Scalero. He considered a career as a singer before settling on composition. Barber wrote in many forms, and chamber music was not his great strength. Only the string quartet, the cello sonata (dedicated to Scalero) and *Dover Beach* (for string quartet with voice) are currently widely heard in chamber music circles.

He wrote the string quartet in the summer of 1936 near Salzburg where he spent a summer holiday. The Pro Arte Quartet first performed it the subsequent winter in Rome. A few months later, the Curtis Quartet presented it at the Curtis Institute. Toscanini, preparing a program for the newly organized NBC Symphony, took the suggestion of Rodzinski that he solicit a work from Barber. Barber submitted the adagio movement of the string quartet, arranged for string orchestra as the *Adagio for Strings*, as well as the *Essay for Orchestra* and both were presented, to immediate acclaim, in November 1938. The *Adagio* movement is now much better known in its orchestral form than in the string quartet setting.

Quartet in B minor, Op. 11 | (1936)

I *Molto allegro ed appassionato.* II *Molto adagio; Molto allegro.*

The *first movement* is an impassioned allegro in sonata form. It is rather operatic in character, a convincing and satisfying movement.

The *second movement,* the famous adagio, contrasts sharply with the first. It is built on a lyrical and sinuous melody, made liturgical in character by the underlying chordal shifts. The theme repeats eight times in increasingly deeper character, remaining simple and striking. An altered and compacted reprise of the *first movement* follows the adagio. With the *first movement,* this terminal section forms a frame around the adagio. Some quartets delete the reprise of the *first movement* in performance.

Commentary. This quartet is wholly accessible to amateurs. It gives a splendid opportunity to address the technique of establishing balance among the voices. Amateurs who know the adagio in its orchestral setting will find it illuminating to play it in the form in which it was originally conceived. All voices have gratifying parts. Pleasure—3; Effort—2.

BEETHOVEN (1770–1827)
Biographical Notes

Ludwig von Beethoven was the son and grandson of musicians of Flemish origin at the Court of the Elector of Cologne at Bonn. At the time of Beethoven's birth, Germany remained a reasonably stable collection of states, regulated separately by Electors or Landgraves but nominally controlled by the Emperor at Vienna. That Emperor, Joseph II, had appointed his brother, Maximilian, to be the Elector at Bonn where an ambitious program of reform in law, education, and the arts was well under way by 1770.

Beethoven's father, Johann, a tenor in the Court choir, saw to it that the Court musicians trained his son. The talented boy became Court organist at fourteen and played viola in the Court orchestra. His abilities led the Elector to send him at sixteen to visit Vienna, the cultural as well as political center of Germany. In his two-week stay, he may have played for Mozart. If so, it was the only time the two met. On his return to Bonn, he found his consumptive mother, Maria Magdalena, dying and he was soon left responsible for the support and care of his siblings,

Caspar Carl, Johann and an infant sister, supplanting his alcoholic and irresponsible father. He resumed his position as Court organist and violist.

He became acquainted with a cultured family, the Breunings and with Count Waldstein, and these intellectual people encouraged his self-education in literature, philosophy, politics and social affairs. When he entered Bonn University at nineteen, he further expanded the range of his knowledge, especially through contact with a professor there, Eulogius Schneider, who was famous for his fiercely anticlerical views and his enthusiasm for the new spirit that was exemplified by the French revolution. Undoubtedly, Schneider was instrumental in developing Beethoven's keen interest in social and political developments that so greatly affected his life work.

The young Beethoven had been composing from his early years, and he continued to do so, writing many small works mainly for the entertainment of the Court. His first step to fame came with an invitation to write a cantata for the memorial services for the Emperor who had died in 1790. Beethoven had admired the great reformer, and he produced a work so notable that, when Haydn saw the score (and probably others) in 1792 while traveling between London and Vienna, he invited Beethoven to come to Vienna as his student.

1792 was a year of turmoil in Bonn, so close to the French revolution and so far from Vienna, and the unsettled environment undoubtedly influenced Beethoven's decision to take up Haydn's invitation promptly. He took letters of introduction from Count Waldstein to two musical patrons in Vienna, Prince Lichnowsky and Prince Lobkowitz. His father's death soon after his arrival in Vienna did not call him back to Bonn.

His studies with Haydn proved unsatisfactory. The two were incompatible. Beethoven neglected Haydn, taking up the study of composition with Schenk, violin with Schuppanzigh, theory with Albrechtsberger, and vocal writing with Salieri.

He introduced himself to Vienna in part with the three piano trios in Op. 1, probably started at Bonn but completed at Vienna. He quickly found himself in demand as a performer and teacher to the nobility of that city.

Vienna was much affected by the troubles of Europe after 1793. Napoleon's army approached Vienna in 1797 and the city was evacuated. After 1799, the danger receded and life returned to normal. The string quartets in Op. 18, 1798–1800, came from this period. Beethoven enjoyed expanding fortunes for a time, but chronic gastrointestinal complaints, tinnitus and depression developed, leading to an emotional crisis marked by the *Heiligenstadt Testament*, the famous personal declaration he wrote in 1802. Thereafter, he rarely expressed such pessimism, expressing his unhappiness more in anger than in depression.

The year 1805 brought recurrent political troubles. Food shortages and riots in the summer of that year were followed by the two-month French occupation of Vienna in that winter. These events profoundly affected Beethoven's political views, and he no longer remained an admirer of Napoleon. The string quartets of Op. 59 came from this period.

With the return of peace, Beethoven entered upon a period of astonishing productivity, but this ended with the second French occupation of the city in 1809. He was deeply affected by this disaster, by the loss of friends and colleagues (Haydn died in May 1809) and by financial hardships. The string quartets of Op. 74 and Op. 95 came from this year of trouble.

After 1810, Beethoven remained ill and uneasy, for the political situation of Vienna remained insecure. Visits to the Teplitz spa from 1810 to 1812 did little to restore his health. In 1813, however, political events changed for the better, and Beethoven enjoyed a restoration of spirits. The year of *Fidelio*, 1814, was a triumphant one for the composer, and he was caught up in the manic celebrations of the Peace Congress in Vienna.

After Napoleon's final defeat in 1815, Vienna entered upon a long period of disillusion under a more and more repressive government. This trouble for Beethoven was compounded by the personal crisis precipitated by his brother's death and the following conflict with his sister-in-law over the guardianship of his nephew, Karl. As a result, the next three years were the least productive of his life.

A means of escape from his depression and preoccupation with his personal problems came with the installation of his patron, Archduke Rudolph, as Archbishop of Olmutz. Beethoven's decision to write a mass in celebration led to a renewal of his creativity. But the mass went slowly, and he was still plagued by illness. In 1823, a cure at Baden did much to improve his health, and a subsequent reconciliation with his brother, Johann, after a long estrangement, improved his spirits.

He was able to complete the mass (The Mass in D) and the ninth symphony, and their enormously successful first performances brought him great honor.

He returned in 1824 to Baden to begin work on the string quartets that had been commissioned by Prince Galitzin. Once started, they occupied his energies exclusively, despite recurrent ill health and the personal disaster of his nephew Karl's attempted suicide. He completed these works at his brother's country estate in the fall and winter of 1826.

On his return to Vienna, he contracted pneumonia. His illness was protracted and he declined slowly, dying on March 17th, 1827.

BEETHOVEN (1770–1827)
The Early Period: Op. 18

For developing players, these quartets normally constitute the first venture beyond the string quartets of Haydn and Mozart, Beethoven's models in writing them. They were written in 1798–1800 when he was twenty-eight to thirty years old. Count Apponyi, a Viennese patron, had suggested to Beethoven in 1795 that he undertake writing string quartets. He did not make a commitment then, but he began to write sketches and preliminary movements, including a version for string quartet of the piano sonata in E, Op. 14, No. 1. Indeed, Nottebohm (an early expert on Beethoven) suggested that that sonata was originally conceived as a string quartet. Other efforts at quartet writing that Beethoven made in this period became the Viola Quintet, Op. 4 and the String Trio, Op. 3, some experts say.

The Op. 18 quartets were thus the result of Count Apponyi's suggestion, but they were finally written for and dedicated to Prince Lobkowitz, another patron. As a result of their success, Prince Lichnowsky (yet another patron) undertook to support the composer with an annual stipend. The quartets were published in 1801.

These six quartets were not written in the order in which they are numbered. The published numbering seems to have been affected especially by Schuppanzigh, a virtuoso violinist, colleague, and friend. The true order of composition was later established or postulated from Beethoven's sketchbooks as well as from the analysis of the works themselves. Most authorities agree that the order of composition is as follows: No. 3 (D major), No. 1 (F major), No. 2 (G major), No. 5 (A major), No. 4 (C minor) and No. 6 (B-flat major). The order of composition is useful to keep in mind because the six works reveal the experimentation and progress that Beethoven made in this form that was to become so important to him. Thus, No. 3 and No. 1 show relatively less that is innovative. No. 2 seems to be a particular effort to model the style of Haydn. No. 5 was probably modeled on the style of Mozart. No. 6 contains an 'extra' movement, the famous *La Malinconia*. No. 4, say some experts, is a pastiche of earlier unused musical ideas, put together with relatively little care in order to complete the set of six. The composition and publication of quartets in sets of six was a convention of the eighteenth century.

Some experts have not been wholly favorable about Op. 18. Haydn is said to have been cool toward them. D'Indy, the great French musicologist of the nineteenth century, was not enthusiastic about them. Now, everyone considers them to be monumental. Ambitious amateurs may be tempted to neglect them in favor of the later quartets of Beethoven. They deserve close attention, however, for they lie at a critical point in the evolution of the form. Beyond that, though, they are magnificent works to play.

Quartet in F major, Op. 18, No. 1 | (1799)

I *Allegro con brio.* II *Adagio affetuoso ed appassionato.*
III *Scherzo: Allegro molto.* IV *Allegro.*

The *first movement*, a sonata allegro, opens directly with an abrupt turn figuration in unison that immediately expands into the principal theme of the movement. This ornamental motif, as the principal theme or in derived forms, dominates the whole of the movement, being deftly manipulated and remade. Viewed overall, the movement has a jagged, fragmentary and abrupt character. The atmosphere is rather cold and unemotional, but brilliant.

The *second movement* is a long and extensively worked-out adagio. It is melodramatic, sentimental and full of grand musical gestures. Beethoven said that he wrote this movement with the Vault Scene from *Romeo and Juliet* in mind, according to Nottebohm, the nineteenth-century expert on Beethoven. That idea is certainly consistent with the melodrama of the movement.

The *third movement* is a true scherzo and called such for the first time in the literature of string quartets. Note that Beethoven evades the minuet-scherzo question altogether in Op. 18, No. 3. This is a small but tidy and effective movement, showing asymmetry in the ten-bar opening theme.

The *fourth movement*, a rondo, is large in scale for the period and full of innovations. Despite that, it seems a little unfocused.

Commentary. In its adherence to established forms and style, this quartet is wholly conventional in the traditions established by Beethoven's predecessors, especially Haydn. Even the rather operatic nature of the slow movement, the most memorable of the quartet, has a precedent, for example, in Haydn's quartet in Op. 20, No. 2. The quartet is fully accessible to experienced players, but it requires well-developed instrumental and ensemble techniques. Pleasure—4; Effort—3.

Quartet in G major, Op. 18, No. 2 | (1799), *The Compliment*

I *Allegro.* II *Adagio cantabile.* III *Scherzo: Allegro.*
IV *Allegro molto quasi presto.*

The *first movement* opens with a courtly two-bar phrase or gesture that immediately expands to become the melody. It dominates the thematic material throughout. The formal nature of this phrase is the origin of the common name that posterity has given to this quartet. The exposition is formal, restrained, and witty. The development, by contrast, is contrapuntal, complex, irregular, and even a little raucous, but the extreme formality returns in the recapitulation. The movement is compact and rather formal throughout.

The *second movement* opens with an adagio theme in 3/4 time that is bland, cool, and a little pretentious. Abruptly, a dance parody in 2/4 time appears, seemingly as a gesture of rejection of the adagio theme. The adagio then recurs in variation from its first statement. This structure exemplifies Beethoven's experimentation with forms. Nottebohm suggested that the allegro section was inserted after the adagio had been completed.

The *third movement* is a clever, quick, comical and kittenish scherzo. The trio section begins with a tune that resembles that of the adagio movement.

The *fourth movement* opens with a theme that is derived from the secondary theme of the *first movement*. Its subsequent treatment is free, complex and highly contrapuntal. The movement is bright and frisky in character throughout.

Commentary. Beethoven consciously modeled the style of Haydn in this witty quartet, according to most commentators. Some see it (the last movement, in particular) as an intelligent, skillful, and rather brutal extension of the Haydn aesthetic, a presentation of the comedy of manners that is such an important element in the classical style. As such, it is a most interesting work for the amateur to learn, for here one can see Beethoven's ideas straining at the bonds of classicism. The quartet requires good instrumental and ensemble technique. It contains good parts in all voices. The first violin part is especially difficult. The cello part is unusually prominent. None of the parts is quite easy. Pleasure—4; Effort—3.

Quartet in D major, Op. 18, No. 3 | (1798)

I *Allegro.* II *Andante con moto.* III *Allegro.* IV *Presto.*

The *first movement* opens abruptly with the principal theme, a broad, bland and soaring ten-bar phrase followed by an unbroken sixteen-bar phrase. This long, lyrical and asymmetric theme, so striking and original a concept, is treated broadly in the exposition. Many experts advise that the exposition should be repeated as written. The development section is rather conventional and not extended, and the recapitulation is truncated. The extensive coda seems to refer to the action of the whole movement. The final few bars bring to mind the corresponding ending of the D major quartet of Mozart, K. 575.

The *second movement* uses a simple and warm theme, worked out contrapuntally. The dense texture of the long movement produces an effect that is both sentimental and moving.

The *third movement* is a tidy, taut and rather inconspicuous scherzo-minuet. Beethoven called it neither, an indication of its ambiguity in this regard.

The *fourth movement*, a presto perpetuum mobile in 6/8, contains extensive contrapuntal writing with a fugato and canons. The treatment is ingenious, and the effect makes a great impression, though the movement is not quite brilliant. The thematic materials bear a family resemblance to those of the earlier movements.

Commentary. One cannot quite understand Schuppanzigh's preference for Op. 18, No. 1 over this work. This quartet may have seemed too adventurous, both because of the remarkable principal theme of the *first movement* and because of the extensive use of counterpoint in the *second* and *fourth movements*. On the other hand, it may have seemed too conventional for it offers few innovations in form and technique over Haydn and Mozart. It presents no major technical or musical problems to skilled amateurs, although the *fourth movement* requires special attention as to instrumental technique. Pleasure—4; Effort—3.

Quartet in C minor, Op. 18, No. 4 | (1799–1800)

I *Allegro ma non tanto*. II *Scherzo: Andante scherzoso quasi allegro*. III *Menuetto: Allegretto*. IV *Allegro*.

The *first movement* is dramatic and stormy, a long sonata allegro of conventional form. Many authorities comment on the relative crudity of the compositional technique, calling the transitions such things as "brutal" and the development "old-fashioned."

The *second movement*, a restrained scherzo in sonata form, opens with a fugato and remains contrapuntal throughout. A half-fast and half-slow movement, it seems to represent an effort at humorous writing to contrast with the storm and drama of the first. The severest critics have called the movement "trifling" and "frigid," though such terms seem unduly harsh.

The *third movement*, an undistinguished minuet, gives a pleasing independence to the second violin.

The *fourth movement*, a rondo with a Gipsy tune as its principal theme and a prestissimo ending, has a somewhat fragmented feeling because of its frequent fermata pauses.

Commentary. Many authorities consider this to be the weakest quartet in the opus. A principal criticism is that it lacks a perceptible overall direction or shape. Some go so far as to suggest that Beethoven, wishing to have a C minor quartet in the set (in admiration of Mozart's successes in that key), patched together old material to form one. Such an explanation would account for the otherwise unexplained diffuse nature of the work and for the strange absence of a true slow movement. Such weaknesses have not impaired its appreciation, and it remains a most popular work both with amateur players and in concert. It offers no major musical or technical problems for experienced amateurs. Pleasure—4; Effort—3.

Quartet in A major, Op. 18, No. 5 | (1799–1800)

I *Allegro.* II *Menuetto.* III *Andante cantabile.* IV *Allegro.*

The *first movement* is bland and unimpassioned. There is a full-scale repetition of the exposition with a full development and recapitulation and a rather brief coda. The bridge passages are perfunctory. The adherence to formality and convention in the structure emphasizes the architectural symmetry of the sonata allegro form at the expense of drama and surprise. The movement is graceful and Mozartean.

The *second movement*, a minuet, is starkly simple, lyrical, graceful and relaxed. It opens with a violin duet. This movement has the character of the German dance, a character that often marks the minuets in the quartets of Mozart.

The *third movement* presents a theme and variations for the first time in these quartets. The simple and graceful theme is followed by five variations, none in the minor mode. Beethoven probably meant this to be the center of gravity of this quartet. The movement may have been modeled on the similar movement in Mozart's quartet in A major, K. 464. That movement, in turn, may have been modeled on the *second movement* in Haydn's quartet in Op. 20, No. 4. Critics have said that this movement shows Beethoven to have been uncomfortable with the form of the theme and variations.

The *fourth movement* is the most Mozartean of the four, having a glossy and relaxed brilliance.

Commentary. Throughout, this quartet is easy and unruffled. It seems clear that Beethoven was here making an earnest effort to write in the manner of Mozart. In doing so, he produced a work that is the least characteristic and personal of his quartets. It offers no major musical or technical problems to experienced players. Pleasure—4; Effort—3.

Quartet in B-flat major, Op. 18, No. 6 | (1799–1801)

I *Allegro con brio.* II *Adagio ma non troppo.* III *Scherzo: Allegro.*
IV *La Malinconia.* V *Allegretto quasi allegro.*

The *first movement*, a sonata allegro, has a flat and drawn-out march-like subject, treated as a dialogue between voices. The expansive and highly contrapuntal development section contains passages of unprecedented flexibility and freedom.

The *second movement* is elementary in plan. A deliberate and studied theme is given interest by rococo ornamentation. Overall, the movement seems tidy and immaculate.

The *third movement*, a skillfully written scherzo, relies upon the hemiola to create interest. The movement is harmonically unsophisticated, but tidy and brilliant. The trio is very difficult in the first violin part.

The *fourth movement*, La Malinconia, is a second adagio, not quite independent but serving as an introduction or transition to the *fifth movement*. In the score, Beethoven advises, "This piece is to be played with the greatest delicacy." Despite the title Beethoven gave the movement, the mood is not so much melancholy as it is mysterious. Some believe it to be the first comment made by Beethoven on his deafness that he first publicly acknowledged in 1801. This little movement is unlike anything Beethoven had written to that time, anticipating the very personal nature of the later quartets.

The *fifth movement* is a single-minded Danza alla Tedesca, quiet, fast and pure, almost a perpetuum mobile. There is little or no development or contrast. The flat running texture is terminated by a penultimate interlude that is a brief recollection of La Malinconia, the *fourth movement*. The dance tune then returns and leads to a prestissimo coda.

Commentary. The sketchbooks indicate that this was the last of the set to be written, and its composition may well have been simultaneous with the piano sonata in B-flat major, Op. 22. Similarities can be seen in the *first movements* of the two works. The whole work exhibits a greater unity and sense of proportion than do the other works of the opus. It is not easy, presenting technical challenges to the first violinist in particular and requiring very careful attention to ensemble playing. Pleasure—4; Effort—3.

BEETHOVEN
The Middle Period: Opp. 59, 74, and 95

It is a convention to divide Beethoven's compositions into three periods. This may be a useful pedagogical device, but it goes against the fact that his creative evolution was continuous. The idea of periods may have been particularly fostered by consideration of the quartets, where an enormous gulf in technique and style separates Op. 18 from Op. 59. Since the former quartets date from 1798–1800 and the latter from 1806, this only means that Beethoven's stylistic evolution was rapid at this time.

The Russian ambassador to Vienna, Count Razoumovsky, commissioned the three quartets in Op. 59. He stipulated the use of Russian tunes in the works, either real or simulated. Beethoven projected them at the end of 1804, probably worked on all three simultaneously and completed them in 1806. Thus, they followed soon after the *Waldstein* and *Appassionata* piano sonatas. His work on them must have coincided with his work on *Fidelio*, the fourth piano concerto, the triple concerto, the piano sonata in F major, Op. 54, the *Leonora* overtures, and perhaps the fourth symphony. Beethoven's capacity for simultaneous work on multiple compositions is well known.

The three "Razoumovsky" quartets, Op. 59, were poorly received after both their introduction in 1806–07 and their publication in 1808. Perhaps for that reason, Beethoven wrote a much less adventurous quartet, Op. 74, "The Harp," in 1809, on commission from Prince Lobkowitz (also the dedicatee of Op. 18). That year, 1808–09, was a thin period for Beethoven. Besides the two quartets, he wrote only the three piano sonatas, those in F-sharp major, G major and E-flat major. This relatively low level of productivity in 1808–09 may be attributed to his many troubles then, including the rejection of his proposal of marriage to Therese Malfatti and circumstances surrounding the second French invasion of Vienna, which greatly affected his personal circumstances.

Beethoven wrote Op. 95, the "Quartetto Serioso," late in 1809 at the same time as the *Archduke Trio*, Op. 97, but he delayed public performance of Op. 95 until six years later, perhaps because it seemed too experimental, eccentric or problematic to be released sooner. Op. 95 is dedicated to Nicholaus Zmeskall. That name also appears in the dedication of the Op. 20 quartets of Haydn (1772). The two dedicatees must have been related if not, in fact, the same person.

Quartet in F major, Op. 59, No. 1 | (1805–06), *The First Razoumovsky*

I *Allegro.* II *Allegretto vivace e sempre scherzando.*
III *Adagio molto e mesto.* IV *Theme Russe: Allegro.*

The *first movement* begins abruptly with the simple statement (by the cello, under a rhythmic pedal point in the upper voices) of a broad declamatory principal subject, resembling that of the *Archduke Trio*, Op. 97. The second subject is extremely dissonant for the period. The development section comprises five episodes in which the principal theme is exhibited in extreme convolutions with much contrapuntal writing. After some bridge passages, the principal theme returns in recapitulation with a majestic and definitive terminal development.

The *second movement*, a huge scherzo, opens with a solo statement (again by the cello) of a monotonic rhythmic substructure that serves to unite the whole movement. This opening closely resembles the opening of the corresponding movement in the *Archduke Trio*. The movement has first-movement form, except that expositions and developments are repeated twice, making this movement both long and complex. The brisk tempo must not be allowed to sag.

The *third movement*, a haunting lament in first-movement form, is long and complex. Beethoven wrote in the margin of his notebook, "A weeping willow tree or acacia tree over my brother's grave," though this inscription does not appear in the score. This phrase indicates the sentimentality of the movement, which some experts characterize as a little superficial or ceremonial. The movement ends with a cadenza-like outburst in the first violin part that leads directly to the *fourth movement*, without pause.

The *fourth movement* opens with a bold statement of a Russian folk-dance theme. Its initial statement in the cello reinforces its resemblance to the theme that opens the *first movement*. This movement is also in sonata allegro form. The development seems at times to treat the Russian theme with good-natured parody. Throughout, the mood is ebullient, spirited, and forthright. Some critics consider the movement inferior to the other three, but not all agree.

Commentary. Taken as a whole, this work is monumental for its innovations in form and style, for its complexity and for its length. Experts compare it to the *Eroica* Symphony. It is not symphonic, however, but well fitted to the quartet idiom and texture. It is difficult in technique, in ensemble and in interpretation. Especially, the first violinist and the cellist undertaking to read it for the first time are well advised to practice many passages beforehand. Newcomers to the work will certainly flag in many places, but repetition and deeper acquaintance can overcome its difficulties, to the great reward of all those who make the effort. Pleasure—4; Effort—4.

Quartet in E minor, Op. 59, No. 2 | (1805–06),
The Second Razoumovsky

I *Allegro.* II *Molto adagio.* III *Allegretto.* IV *Finale: Presto.*

In mood, the *first movement* is the antithesis of the *first movement* of Op. 59, No. 1. It opens with two sharp questioning chords that lead, after a measure of rest, to a fragmentary reply. The rest of the movement repeats the pattern. The whole exposition is suffused with these fragments and the development similarly rests upon them. The mood throughout is brusque, interrogatory and tense.

The *second movement* adagio occurred to Beethoven " . . . when contemplating the starry sky and thinking of the music of the spheres . . ." said Carl Czerny, one of his pupils. Beethoven himself says only, "This piece is to be played with great feeling," in the score. The broad hymn-like opening theme is succeeded by a second subject that exhibits a vague uneasiness produced by the rhythm. A subsequent development section projects a mood of sorrow. The movement ends in a tranquil but joyless atmosphere.

The *third movement* is unusual in form in that the scherzo allegro is repeated three times and the trio twice, in alternation. The scherzo allegro is made restless by its unrelenting syncopation. The five-bar Russian theme of the trio (introduced by the viola) is treated rather waggishly. Some experts find the treatment heavy-handed, even brutal (some suggest contemptuous). At least there is little humor in it. This same theme appears prominently in Moussorgsky's opera, *Boris Godounov* and in other Russian compositions. This movement does little to relieve the tension of the *first movement* and the sadness of the second.

The *fourth movement* combines sonata and rondo forms in a galloping and cheerful way. An obsessive pulse drives the whole.

Commentary. Structurally, this work resembles the First Rasoumovsky in the persistent use of sonata form, including the innovative combination of sonata and rondo forms in the last movement. The structure of the scherzo is unique. The delay of the release in tension until the last movement is notable. The work is shorter than Op. 59, No. 1, and it is technically and musically less taxing. Still, it requires well-developed skills. It is the best introduction to the opus for amateurs. Pleasure—4; Effort—3.

Quartet in C major, Op. 59, No. 3 | (1805–06),
The Third Razoumovsky

I *Introduzione: Andante con moto; Allegro vivace.* II *Andante con moto quasi allegretto.* III *Menuetto: Grazioso.* IV *Allegro molto.*

The *first movement* opens with a long andante introduction characterized by dissonance, ambiguity of key and seeming suspension of forward movement. A sharp declamatory figure then leads to a cadenza-like expression of the rhythmic first theme in the first violin. The initial declamatory figure persists throughout the movement, intruding on the subsequent exposition and development sections. The same figure dominates even the modest coda. The liveliness and the decorative theme make this movement rather Mozartean.

The *second movement*, opening in A minor, forms the center of gravity of the work. The opening theme is a *Lied* (possibly based on a Russian tune) that is soon steered into somber moods and shadowy corners over a pizzicato pedal point in the cello. The movement shows few internal contrasts in spirit, having an unrelieved moody complexity as it evolves through six keys before emerging into A major.

The *third movement* represents a return to the style of Mozart. A symmetrical rococo minuet, elementary and simple, seems to have been put here to relieve the somber mood left by the *second movement.* The unusually long trio and coda seem to anticipate the massive movement to follow.

The *fourth movement*, an emphatic fugue, boisterous, ebullient, complex, and noisy, is the first complete fugue in the Beethoven quartets.

It is certainly powerful, but a little long-winded and perhaps superficial as compared to the other final movements of this opus. It benefits from being played as marked, allegro molto rather than presto.

Commentary. This quartet shows more variety of moods among the movements than the others do in the opus. It is most memorable for the slow movement. Some consider the heroic fugue in the *fourth movement* to be its apex. It requires good players, but its difficulties are neither taxing nor insurmountable for accomplished amateurs. Pleasure—4; Effort—4.

Quartet in E-flat major, Op. 74 | (1809), *The Harp*

I *Poco Adagio; Allegro.* II *Adagio ma non troppo.* III *Presto.* IV *Allegretto con Variazione.*

The *first movement* opens with a long and contemplative introduction characterized by an interrogative phrase ('Möchte es sein?' suggests Kerman). This leads to an affirmative response in the theme of the subsequent allegro with a cheerful and relaxed mood throughout the exposition and development sections. The extensive use of pizzicato arpeggios in this movement gives the work its common name. Players particularly remember the brilliant virtuosic outburst in the first violin that leads to the broad peroration of the coda. The whole movement is genial and joyful, yet serene.

The *second movement* opens with a noble and grand melody that is then treated in more complex episodes, alternating with other episodes built on equally majestic melodies. A brief evocation of the *first movement* ends this movement.

The *third movement* is a typical Beethoven scherzo with the trio repeated twice. The scherzo allegro is furious with a hammered motive and the trio ebullient, even raucous. The tempo must be such that a single bar of the scherzo allegro equals two bars of the trio.

The *fourth movement*, eight variations on an elegant theme, is pleasant and ingratiating, but it contains little that is novel or characteristic in dramatic terms. Rather, it seems introspective, concentrating on the technique of composition rather than on effects. Some experts comment that it is less interesting than the other movements.

Commentary. This pleasant and beautiful work, light and elegant for the most part, seems at first to lack much that is new. It is great fun to play for it is not really difficult, though the first violin must study the famous virtuosic passage in the *first movement*. All voices have rewarding parts. Pleasure—4; Effort—3.

Quartet in F minor, Op. 95 | (1809), *Quartetto Serioso*

I *Allegro con brio*. II *Allegretto ma non troppo*. III *Allegro assai vivace ma serioso*. IV *Larghetto espressivo; Allegretto agitato*.

The *first movement* opens abruptly with the peremptory first subject stated in unison. The abrupt and stark exposition, the spare development, and the truncated recapitulation and coda give the movement a feeling of brusqueness. The movement ends abruptly, almost rudely. The atmosphere throughout the movement is one of anger and impatience. The starkness of the material is supported by the way in which the sonata allegro form is reduced to its bare essentials.

The *second movement* opens with a descending scale in the cello. A melancholy aria is here treated in several varied episodes along with other material. The movement displays, overall, a restless lyricism and tense melancholy.

The *third movement*, a driving grand scherzo is agitated, dry and symmetrical. The two trios are hesitant and spare, consisting of block chords. They are not quite identical.

The *fourth movement* is introduced by a five-bar larghetto, a relaxation that obliterates the agitation of the dotted rhythm in the scherzo allegro. The rondo that follows maintains the taut and spare character of the preceding movements. The three statements of refrains and couplets terminate abruptly in an alla breve coda in which all of the anxiety and pathos of the work seem to explode and fly away. This ending is like that of a comic opera, quite out of character with the rest of the work and an obvious attempt to provide a release of the tension of this most stark, spare and taut work.

Commentary. This is a wonderful quartet to get to know really well. It is certainly accessible to amateurs both in the technical sense and musically. All amateurs should know it. Beethoven himself gave the quartet its common name. Pleasure—4; Effort—3.

BEETHOVEN
The Late Period: Opp. 127, 130, 131, 132, 133, and 135

Now universally admired, these last quartets were not accepted well at the time of their first presentation. In the fifteen years after Beethoven's death, for example, Vienna heard only seven performances of any of them. The *Great Fugue* waited twenty-seven years for its second public hearing, and it had only fourteen public performances up to 1875.

Beethoven received a commission in late 1822 from the Russian Prince Galitzin for three quartets. He finished all six in the set in about three years. He completed Op. 127 in February 1825, Op. 132 in July, and Op. 130 in November. Op. 131 was finished in July 1826 and Op. 135 in October. The new finale for Op. 130 was finished in December 1826. The opus numbers, thus, do not reflect the true order of composition.

The delay between the commission in 1822 and his start of work on Op. 127 was forced by Beethoven's concentration on the ninth symphony. Once begun, the quartets occupied his full attention. They represent the last major effort he made in composition before his death in 1827.

These quartets are the sacred canon of the literature. They have been so much studied, analyzed and described that the brief notes offered here might seem fatuous. Still, amateurs often fear to undertake them, and so they do not get to know them from the inside, from actually reading them. These superficial notes are meant only to serve as guides to encourage players to venture these grand works.

Their difficulties are as much musical as technical. The instrumental parts are more difficult to play than those of the earlier Beethoven quartets, but these quartets also require a highly-developed sense of ensemble playing. The real difficulties are in interpretation, and it is the faculty for interpretation that can be particularly learned from playing them.

Op. 127 was written at Baden, which accounts, possibly, for its rather pastoral nature. Op. 132 was written after Beethoven had recovered from a three-month illness, with one month spent in bed. This accounts for its religious nature, as expressed in the superscript to the *third movement* in the score. Op. 133, the *Great Fugue*, was originally the last movement of Op. 130, later replaced by another movement and published as a separate work at the advice of a publisher and probably others.

Quartet in E-flat major, Op. 127 | (1824–25)

I *Maestoso; Allegro.* II *Adagio, ma non troppo e molto cantabile.* III *Scherzando vivace.* IV *Finale.*

The *first movement* opens with a maestoso introduction. The allegro themes that follow are somewhat monotonous because of the persisting single rhythm. The monotony is broken by the repeated reappearance of the maestoso, which thus becomes not simply an introduction but a motivic means for supplying contrast to the placidity of the allegro. The movement is lyrical, pastoral and calm.

The *second movement* is a set of variations on a splendid melody that resembles that of the *Benedictus* from the *Mass in D.* The melody is treated to five non-programmatic variations of progressively greater splendor and ingenuity. The movement projects an incomparable religious peace throughout.

The *third movement* scherzo is playful and joyful, with tempo interruptions in different meter. The dotted-rhythm allegro is contrasted with a droll trio, called recitativo, that is expressed mainly by the viola and cello.

The *fourth movement* returns to the pastoral mood of the first. A fully developed sonata form precedes a new section, a dream-like development in a new key and meter. The serenity of the ending seems to erase all that has gone before.

Commentary. One cannot admire this work enough. It is most approachable and understandable, both to the player and to the listener. Its pastoral nature may make it seem earlier than it is. There is little storm or anxiety here. No truly massive technical problems exist, but the interpretation of the slow movement adagio variations is a major challenge for all players at any level. Pleasure—4; Effort—3.

Quartet in B-flat major, Op. 130 (1825–26)

I *Adagio ma non troppo; Allegro.* II *Presto.* III *Andante con moto, ma non troppo.* IV *Alla danza tedesca: Allegro Assai.* V *Cavatina: Adagio molto espressivo.* VI *Finale: Allegro.*

The *first movement* opens with an adagio theme that is no mere prelude, but reappears seven times in the movement. This structure contrasts adagio gentleness and allegro violence alternatively.

The *second movement* is a fanciful scherzo with a quick restless little tune and rather comical effects.

The *third movement*, andante, is a sonata with little development. It has what seems to be an intentional monotony that supports the intimate and touching character of the movement. Interpretation is difficult in this movement.

The *fourth movement* is a slow waltz, the second minuet-scherzo of the work, lilting and light, yet strangely abstract.

The *fifth movement*, an aria written in three sections, is like a memory, restrained, mournful and poetic.

The *sixth movement*, a combination of sonata and rondo forms, was the last composition of Beethoven, having been substituted for the movement that became the *Great Fugue*. The mood is one of restlessness and cheerful agitation.

Commentary. This difficult quartet is relatively unplayed by amateurs, perhaps not so much because of its great technical demands as because the succession of relatively small movements of highly contrasting character seems a little odd. The deficiency in a unifying structure or character in the work may mean only that Beethoven intended it as a sort of divertimento. The lovely cavatina is justly famous and cherished, and all amateurs should know it. The finale is very difficult. Pleasure—4; Effort—4.

Quartet in C-sharp minor, Op. 131 | (1826)

I *Adagio ma non troppo e molto espressivo.* II *Allegro molto vivace.* III *Andante ma non troppo e molto cantabile.* IV *Presto.* V *Adagio quasi un poco andante.* VI *Allegro.*

The *first movement*, a melancholy and majestic fugue on a subject that resembles that of the trio of the *second movement* of Op. 132, maintains a restrained anguish throughout.

The *second movement* is a sprightly and impelling vivace, contrasting sharply with the melancholy grandeur of the *first movement.*

The *third movement* andante presents, after a short recitative, a theme expressed in dialogue form and then treated to seven variations, each a sort of fantasia on the theme. Some see the theme as a tribute to Haydn's last string quartet, Op. 103.

The *fourth movement,* a long and joyous scherzo in five sections, uses folk material to form a massive structure.

The *fifth movement* is a brief aria with a mood that resembles that of the cavatina of Op. 130, but less expansive. It is an intense, concentrated and direct expression of grief.

The *sixth movement,* a complete sonata form, opens with a fugue subject and ends with an extensive terminal development. It is full of contrasts but the overall mood is one of tragedy.

Commentary. Beethoven is said to have considered this his greatest quartet. He wrote on the manuscript, "made of bits and pieces, stolen from here and there", probably as a joke. It is the eighteenth-century divertimento "raised to sublimity" according to Lam. Many amateurs hesitate even to try to read this most difficult work. Certainly, awe is justified. Still, all serious amateurs must sometime venture it, for it is the supreme achievement of the form. Pleasure—4; Effort—4.

Quartet in A minor, Op. 132 | (1825–26)

I *Assai sostenuto; Allegro.* II *Allegro ma non tanto.* III *Molto adagio.* IV *Allegro marcia; Assai vivace.*

The *first movement* opens with a brief introduction that sets the tonal structure of the movement in the simplest possible manner. The allegro contains three successive expositions, interrupted by developments of the introductory theme. The mood is one of suffering, interrupted and relieved by hope.

The *second movement* is a rather conventional scherzo with a pastoral or bucolic trio. Lam calls it the "ghost of a Mozartean menuetto." This movement was substituted for the one originally conceived which became the Alla Danza Tedesca (the *fourth movement*) of Op. 130.

The *third movement*, the centerpiece of the work, bears the super-script "Holy song of thanks to the Godhead from a convalescent, in the Lydian mode." The hymn tune is treated in five sections of progressive ingenuity. The mood is sublimely prayerful, unparalleled in the quartet literature.

The *fourth movement* is a little military march, breaking the religious mood left by the *third movement*.

The *fifth movement* opens with a recitative leading to the radiant joy of the rondo that constitutes the finale.

Commentary. The quartet as a whole is striking for the contrasting moods of the five movements: hopeful suffering, bucolic cheer, prayerful thanksgiving, sprightliness and radiant joy. The *third movement* hymn is the perhaps most profound such movement Beethoven ever wrote, and it is exceedingly difficult to play, not so much technically as interpretatively. Close study and much repetition of this movement is advised, for its rewards do not come with casual readings. The quartet as a whole is more difficult and less accessible than Op. 127. Pleasure—4; Effort—4.

Quartet in B-flat Major, Op. 133 | (1825), The Great Fugue

I *Overture; Fugue.*

The first twenty-nine bars constitute an introduction, displaying the theme and previewing its treatments to come. The fugue that follows has two subjects, one gentle and melancholy, the other gay and exuberant. These are treated antagonistically in three sections. The first section exclusively treats the joyous subject. The second section treats the serious subject. The two subjects are treated simultaneously in the third section in contrast and conflict.

Commentary. This is the original finale for Op. 130, replaced at the advice of Beethoven's publishers and others. It is a formidable work both technically and musically, not often undertaken by amateurs. Many believe that it should not be performed by a quartet at all, but by a string orchestra. Keller suggests that Beethoven may have thought so too, and that that accounts for his willingness to see it separated from Op. 130. Still, amateur quartet players can best learn to understand it by reading it. It is so intensely intellectual and so complex that amateurs may, for a long time, come to find satisfaction only in having gotten through it at all. Pleasure—2; Effort—4.

Quartet in F major, Op. 135 | (1826)

I *Allegretto.* II *Vivace.* III *Lento assai e cantante tranquillo.*
IV *Grave ma non troppo tratto: Allegro.*

The *first movement*, a straightforward and pithy sonata allegro, is witty, cheerful and charming, with touches of humor and surprise.

The *second movement*, a humorous and rollicking vivace, provides violinistic showmanship over a three-part ostinato.

The *third movement* is a simple and peaceful aria, reminiscent of the cavatina of Op. 130, but more succinct. It is a wonderfully condensed song.

The *fourth movement* opens with a theme introduced in a grave recitativo to the words written in the score, "Must it be?" The allegro that follows provides the answer repeatedly, "It must be," emphatically and cheerfully. The origin of the question is alleged to have been a mundane domestic incident having to do with the rent, but that story is apocryphal. Beethoven himself said that the answer refers to his production of the quartet from a need for money. Whatever the meaning of the programmatic statements provided, this allegro is a dramatic and rather operatic answer to a serious question, an answer of triumph without solemnity or pretentiousness.

Commentary. D'Indy and others find it puzzling that this quartet is so simple in comparison with the others in the group. It is, but that simplicity should not detract from its performance. Because of its brevity and clarity, it is readily accessible to amateurs. It is a fine work to undertake as the first effort in approaching these late quartets, but it is still a difficult work. Pleasure—3; Effort—3.

BLOCH (1880–1959)

Ernest Bloch had established his reputation in his native Switzerland before he immigrated to the United States in 1916. He became a citizen of the United States in 1924 and remained here until about 1930, when he returned to Switzerland. He came back to the United States in 1941 to stay for the rest of his life. In the United States, he served as Director of the Cleveland Institute of Music, Director of the San Francisco Conservatory, and faculty member at the University of California. Chamber music constituted a large part of his work. There are five full-

scale string quartets and five smaller pieces for string quartet,
besides other forms for other combinations of instruments. The
five full-scale quartets date from 1916, 1945, 1952, 1953 and 1956.
The latter four, coming so much later in his career, are more difficult than the first. They contain greater harmonic and rhythmic
complexities, including the use of dodecaphonic technique. The
first quartet, accordingly, is the one most suited to amateurs who
seek an introduction to the Bloch quartets. It was composed just
after *Schelomo*.

Quartet, First, in G major | (1916)

I *Andante moderato; Lamentoso.* II *Allegro frenetico.* III *Andante
molto moderato (Pastorale).* IV *Finale: Vivace; Assai lento; Tempo
dell'andante; Agitato molto; Allegro con fuoco.*

The *first movement* opens with a brief andante introduction. The phrase
that opens the following Lamentoso is a motto theme, one that appears
in modified form throughout the work. The movement proceeds in
sonata form with rather frequent tempo changes consistent with the
Hebraic quality of the material. A fine coda ends the movement.

The *second movement* opens with a ferocious frenetico section, exhilarating in rhythm and in harmony. Time-signatures change at short
intervals, but these are not problematic. A contrasting middle section
follows, sultry music said to have represented Bloch's impression of
Gaugin's paintings, after which the Allegro frenetico returns. The
movement ends with an abrupt presto flight.

The *third movement* opens in the viola with a dreaming phrase that
then passes to the other instruments. A bariolage in the cello and
the introduction of a second theme in the viola produce a sense of
mystery and sadness. Progressive animation appears and, with the
introduction of some new material, leads to a climax after which
the melancholy of the opening returns. The movement has great
beauty and simplicity. Bloch himself described a depiction of primitive hunters returning at the end of the day to a woman and
child.

The *fourth movement* begins with an introduction that reviews thematic fragments from the previous movements. The main subject of
the finale begins at the Allegro con fuoco. This forceful subject and a
strongly rhythmic second subject (ben ritmato) are continued in devel-

opment with other material through passages of contrasting mood. After a lento, brief grave reminiscences of the earlier movements end this movement in a quiet mood.

Commentary. This quartet has great power, imagination and beauty. It was once much admired, but it is no longer often heard. Its complicated and rather daring effects certainly require technical expertise, and amateurs approaching it for the first time will not find it to be easy. It should attract violists in particular, but all voices have good parts. Pleasure—2; Effort—4.

BORODIN (1833–1887)

Alexander Porfiryevich Borodin was the illegitimate son of Prince Luka Gedianov, one of a line of princes of Tatar origin that was established under Ivan the Terrible. The family, once prominent, was much reduced in circumstances. Prince Luka was a well-educated, literary and mystical man who lived off his inheritance, one of the landed gentry. Unhappily married, he had a long relationship with the daughter of a soldier, Avdotya Antonova, living with her and fathering children.

Alexander, following the local custom for illegitimate children, was registered at birth as the legal son of Porfiry Borodin, a servant of the Prince, but he lived as a son with his natural parents in St. Petersburg. After his biological father's death in 1843, he continued living with his mother through adolescence. His musical gift became clear early in life, and he was composing by the age of nine and studying the piano and cello. At the same time he developed a keen interest in chemistry and the natural sciences.

He entered the Academy of Physicians in St. Petersburg in 1850, graduating in 1855 with honors. There, he became fascinated with many areas of science but he also continued his activity in music, composing and playing the cello in amateur chamber music groups.

After graduation, he became a medical practitioner in a military hospital. He soon found the practice of medicine not to be to his liking, but he persisted, completing the research and dissertation required for the degree of Doctor of Medicine.

The Academy of Physicians was so impressed with his scientific abilities that the Academy sponsored further training abroad to prepare him for a faculty post. He gave up his career as a physician and went to Heidelberg where he studied with some of the great scientists of the day, Bunsen, Helmholtz, Kirchoff, and Erlenmeyer. In Heidelberg he continued his musical activity, composing and playing in amateur groups. He went on to Paris for more training and visited Italy. Late in this tour abroad, he met Catherine Protopova, a gifted amateur pianist. After a winter spent at Pisa, where Borodin had further training in science, the two returned to St. Petersburg where he took a position at the Academy of Physicians. He and Catherine were married in 1863 and settled into the circumstances that they were to occupy permanently. Though they had no natural children, they adopted two daughters.

Borodin settled into a busy and regular pattern of work in teaching and research in biochemistry where he soon made important contributions. He also took a special interest in the medical education of women, becoming a leader in the development of programs for teaching women in medicine.

Borodin had met Moussorgsky before he left St. Petersburg. After his return, he developed a close relationship with other composers in St. Petersburg: Balakireff, Rimsky-Korsakov, Stassov, and Cui. Fully accepted by them as a composer, he wrote steadily, producing operas and symphonic forms as well as songs and smaller pieces. He gradually adopted the nationalistic style for which he is now known. He worked constantly and steadily at both his vocations, achieving fame in both. His work was rarely interrupted except by his mother's fatal illness in 1873 and by trips he took abroad in connection with his profession in biochemistry. His chief musical contacts were in Russia, though he visited Franz Liszt at Weimar in 1876 and in 1881.

His wife's chronic illness with pulmonary disease troubled his last years. Also, in 1886, he began to suffer chest pain, recognized as cardiac in origin. Such problems slowed his progress in writing the opera, *Prince Igor*, on which he labored for a long time, but he continued to work at his accustomed heavy pace. He died suddenly of a myocardial infarction in February 1887. His wife survived him only a short time, dying of heart failure in June of that same year.

Borodin was a remarkably amiable and even-tempered man with the capacity to pursue two parallel careers. The fact that he is now remembered more for his music than for his science testifies to his musical gift. His contributions in medicine were also considerable, noteworthy especially for the work he did to advance the possibilities for medical careers for women.

This Russian master earned his place in history with a remarkably small output and his major chamber music is small indeed, two string quartets and one movement of a quartet written in company with Rimsky-Korsakov, Liadov and Glazounov. Both of his own string quartets are masterpieces and show what more he might have done had his vocation been composition rather than biochemistry.

The first string quartet was begun in 1875, to the dismay of Moussourgsky and Stassov who thought he should emphasize larger forms. It was completed in 1878 and first performed in St. Petersburg in January 1881, but not published until four years later, dedicated to Rimsky-Korsakov's wife. Both performers and the public instantly acclaimed the work. The title page stated that the work was inspired by a theme of Beethoven. The Beethoven-derived theme, the opening of the allegro section in the *first movement*, is only remotely derived from that theme, which occurs in the finale of Op. 130 beginning at bar 118. The theme is also said to be the source of the second subject of the andante and of the first subject of the finale. The work is acclaimed for its eloquence, sonority, passion and sincerity. It uses the best of the established German techniques to achieve a Russian masterpiece.

The second quartet was written in a single creative burst, between July 23rd and September 19th, 1881. It had its first performance in St. Petersburg on January 26th, 1882, only one year after the premiere of the earlier quartet. It was not published until 1888 (after Borodin's death) and dedicated to his wife. Both quartets were soon known throughout Europe and in North America.

Experts believe that these works were especially influential in the writing of string quartets by Debussy and Ravel. Both the latter composers are known to have admired the Russian composers, as did most of the young French composers of the period who saw in the Russians an escape from the dominance of German intellectualism.

Quartet, First, in A major | (1878)

I *Moderato; Allegro.* II *Andante con moto; Fugato.* III *Scherzo: Prestissimo.* IV *Andante; Allegro risoluto.*

The *first movement* opens with a long Moderato introduction. The following Allegro begins with the theme derived from Beethoven's Op. 130 finale played by the first violin. Later it is given to the second violin. The theme is treated contrapuntally along with the second subject, which resembles the first in character. The development is ingenious and thorough, with a fugato that anticipates that of the next movement. The theme of the introduction reappears, and a cantabile passage follows. A new theme leads to the recapitulation. This is a long movement, but it does not seem so from its grace, simplicity, and variety.

The *second movement* opens as a lovely, dreamy and meditative *Lied* in the first violin and viola. The second subject soon appears, heralded by an impassioned triplet figure in the first violin, più vivo, and the cantabile mood continues. A central section, Fugato, ends with another triplet figure in the first violin, and the andante cantabile returns to close the movement.

The *third movement*, a whimsical scherzo with a sustained rhythm and velocity, is delicate and ingenious. The much slower trio, which makes good use of harmonics, is dreamy and contemplative.

The *fourth movement* opens with a short andante introduction whose motive arises from the first subject of the *first movement* and is modified further here to form the first theme of the following energetic Allegro risoluto in A minor. The second subject derives from that of the *first movement*. The substantial and contrapuntal sonata movement ends brightly in A major.

Commentary. This is the lesser known of the two quartets, but it has been much admired by experts because it is a fuller exposition of Borodin's style and technique. It is a large work, but remarkably even, all movements being quite splendid. It is fully accessible to experienced amateurs. All parts have fine passages. Pleasure—3; Effort—2.

Quartet, Second, in D major | (1881)

I *Allegro moderato.* II *Scherzo: Allegro.* III *Notturno: Andante.*
IV *Finale: Andante; Vivace.*

The *first movement* sonata allegro opens with a happy lyrical theme in
the cello, which is then continued in the first violin. The theme dominates the whole movement, the second subject being treated less
fully. The development is uncomplicated, and the mood throughout is
calm and cheerful.

The *second movement* scherzo has two subjects, one breezy and
bustling, the other lyrical and sensuous. These are treated in contrasting alternation, creating a combined scherzo and intermezzo. There is
no trio.

The *third movement*, a tuneful and expressive cantilena maintaining
the character of a nocturne throughout, is especially fine. The cello
opens with the wonderful melody that then passes among all voices,
with much antiphonal imitation. It was once heard often in orchestral
transcription.

The *fourth movement* is a rondo, introduced by an andante statement
of its pithy and enigmatic tune. The subsequent episodes that treat this
motive are highly varied and always interesting. This movement seems
somewhat less appealing, perhaps a little more studied, than the earlier movements.

Commentary. The comparative simplicity, lucidity, and intimacy of
this quartet make it the more accessible and popular of the two. The
use of some of its themes in *Kismet* (the stage musical) and their subsequent entry into the realm of classic popular songs make them now
universally recognized, even to the point of parody. The work is a
delight to play, and fully within the scope of reasonably experienced
players. Its popularity among amateurs makes them neglect the more
substantial first quartet. Pleasure—3; Effort—2.

BRAHMS (1833–1897)

Johannes Brahms's roots were not wholly in Hamburg, the great
seaport of his birth, for his father, Johann Jakob, came there from
the village of Heide in Holstein. There the Brahms family had
long lived by the trades and crafts of village life. Johann Jakob,

determined to be a musician, left Heide at nineteen to find a career playing the flute, French horn, and stringed instruments in the dives of the Hamburg dockside. He moved out of the slums as his fortunes improved, ultimately taking rooms in the house of a seamstress and her husband where the wife's sister, also a seamstress, lived. A week after moving in, he proposed marriage to the sister. He was twenty-four and she was forty-two.

His fiancée, to be Johannes Brahms's mother, was descended from a Hamburg family that had lost its former social position. She had earned her living as a seamstress from the age of thirteen. Biographers have commented on her intelligence, domesticity, even temper, kindness, and interest in the arts.

The marriage in 1830 of the young, healthy, and handsome musician and his frail older wife produced three children. Their first, Elizabeth (Elise) was soon followed by a son, Johannes, and by a second son, Fritz, in 1835. The couple sought the best educations they could for their children. Johannes began school at six and studied piano at seven. His piano teacher, Friederich Wilhelm Cossel, took great pains to develop the talent that he quickly recognized, and the Cossel and Brahms families became enduring friends. Johannes made his first public appearance at ten. He became a pupil of Eduard Marxen soon after, and Marxen encouraged his interest in composition as well as in the piano.

The Brahms family, never well off, found it difficult to support Johannes's musical education, so the boy began to play in taverns and restaurants to support his education from the age of thirteen. In his adolescence, he became solitary, engaging in an intense focus on composition and reading, especially in romantic literature.

A long period of inner growth but outward immobility ended in 1853 when Brahms came to the attention of the virtuoso violinist, Eduard Remenyi, who invited him to join him in a concert tour. Brahms left Hamburg in April, an unknown, and returned seven months later, a celebrity. The tour took them to the major cities of the German states where Brahms met many of the great musicians of the day, including the Hungarian violinist, Joseph Joachim, and Robert and Clara Schumann. The enthusiasm of Robert Schumann for the young genius was critical in the immediate celebrity that Brahms enjoyed.

At the end of the tour, Brahms returned to Hannover to work with Joachim. This peaceful interlude in his life soon ended, however, for in February 1854, Robert Schumann experienced the catastrophic crisis in his mental disorder that led to his death. Brahms had become close to the Schumanns in his brief acquaintance and he was deeply affected. The following two years were agonizing for Brahms as he tried to provide emotional support to the beautiful and gifted Clara Schumann and her five young children. Part of the Op. 60 piano quartet was written during this period of his anguish.

In 1857, he took temporary employment at the little Court at Detmold where he had much time for composition. Here he wrote the string sextet, Op. 18. He had much time free for touring as well. In Gottingen, he fell in love with Agathe von Siebold, the daughter of a professor in the university there. His romance with this beautiful young singer lasted for some time, and after it ended he was left with an enduring sense of loss. He remembered her in the Op. 36 string sextet.

Brahms first visited Vienna in 1863 and began then to consider moving there from Hamburg. Until 1869, the year he finally settled permanently in Vienna, he shifted his home between the cities. His ties to Hamburg loosened after the death of his mother in 1865 and his father's prompt remarriage. After he accepted the position of director of the Gesellschaft der Musikfreunde in Vienna, he lived a calm and organized life in Vienna. The three string quartets came from this period.

After 1876, Brahms began a long period of touring, conducting and performing his works throughout Europe, but continuing to compose as well. In 1890–91, with the composition of the Op. 111 viola quintet, he ceased writing and set about to prepare for his retirement, reviewing unpublished and unfinished works and writing a will.

This pause was brief, however. Hearing a performance by the virtuoso clarinettist, Richard Muehlfeld, in 1891, he enjoyed a renewal, notable to chamber musicians for its fruits, the two works for clarinet with strings and the two clarinet (or viola) sonatas. He resumed travel as well, both to perform and to receive honors.

Clara Schumann's death in 1896 greatly affected his spirits. Very soon after, he developed the jaundice that was the first sign of his own fatal illness. Though he continued to work, his course was one of steady decline. He died in coma on April 3rd, 1897.

Brahms wrote and destroyed many string quartets (one authority says as many as twenty) before he released those that constitute Op. 51. He was a serious student of the form and he owned the autographs of Haydn's Op. 20 string quartets and of Schubert's C minor quartet movement (D. 703). His selection of that same key for his first quartet and for the first symphony indicates his view of C minor as the choice for dramatic agitation.

The two quartets in Op. 51 were completed on a summer holiday in 1873 spent at Tutzing, near Munich. The same summer also saw the completion of the Haydn Variations, Op. 56 and most of the songs in Op. 59. These quartets are dedicated to Brahms's close friend, Dr. Theodor Billroth, a Viennese surgeon of renown and an enthusiastic player of chamber music. The correspondence between this remarkable surgeon and Brahms has been published and it should interest all those who cherish Brahms's chamber music.

The third quartet, Op. 67, was completed two years later, in 1875, also when Brahms was on a summer holiday. Summer was usually the most productive time for him. That summer, spent at Ziegelhausen near Heidelberg, was an especially contented one, for he had just resigned a duty that had become troublesome, that of Director of the Gesellschaft der Musikfreunde. That summer saw also the completion of the duets of Op. 66 and of the piano quartet, Op. 60. It was that summer that he grew his beard. The dedicatee of Op. 67, Professor Engelmann, was a physician in Utrecht, an enthusiast about music, and a friend. Brahms made a transcription of this work for piano, four hands, and he played it in that form with Dr. Billroth. The Hellmesberger Quartet, which introduced the quartets of Brahms, rehearsed this work in the home of Dr. Billroth for its premier performance.

Quartet in C minor, Op. 51, No. 1 | (1873)

I *Allegro*. II *Romanza: Poco Adagio*. III *Allegretto molto moderato e comodo*. IV *Allegro*.

The principal theme of the *first movement* is an ascending dotted-rhythm arpeggio, dark and gloomy. The second theme is no less shadowy, and so the whole movement is somber and stormy.

The simple structure of the *second movement*, an ABA form, and the spareness of the treatment may be what Brahms meant to indicate in calling this a romanza. Nevertheless, the compositional technique belies the title, producing an effect of complexity. The beautiful movement continues the dotted rhythm of the first.

In the *third movement*, a whimsical, a scherzo-like movement with an obscured tonality, the viola first speaks the tune. The trio, featuring a bariolage, offers a contrast in the shift to a faster triple time from the duple time of the scherzo. The mood, overall, is rather dark.

The *fourth movement* allegro opens with a theme that is derived from those of the *first* and *second movements*. The tragic and stormy music remains steadfast in mood and tonality.

Commentary. This quartet, so full of tragic passion, is more notable for its sonority and harmonic richness than for its tunefulness. It is technically and musically rather difficult. All parts require fine instrumental technique. The parts for the middle voices are not wholly gratifying. Pleasure—3; Effort—3.

Quartet in A minor, Op. 51, No. 2 | (1873)

I *Allegro non troppo.* II *Andante moderato.* III *Quasi Menuetto: Allegro Vivace.* IV *Finale; Allegro non assai.*

The *first movement*, a sonata allegro, opens with a rising lyrical theme, A-F-A-E. Some see in this a reference to Joachim's motto ("frei aber einsam"), despite the absence of any objective evidence for such. The second subject is exceedingly attractive and graceful. Despite this, the overall mood is sad if not tragic. The coda contains a very difficult passage in which there is a three-fold conflict of rhythms.

The *second movement*, an ABA form with an involuted, rhythmically sophisticated and rather solemn melody, contains a wonderful violincello canon to a theme that was later used by Richard Strauss in *Don Juan*. The mood continues to be autumnal.

The *third movement* is a slow minuet, ingenious and wistful, with drooping cadences. The polyphonic vivace in duple time with a running rhythm provides a striking contrast.

The *fourth movement* is a vigorous and gay brio movement with a Hungarian flavor. There is no tragedy here, only high spirits and exhilaration.

Commentary. Brahms wrote Dr. Billroth that this quartet arose out of Op. 51, No. 1. It is not conspicuous that it did. The work is more pleasing to play than No. 1, mainly because of its more melodic character. Like No. 1, it seems a little pedantic, but it is a splendid and masterful treatment of the form. It is not an easy work for amateurs but very satisfying once gotten in hand. Pleasure—3; Effort—3.

Quartet in B-flat major, Op. 67 | (1875)

I *Vivace.* II *Andante.* III *Agitato: Allegretto non troppo.*
IV *Poco allegretto con variazione.*

The *first movement,* in which the viola has prominence, is light-hearted, teasing and cheerful. It mingles horn-calls in 6/8 meter with Czech dances in 2/4 meter. Some see the horn-calls as a reference to Mozart's "Hunt" quartet, K.458, in the same key.

The *second movement,* a freely conceived andante in ABA form, opens with a religious theme. The central section modulates widely and restlessly, after which the reverent melody returns in an even richer context. The mood is serene and tender.

The *third movement* is a *tour de force* for the viola, scherzo in form and lyrical in style, but having the tempo of a waltz. The instruments other than the viola are muted, a requirement when most of the action is in a middle voice. This partial muting provides a very unusual texture. Brahms called the movement amorous and affectionate.

The finale, eight Mozartean or Haydnesque variations on a plain melody that resembles a folk-song, projects a mood of serenity and happiness. Thematic material from the *first movement* is brought into the melodic content of the last two variations.

Commentary. This quartet is a sharp contrast to those of Op. 51. Where they are studied, pedantic and a little heavy, this is relaxed and light. Both the style and the content seem clear references to Haydn and Mozart. Even the great prominence given the viola may be seen as a tribute to Mozart. This is the easiest of the Brahms quartets to play if the violist is up to a demanding part. Perhaps the relative neglect of this work is due to its rather unusual character for Brahms. All amateur quartets should play it. Certainly no violist will turn down the chance! Pleasure—3; Effort—3.

DEBUSSY (1863–1918)

Achille-Claude Debussy's chamber music came in two small episodes, the string quartet from 1893, and the three sonatas "pour divers instruments" from 1915–17. He finished the quartet when he was thirty, just after starting the *Prelude to the Afternoon of a Faun* (1892) and just at the time he was beginning *Pelléas et Mélisande.*

The quartet is more formal and academic than anything Debussy had written until then. This formality may reflect the influence of Chausson, a disciple of Franck (which Debussy was not) who was then the academic master of French composition. Chausson's friendship with Debussy was very close, and Debussy regarded him almost as an older brother. The rather academic nature of the quartet is evident in its formal structure, in the use of Franck's then-popular cyclical form, in the fact that titles were given to the movements and in the assignment by Debussy of an opus number, which he did for no other work. Its key designation refers to its opening in the Phrygian mode on G with the flatted supertonic.

Chausson did not view the quartet kindly, and this may have contributed to the abrupt severance of his friendship in 1894. Debussy, in an effort at conciliation, told Chausson that he would write another quartet "in a more dignified form," but he never did. This promise accounts for the fact that it was called "first quartet" when it was published. No other hints of a second have ever come up. This quartet was well received by the public at its premier by the Ysaye Quartet in December 1893, the group to which it is dedicated.

Experts see Russian influences in the quartet, especially the influence of Borodin. Like many French composers of the period, Debussy studied and admired the Russians, especially after he visited Russia in 1880. The pizzicato scherzo in this work is seen as a reference to the pizzicato scherzo of Tchaikovsky's Fourth Symphony.

Quartet in G minor, Op. 10 | (1893)

I *Animé et tres décidé.* II *Assez vif et bien rhythmé.* III *Andantino, doucement expressif.* IV *Tres modéré; Tres mouvemente et avec passion.*

The *first movement* opens directly with a generating or motto theme, a square and solid declamation that comes to dominate the whole work in derivative forms. A flowing second subject follows and continues with a long sequence until, after a pause, there is a development. The recapitulation omits the second subject. The spirit throughout the movement remains like a declamation, a sort of exposition of what is to follow.

The *second movement,* a scherzo, gives a sprightly derivative of the generating theme of the *first movement* to the viola, the other voices accompanying in pizzicato. Later, the generating theme appears in other modifications, including compression and augmentation, in the other voices.

The *third movement,* a funereal andantino, uses thematic material that is only remotely related to the generating theme of the *first movement.* The opening theme, entering at the fifth bar, is suave and lyrical. A middle section is notable for its subdued beginning with a sustained building to a tremendous climax, after which the opening melody reappears.

The energetic *fourth movement* begins with an introduction, again presenting the generating theme in modified form. The following allegro uses yet another modification of the generating theme as its second subject, and the generating theme itself returns in the coda.

Commentary. Amateurs avoid this work because it sounds so difficult. Its difficulties are largely harmonic, however, and to some degree rhythmic. It is quite easy music to grasp, and the rather classical form makes it seem even familiar. The work is not really difficult in the technical sense either. Accomplished amateurs should not hesitate to undertake it. Knowledge of this quartet from the inside vastly enhances appreciation of this masterpiece. Pleasure—4; Effort—3.

DVORÁK (1841–1904)

Bohemia, the part of the Czech Republic centered on Prague, is an ancient national entity that has long struggled to preserve its identity in the troubled history of central Europe. Antonin Leopold Dvorák's roots were thoroughly planted in Bohemian tradition. His native village, Nelahovezes, is located in an agricultural district not far from Prague. His father, from an old local family, was an innkeeper and butcher there as well as a good amateur musician. His mother, also of local origin, was a domestic servant to a local nobleman, Prince Lobkowitz.

Antonin was their first child, but four more sons and three daughters followed. The boy's early years were spent in the pub atmosphere of the inn in a stable society where Bohemian traditions persisted relatively free of foreign influences. He began school at the age of eight, where he soon took up the violin under the instruction of the musical schoolmaster.

Austria then dominated Bohemia, and German was the language of commerce. Accordingly, his father determined that Antonin should learn German, sending him at the age of twelve to Zlonice, a nearby town, where he was to continue his education while living in the home of an uncle. The headmaster of the Zlonice school, Antonin Liehmann, was a musician, and so Dvorák studied not only German but also the organ, piano, violin, viola, and composition. He probably neglected his German studies for, when the whole Dvorák family moved to Zlonice two years later, Antonin was sent on to Boehmische-Kamnitz (in the Sudetenland) to concentrate on German as an apprentice to a miller. A year later the youth returned to Zlonice, now apprenticed to a butcher but putting his real energies into music, with Liehmann's support. After considerable pressure, the elder Dvorák relented in his efforts to make his eldest son a butcher and allowed him to enter the Organ School in Prague at the age of sixteen. Here he became an enthusiast for the German romantic tradition, especially for the music of Wagner. At the end of the two-year curriculum, he graduated second in the class of twelve, being considered as proficient in performance but weak in theory.

The Organ School graduates mainly found posts as church musicians, but the young Dvorák rejected that course to become a violist in a popular orchestra. That orchestra soon became the nucleus of a new Czech National Orchestra, formed to support a new indigenous opera house. Bedrich Smetana, the conductor of the opera orchestra, was then involved in his project to express the spirit of Czech nationalism in operatic composition. As an orchestra player, the still impressionable young violist thus directly confronted the contrast between the new Czech spirit expressed by Smetana and the German romanticism of his training. His response was to compose tirelessly.

In the twelve years from 1859, when he left the Organ School, until 1871, when he emerged as a composer, he wrote and destroyed many works. Those that survive betray the continuing influence of German models, Mozart, Schubert, Beethoven, and Wagner. The chamber music of this period is now rarely heard.

1871 saw his first public appearance as a composer with the performance in Prague of an overture he wrote for a comic opera. The performance of his *Hymnus* for choir and orchestra in 1872 further established his career as a composer.

Dvořák had taken students to support himself in part, and thus he met the daughters of a goldsmith named Cermakova. In a history reminiscent of Mozart's involvement with the Weber family, he first made advances to one daughter, Josefa, but married another, Anna, in 1873. Now established, he gave up his job as a violist and became a church organist.

He began to submit works in a competition for a state grant established in 1863 by the Austrian government for the support of artists. Among the judges were Hanslick, the noted music critic, Johan Herbeck, conductor of the Vienna State Opera, and Johannes Brahms. Their recognition of his gifts and their support soon brought him to the attention of a wider public.

Dvořák remained in Prague, increasingly supporting himself and his family by composing. Two family tragedies, the death of an infant daughter in 1875 and the death of his mother in 1882 disturbed the even course of his life over the next many years. His spreading fame brought him to visit England in 1884 where an enormous success produced further commissions. He undertook further tours to London and to Berlin in the next few years, and he received honorary degrees from the Czech University at Prague and from Cambridge University in 1891. That year he accepted a post as professor of composition at the Prague Conservatory, which had recently amalgamated with his alma mater, the Organ School. The next year he went to the United States for his notable American visit.

A wealthy New Yorker, Mrs. Jeanette Thurber, invited him to be director of a National Conservatory of Music which she had established there in 1885. Besides money, Mrs. Thurber possessed energy and ambition. Dvorák finally yielded to her entreaties and embarked with his wife, two of his children and a young friend, Joseph Kovarik, arriving to a warm reception. Dvorák was not altogether happy in New York, and at first he intended to return to Bohemia at the end of the term. For various reasons, however, he chose instead to spend the summer at Spillville, Iowa, a Bohemian community where Kovarik's father was church choirmaster.

The Dvoráks sent for the remaining children from Prague, and the whole family arrived in Spillville in June 1893. At the end of that happy summer, Dvorák returned with his family to New York. When he returned to Bohemia in May 1894, he promised the persistent Mrs. Thurber to return to New York after a five-month leave. His third visit to New York, begun that autumn, was no happier than the earlier two visits had been. This American period is notable for the great works that it produced, including the *American* Quartet, the *New World* Symphony, and the Cello Concerto.

Back in Prague, the fifty-four-year-old composer resumed his post at the Conservatory and continued composing, soon completing the last two string quartets. He gave much time to his long ambition to write a really successful opera, producing *Rusalka*, the only one of his several operas to achieve much renown. He slowly declined from the effects of general arteriosclerosis and uremia, dying on May 1st, 1904, of a stroke.

A problem exists for the Dvorák string quartets in that the opus numbers do not represent the order of composition. One must think of the quartets chronologically in order to gain a sense of the whole body of work. Dvorák's compositional style and technique evolved continuously, but one can cluster his quartets in two groups, the formative quartets and the mature quartets.

The formative quartets, written from 1862 through 1874, are either not surviving or not much played currently. They are said to reflect the sequential study of stylistic models, first the classic school, then Wagner, then Liszt and Smetana. The period

1876–77 was a turning point in Dvořák's life, for he was bereaved at that time and made the acquaintance of Brahms. The results of the emotional maturation that comes with bereavement together with Brahms's support soon led to works that made Dvořák internationally famous. Thus, the mature quartets, written from 1876 through 1895, constitute the more important works, but not all of them remain in the current popular repertoire.

The last three quartets are closely related to Dvořák's time spent in America. The *American* Quartet (Op. 96) was written during the summer spent in Iowa in a Czech community. Opp. 105 and 106 reflect his feelings upon his return to Bohemia after what had not been a wholly happy visit to the New World.

Aside from the *American* Quartet, the Dvořák quartets are not widely familiar among concertgoers and amateur players. They deserve a broader acquaintance, and amateur players would be well served by getting to know them. The following list of works from 1873 and later is chronological. It may help to allay the confusion created by the opus numbers, which were given in order of publication.

Quartet in F minor, Op. 9 (1873).
Quartet in A minor, Op. 12 (1873).
Quartet in A minor, Op. 16 (1874).
Quartet in E major, Op. 80 (also called Op. 29) (1876).
Quartet in D minor, Op. 34 (1877).
Quartet in E-flat major, Op. 51 (1878-79).
Two Waltzes, Op. 54 (1880).
Quartet Movement in F major, no opus (1881).
Quartet in C major, Op. 61 (1881).
Evening Songs ("Cypresses"), no opus (1887)
Quartet in F major, Op. 96, "The American Quartet" (1893).
Quartet in G major, Op. 106 (1895).
Quartet in A-flat major, Op. 105 (1895).

Quartet in E major, Op. 80, also called Op. 29 | (1876)

I *Allegro.* II *Andante con moto.* III *Allegretto scherzando.*
IV *Finale: Allegro con brio.*

The *first movement*, in sonata allegro form, uses Slavonic coloration to deal with expressive thematic material that is pervaded by tender sadness.

In the *second movement*, in A minor, two themes, both somber and touching Slavonic songs, create a miniature that is noble and full of pathos. Elements of the dumky (elegy) form are incipient in this poignant movement.

The *third movement* has a Schumannesque melancholy and a romantic waltz theme. The trio, in C-sharp minor, features strong dynamic contrasts.

The *fourth movement* is a remarkably agitated allegro with extensive triplet figures. The opening theme of the *first movement* reappears at the end.

Commentary. The prevailing tone of this quartet is a gentle melancholy, probably reflecting Dvořák's recent bereavement. The slow movement has occasioned particular enthusiasm. The fine technique of composition reflects the composer's study of Beethoven. The quartet was written immediately before the *Stabat Mater.* It is a fine and serious work. Amateurs should not hesitate to undertake it. Pleasure—2; Effort—2.

Quartet in D minor, Op. 34 | (1877)

I *Allegro.* II *Alla Polka: Allegretto scherzando.* III *Adagio.*
IV *Finale: Poco Allegro.*

The *first movement* uses two closely related themes that also influence the theme of the slow movement. The mood is melancholy, and the style is Schubertian.

The *second movement* scherzo presents an idealized polka. The trio is a smooth Czech version of the Ländler with a tender theme, partly in the bass.

The *third movement*, a hesitant song that forms the climax of the work, is broad, profound, warm and noble. The scoring is rather orchestral with the strings muted. The first theme of the *first move-ment* returns at the end.

In the agitated *fourth movement*, the pervasive melancholy is not dissipated.

Commentary. Although Dvořák dedicated this melancholy quartet to Brahms, he did not imitate him. Its mood reflects the recent family tragedy, like the preceding E major quartet, but this work is even more serious, intimate and original. The slow movement is especially admired. Pleasure—2; Effort—2.

Quartet in E-flat major, Op. 51 | (1879)

I *Allegro ma non troppo.* II *Dumka (Elegie): Andante con moto.*
III *Romanze: Andante con moto.* IV *Finale: Allegro assai.*

The *first movement* has a warm and happy first theme and a polka sec-ond subject. It presents a Bohemian mood of optimism and cheer throughout.

The *second movement*, a dumka (elegy) in G minor, features sections of strongly contrasting mood. The two sections here grow out of the same thematic material. The theme in the andante is a melancholy dia-logue in the violin and viola over a pizzicato accompaniment. In the furiant, it appears as a wild dance.

The *third movement*, a noble romance, is a tender and poetic nocturne.

In the *fourth movement*, based on a Czech dance called the scocna, a sort of reel, a wanton and sportive tune is contrasted with another more meditative tune. Material from the *first movement* appears as a contrapuntal element. The movement ends in a furiant.

Commentary. This quartet was Dvořák's response to a request from the Florentine Quartet for a work in the Slavonic style. It is one of the most attractive and individualistic of his quartets. The mood through-out is one of frank cheer and good humor. Accomplished amateurs can readily play it. Pleasure—3; Effort—2.

Quartet in C major, Op. 61 | (1881)

I *Allegro.* II *Poco adagio e molto cantabile.* III *Allegro vivace.*
IV *Finale: Vivace.*

The *first movement*, in sonata form, opens with a beautiful theme that
might have been conceived by Beethoven, but the second theme is
less expressive. The beginning of the movement owes much to
Beethoven in style with Dvorák emerging more as himself in the closing sections.

The *second movement*, a ternary adagio in F major, involves a tender
dialogue between the two violins alternating with a dreamy, mournful melody. The mode fluctuates often from major to minor. Some see
a mixture of the styles of Beethoven, Schubert, and Chopin in this
movement.

The *third movement* is strictly classical in form. The style in the first
and last sections, in A minor, resembles that of Beethoven, while the
trio, in A major, is Schubertian.

The *fourth movement* is resolutely Slavonic. This is a joyous and bright
movement, bold and extended.

Commentary. This quartet was so eagerly awaited that its advent
was announced by its dedicatee, Hellmesberger, even before it was
composed! It is deficient in nationalistic character, being rather imitative in its style. Despite that, it is a finely made work, charming, poetic
and strong. It is a fine work in the Germanic tradition, worthy of a
reading. It is, however, not really characteristic Dvorák but a well
crafted rather pedantic work. Pleasure—3; Effort—3.

Quartet in F major, Op. 96 | (1895), *The American Quartet*

I *Allegro ma non troppo.* II *Lento.* III *Molto vivace.* IV *Finale: vivace
ma non troppo.*

The *first movement* opens with a calm and lyrical theme. Two other
themes of similar character follow and the three are treated in characteristic style to produce a uniform mood of calm and placid
reflection.

The *second movement* is a rhapsodic lento, a poignant melody soaring over a rocking rhythmic figure. This is Dvorák at his most lyrical.

The *third movement* is a set of miniature variations on a simple bright theme. Dvořák said that the theme was inspired in part by the singing of a red and black bird, probably a scarlet tanager. The brusque rhythms, the abrupt and violent outbursts, and the open fifths give this movement a somewhat exotic character.

The *fourth movement* is a gay rondo, a Bohemian hoedown, alternately humorous and passionate. It contains a short imitation of a chorale, possibly an allusion to the church at Spillville, Iowa, where Dvořák played the organ.

Commentary. This inspired work, finished in only fifteen days, is justly popular for its spontaneity, simplicity, and unity of character. It is highly individualistic but not especially difficult, and so it should be a favorite of all amateur players. It reflects Dvořák's mood during a summer spent in the rural Czech community in Iowa after a trying season in New York. Pleasure—4; Effort—3.

Quartet in G major, Op. 106 | (1895)

I *Allegro moderato.* II *Adagio ma non troppo.* III *Molto vivace.*
IV *Andante sostenuto; Allegro con fuoco.*

The *first movement* opens with a simple joyous theme, a rich subject in broad-based triplets. The cantabile second theme, more nationalistic in character, recurs again in the finale. This bold and large-scale movement is persistently warm, joyous, highly original and characteristic.

The *second movement* is built on a single broad and intimate theme. The character is grave at first, then more agitated, and finally strongly hymnal. This movement has a massive architecture. It is considered by some to be the finest slow movement in the Dvořák quartets.

The *third movement* begins as an ingenious scherzo marked by a roughness that contrasts strongly with the antecedent monumental adagio. The rich triads and pedal point of the trio contrast strongly with the Bohemian spirit of the molto vivace.

The *fourth movement*, after a slow introduction, presents a joyful leading theme that is then treated in contrast with a melanchology quotation of a theme from the *first movement*. These episodes present a conflict in which warmth and brightness win at the end.

Commentary. Some critics consider the first two movements to be the finest movements of Dvorák's chamber music. The last two movements are by no means weak. The work, overall, reflects Dvofiák's joyful mood upon his return to his homeland from America. It is a difficult work, not to be undertaken by amateurs casually. It is, however, a landmark that ambitious amateurs should undertake sometime. Pleasure—4; Effort—4.

Quartet in A-flat major, Op. 105 | (1895)

I *Adagio ma non troppo: Allegro appassionato.* II *Molto vivace.*
III *Lento e molto cantabile. I Allegro non tanto.*

The slow introduction of the *first movement* gives no hint of the sunny spirit of the allegro that follows, although it provides the basis for the principal theme of the *first movement* and the opening theme of the *second.* The sonata allegro is structurally conventional. The mood is idyllic and cheerful throughout.

The *second movement* is considered by many critics to be the finest scherzo that Dvorák wrote. The first and last sections have the nature of a furiant. The suave middle section has a more lyrical theme treated canonically in the violins.

The *third movement* begins with a simple folk melody that expands to become rich and warm. After an agitated middle section, the folk song returns to be treated with figuration.

In the joyful *fourth movement,* highly ingenious devices produce a rondo of great interest and excitement. The movement is very long.

Commentary. Some critics consider this an inferior work to Op. 106, but others do not. All movements are fine, especially the scherzo. Written just after Op. 106, it also reflects Dvorák's mood on his return to his home. It is not at all easy, but it is a quartet that prepared amateurs should undertake. It is warmly recommended. Pleasure—4; Effort—4.

FAURÉ (1845–1924)

Gabriel-Urbain Fauré's antecedents in the region where he was born, in the little town of Pamiers near Carcassone, were butchers. His father, Toussaint-Honoré, abandoned the family trade to be a schoolmaster and he was already employed as such when he married, at nineteen, Marie-Antoinette-Helen Lalene, daughter of a retired army officer. Gabriel was the last of six children, born on May 12th, 1845. He was "put out to nurse," that is, raised in a foster home, until the age of four when he returned to his family, now living at Montgauzy near Foix, where his father had a post as director of a teachers' college.

A silent and thoughtful child, he was attracted to music early, frequenting a local chapel where he taught himself to play the harmonium. His gift was so clear that he was sent, at the age of nine, to a music school operated by Louis Niedermeyer in Paris that trained church organists, choirmasters and music teachers. The boy's talents and the family's reduced circumstances led to the waiver of the usual fees. In this school the young Fauré met Saint-Saens, a teacher only ten years older than his pupil, and the older man did much to foster the boy's education.

Fauré graduated in 1865, at the age of twenty, with many distinctions and he quickly found a position as a church organist in Brittany. A short time later he returned to Paris as an organist in various Parisian churches. He also returned to the Niedermeyer school on the teaching staff.

Fauré had been composing from his student years and by 1878 he had begun to publish some works, though not always with a profit. The two piano quartets from 1879 and 1886 were quickly published though he was paid nothing for them.

His engagement to Marianne Viardot was broken off after four years in 1877, despite, or perhaps because of, her own musical abilities and her family connections to prominent musicians and artists of the day. Instead, he married a woman of more domestic temperament, Marie Fremiet, the daughter of a celebrated sculptor.

He advanced to be a principal organist at the Madeleine in Paris and he pursued his career as a composer quite slowly, supplementing his income by teaching privately. Success came gradually. In 1892 he became an inspector of music instruction in state-supported music schools, and in 1896, after the age of fifty, he finally became a professor of composition at the Paris Conservatory, a post for which his applications had previously been rejected. He occupied a chair left by Massenet who had resigned in a pique over not being appointed to succeed Ambroise Thomas as Director of the Conservatory.

In his new post, he educated a whole generation of French musicians, including such giants as Nadia Boulanger and Maurice Ravel, and he indirectly influenced many others. His position and fame also brought him occasions to travel, and they allowed him to pursue composition more enthusiastically than ever before.

In 1905, the Director of the Conservatory resigned and Fauré was appointed to replace him. His appointment to the director-ship was a part of a far-reaching program of reform in the cur-riculum of the Conservatory, one designed to broaden the scope of training, in contrast to the narrow focus on purely technical instruction which had come to characterize its curricu-lum. In his role as a reformer, he found himself at the center of a conflict that lasted a long time, but he remained, ultimately to succeed in bringing about the needed changes. He also came to other positions of great responsibility in the musical life of Paris.

His deafness had begun to be appreciable in 1903, and it had become severely limiting by 1910. It was probably a familial affliction. For a long time, he did not allow it to limit him, but it finally led to his resignation from the directorship of the Conservatory in 1920.

He led a life of semi-retirement in his last years, often win-tering in the South, partly because of his chronic bronchitis. He slowly declined, dying at his home in Paris (Passy) on November 4th, 1924, shortly after completing work on his string quartet.

The string quartet was quite likely meant for a final revision that was precluded by his death. It was written at the request of his publisher, Jacques Durand. Fauré had doubts about his abil-ity to deal with the technical problems of composing for four stringed instruments alone, and he left the decision about the publication of the quartet to be made after his death by a small group of his students and friends. The quartet was not received well by the public, and it has never firmly entered the standard repertoire. It is a serene and peaceful work, exhibiting Fauré's mature idiom and technique. Some see it as having imperfections owing to the fact that he had no time left to revise it. Sentimental commentaries have been made that claim to find in it evidence of a last testament, of melancholy, renunciation and farewell. It is not a last testament, but rather the last mature work by a revered composer.

Quartet in E minor, Op. 121 | (1924)

I *Allegro moderato.* II *Andante.* III *Allegro.*

The *first movement,* a brief sonata allegro, opens with a thematic dialogue between violin and viola. The themes are borrowed from his unfinished and unpublished concerto for violin written forty-five years earlier. Major and minor modes are gracefully opposed and superimposed throughout. A serene coda leads to an unexpectedly lush ending.

The *second movement* is a peaceful andante, generously melodic and harmonically spare, with chains of unresolved discords. Three themes are treated extensively before a coda ends the movement. The movement places the viola in special prominence.

The *third movement* is a scherzo, "of a light and pleasant character," said the composer. The first theme at the opening passes from cello to viola to first violin, with a pizzicato accompaniment. A second lyrical theme appears in the cello. The two themes are treated in quasi-rondo form and in counterpoint, the whole being held together by pizzicato passages.

Commentary. This interesting work lacks extreme contrasts of mood. This characterizes many of Fauré's compositions. It is a fine example of Fauré's work, and it should interest those who are endeared to the idiom or who wish to explore the development of French chamber music. It is fully accessible to amateurs technically, but it will be difficult musically for those who are not attuned to Fauré's serene lyricism and harmonic subtlety. Unfortunately, many are not. Pleasure—2; Effort—3.

FRANCK (1822–1890)

César Franck, a prodigy, entered the Paris Conservatory at fifteen, but after his graduation at twenty he led a life of some obscurity for thirty years, teaching, performing and composing. In 1872, at fifty, he became professor of organ at the Paris Conservatory where he soon attracted a devoted following of students to his classes in organ and composition. He, along with Fauré, established a new direction for French music by the compositions of his later years, helping to free it from its operatic traditions. It is remarkable that this development fell to a man of such serene and unprepossessing temperament and so late in his life. His few pieces of chamber music were the first important body of such work written in France in the nineteenth century. They constitute the following major works:

> Piano Trio in F-sharp minor (1840).
> Piano Trio in B-flat major (1840).
> Piano Trio in B minor (1840).
> Piano Trio in B major (1842).
> Piano Quintet in F minor (1879).
> Sonata for Violin and Piano in A major (1886).
> String Quartet in D major (1889).

Of the last three works, written after his major period of composition began, the string quartet is the least known today. It was well received at its premier performance in 1890.

Quartet in D major | (1889)

I *Poco lento; Allegro.* II *Scherzo: Vivace.* III *Larghetto.*
IV *Finale: Allegro molto.*

The *first movement* opens in lento with a grand *Lied* theme treated fully and chromatically for some eighty bars before the sonata exposition. There is then a return to the *Lied* theme of the opening lento, now treated fugally, followed by the bright sonata allegro again. The lento *Lied* theme appears again to end the movement. This large movement repeatedly contrasts the mysterious and majestic spirit of the lento with the brighter mood of the allegro.

The *second movement* is Mendelssohnian in spirit, an elfin and muted dance. The quiet contrasting mood of the trio contains a brief fragmentary reference to the lento *Lied* theme of the *first movement*. This is a most charming movement.

The *third movement*, larghetto, is an extended *Lied* in five sections, one of which refers to a theme from the trio of the preceding scherzo. D'Indy considered this movement to be as noble and lofty as any of the great Beethoven quartet andantes.

The *fourth movement*, a sonata allegro, begins with an introduction in which themes from the previous movements are offered in little episodes. The choice settles on the lento *Lied* theme that opens the *first movement*, and a monumental finale follows. The movement is as grand in scope as any similar movement is in Beethoven, and as deeply felt and personal.

Commentary. It is hard to understand the neglect of this wonderful work by amateurs. It is by no means easy to play but it is fully accessible to experienced amateurs, both musically and technically. Franck's idiom is familiar from the Symphony, and that idiom characterizes this work, with its thickly held chords, its tonal shifting and its cyclic interlocking of movements. D'Indy praised this work mightily, but his praise may reflect a degree of chauvinism. Amateurs should not undertake this work lightly. Modern players may find it to be long, complicated, and a bit too much to undertake for an evening of casual reading. It is massive, just as the late Beethoven quartets are massive, and it bears just as much study. Pleasure—2; Effort—4.

GRIEG (1843–1907)

Chamber music was not an important medium for Edvard Hagerup Grieg. His German education at Leipzig had acquainted him with the character of chamber music, but the nationalistic and impressionistic style he developed after he returned to Norway did not easily fit the requirements of the German quartet tradition. Aside from the three sonatas for violin and piano and the one for cello and piano, the single completed string quartet is his only piece of chamber music. A second quartet was uncompleted at his death.

He wrote his string quartet during the winter of 1877–78 in a remote district where he had built a hut on an isolated hillside in which to compose in solitude. He projected the work in the summer of 1877 and reported it as complete one year later. It required great time and effort to write, and part of the delay resulted from a voluminous correspondence he had with a violinist, Robert Heckmann, about problems of instrumental technique. He wrote to a friend, "You have no idea what a job I have had with the modeling—but that is because I had been near stagnation and that again was the result partly of many 'occasional' works (Peer Gynt, Sigurd Jorsalfar), and other such stupidities, partly of too much popular stuff." He wrote to the same friend that he regarded the work as a preliminary study for another piece of chamber music, the uncompleted second quartet.

The string quartet shows a strong break with the German tradition, a departure which did not go unnoticed by Debussy when he began writing his own string quartet fifteen years later. Polyphony is abandoned here in favor of a strict melodic-harmonic technique. The material is highly nationalistic and has personal reference. Its texture is orchestral, for which it has been criticized, and the intimacy of chamber music is absent. Perhaps these features explain why it is not often heard now and never occupied a central place in the repertoire, though it was much admired by some at one time.

Quartet in G minor, Op. 27 | (1878)

I *Un poco Andante; Allegro molto ed agitato.* II *Romanze: Andantino.* III *Intermezzo: Allegro molto marcato.* IV *Finale: Lento; Presto al Saltarello.*

The *first movement* opens with a powerful slow introduction that presents a motto theme, one that recurs in various forms throughout the whole work. This theme comes from "The Minstrel's Song," a lyric that deals with a Norse legend about a spirit who lures minstrels with the promise to reveal the art of music, only to rob them of happiness and peace of mind. This introduction, in bold unison, is followed by an agitated sonata allegro. Its texture is thick and orchestral, with much double-stopping. The cello states the motto theme again before the coda.

The *second movement* opens with a lyrical passage that features the cello and viola. A sharply contrasting agitato follows. The lyrical and agitato passages are treated in alternation with modifications. The agitato passages contain thematic material derived from the motto theme.

The *third movement* is like a scherzo in form. Both the scherzo and the contrasting trio equivalent are based on dance tunes having the character of folk music. The motto theme, modified, appears at the opening of the movement.

The *fourth movement* features the motto theme in the lento introduction and in the coda. The main body of the movement is a saltarello, a leaping Italian dance form.

Commentary. In this pleasing work, it is interesting to see how the mature Grieg solved the problem of adapting his gift to the restrictions of the string quartet. Traditionalists may not like it, for it lacks the intimacy and the special texture of the string quartet with its dramatic language and heavy scoring. It thus seems an oddity in the context of string quartets, but it represents exactly what one would expect Grieg to do with the form. It offers no major obstacles to experienced amateurs. Pleasure—2; Effort—3.

HAYDN (1732–1809)
Biographical Notes

Eastern lower Austria, where Franz Joseph Haydn was born in the village of Rohrau, is a region of mixed traditions and peoples: Germans, Croatians, Hungarians, and Gipsies. Haydn was of German and Croatian ancestry but he was first exposed to life in a village of heterogeneous character.

Haydn's ancestors were farmers and craftsmen. His father, Mathias, was a wheelwright and an amateur harpist who also owned some land and served as a civil official responsible for overseeing certain activities of the community. His mother, Maria, was a cook in the household of the local gentry before her marriage to Mathias.

Franz Joseph, their second child, was born on March 31st, 1732. His musical gift was apparent early, and his parents sought a musical education for him beyond that available in Rohrau. The opportunity came when a relative, Johann Matthias Franck, offered to take the boy into his home in the nearby town of Hainburg where Franck was a schoolmaster and church choir director.

At Hainburg, the five-year-old boy studied in Franck's school and received his first instruction in the clavier and violin. He also sang in the church choir and helped with domestic duties in the large Franck household. After two years, he left to become a chorister and student at St. Stephen's cathedral in Vienna, recruited there by Karl George Reutter, the chapel master at the cathedral and a Court composer, who had heard the boy soprano on a visit to Hainburg.

Reutter, responsible for Haydn's full maintenance and education, proved to be a stern taskmaster but a negligent guardian. The boy studied singing, the keyboard and the violin, but his general education and that in music theory was neglected. His living conditions were hard and his duties to the church were great. Still, he rose to become a favorite soloist in the cathedral. When his voice changed, a newcomer, his gifted brother, Michael, challenged his eminence in the choir. The end of his schooling came abruptly when he was expelled from the cathedral school as a result of a prank.

Haydn, now seventeen, homeless, penniless and jobless, was taken in by a young church musician and he began to support himself with small jobs playing and teaching. Within a year, a generous loan from a tradesman enabled him to take private quarters where he could follow a program of practice and self-directed study. Soon after, he became the accompanist of a once famous Italian composer and singer in Vienna, Niccolo Porpora, from whom he received instruction in Italian and composition. Nine years of virtually unguided career building ended when he came to the attention of the musically sophisticated aristocratic circles of Vienna.

He found fixed employment as a musician to the household of Count von Morzin where he remained for three years, playing and composing. Thus settled, he married Maria Anna Keller. When the Count gave up his expensive musical retinue, Haydn accepted a similar position with Prince Eszterhazy, thus coming before he was yet thirty to the position he was to occupy for most of the rest of his life.

The influential Eszterhazy Prince, Paul Anton, died soon after Haydn joined the household, but the musical tradition of the family was continued and extended by his successor, Prince Nicolaus. After five years, in 1766, the new Prince built a new palace at Eszterhaza, near Vienna, and Haydn spent the next twenty-three years there as Court musician. This long period was productive and happy, and Haydn's fame slowly spread beyond the German states. The string quartets of Op. 17 through Op. 64 came from this long period. Haydn's friendship with Mozart began in 1781 when Haydn was forty-nine and Mozart was twenty-five.

As time passed, Haydn became dissatisfied at Eszterhaza, probably feeling that he had outgrown the position and needed new challenges. With the death of Prince Nicolaus in 1790, Haydn felt free to leave the post that he had held for so long. The new Prince, Anton, did not share his predecessor's passion for music. Haydn was now financially secure and free of family encumbrances. He had long since adjusted to his unsatisfactory marriage and he and his wife lived separately. He accepted an offer to visit England from Johann Peter Salomon, a German-born violinist and impresario, and he left Vienna in December 1790, for his first London tour.

The first London tour was a great success and Haydn stayed for many months. At the end, he returned to Vienna, having been called home by the Prince, stopping in Bonn where he met the twenty-two year old Beethoven whom he invited to follow him to Vienna as a student. Back in Vienna in July 1792, he was let down. Mozart had died and Beethoven proved to be a difficult student. For these and other reasons he accepted Salomon's invitation for a second London tour and returned in January 1794. The second London tour proved even more triumphant, and Haydn considered staying in England permanently. He did not, however, returning to Vienna after a year and a half, in part because Prince Anton had died and the new Prince Nicolaus wished to re-establish the musical Court of his grandfather. The quartets of Op. 71 through Op. 76 came from the years surrounding the London tours.

Back home, Haydn was disappointed with the new Prince. He had unusual musical tastes and a tyrannical manner. Though Haydn felt ill-used, his duties were not burdensome and he had much time for composition.

In the spring of 1800, Haydn suffered his first serious illness since childhood. With his recovery after several months, he found his powers diminished. After 1803, when he was unable to complete his last string quartet, he virtually ceased efforts at composition. He reviewed his life work, compiling a catalog in

1805. He made his last public appearance in 1808, becoming house bound and then bedfast, dying on May 31st, 1809, shortly after the second French occupation of Vienna.

HAYDN, Opp. 1–3

These early Haydn quartets are little played today. They interest mainly those who are devoted to the study of the evolution of the modern form. An "Op. 0" in E-flat that was discovered late is not generally known. The sets that we now know as Opp. 1 and 2 display the evolution of the quartet form from that of the symphony. Opinions as to the dates of their composition vary from 1750 to 1760, but it was probably late in that decade. The six quartets in Op. 3 are not now considered by everyone to be authentic. Some experts say that they are probably the work of a Benedictine monk, Romanus Hoffstetter, who was an admirer of Haydn, but that contention remains controversial.

There was some confusion created by the first publication of Opp. 1 and 2 since the works published then as sets were not consistent in their groupings. There is no reason to regard these twelve quartets as having been written as sets, like the sets of the later opuses, nor is it necessarily true that the set we now know as Op. 2 is later than the set we now call Op. 1. Indeed, the provenance of these works remains so controversial that we, as players, can only deal with them as though they were unquestioned, in their order as published in the prevalent modern editions. Since the numbering of these works may vary among editions, this book follows that given in the Eulenberg scores, which corresponds to that in the Peters editions.

These early quartets are now collectively called the quartet-divertimenti or the quadri-cassazione. Derived in form from the baroque suite, they are written typically in major keys, and they usually contain five movements, two of them minuets, following the order of allegro, minuet, adagio, minuet, and presto or allegro. All movements generally have the same key, except that the trios of the minuets lie usually in the minor, and the adagio in the subdominant or tonic minor.

In character, these quartets are simple and cheerful, having roots in folk music and having been written as popular entertainments. They often lack the melodic interplay among the instruments characteristic of the later quartets, and the simple writing often includes octave doubling to achieve two-part harmony. They contain fine melodies, however, and amateurs can enjoy them as showing early evidence of the use that Haydn was later to make of the form.

Quartet in B-flat major, Op. 1, No. 1

I *Presto.* II *Menuetto.* III *Adagio.* IV *Menuetto.* V *Presto*

Quartet in E-flat major, Op. 1, No. 2

I *Allegro molto.* II *Menuetto.* III *Adagio.* IV *Menuetto.* V *Presto*

Quartet in D major, Op. 1, No. 3

I *Adagio.* II *Menuetto.* III *Presto.* IV *Menuetto. Trio.* V *Presto*

The *first movement* resembles a baroque trio sonata, with the violins in dialog and the two lower strings providing a continuo.

The *third movement*, a ternary presto, constitutes the center of gravity of the work.

The *fourth movement* minuet consists of two lines (two voices to each line) working in contrast. Its trio in the tonic minor has the same simple plan.

Quartet in G major, Op. 1, No. 4

I *Presto.* II *Menuetto I.* III *Adagio.* IV *Menuetto II.* V *Presto*

Quartet in B-flat major, Op. 1, No. 5

I *Allegro.* II *Andante.* III *Allegro molto.*

This work was written originally as a symphony. The string parts, minus the wind parts, were substituted for a quartet in E flat major that was originally in this place in the opus.

Quartet in C major, Op. 1, No. 6

I *Presto assai.* II *Menuetto.* III *Adagio.* IV *Menuetto.* V *Finale. Presto.*

Quartet in A major, Op. 2, No. 1

I *Allegro.* II *Menuetto.* III *Poco Adagio.* IV *Menuetto.* V *Allegro molto.*

The *third movement* poco adagio is notable.

Quartet in E major, Op. 2, No. 2

I *Allegro.* II *Menuetto.* III *Adagio.* IV *Menuetto.* V *Finale. Presto.*

The *third movement* adagio is particularly fine.

Quartet in E-flat major, Op. 2, No. 3

I *Allegro molto.* II *Menuetto.* III *Adagio.* IV *Menuetto.* V *Finale. Allegro.*

This work was first written and published as a sextet with two horns. Publishers simply dropped the horn parts in later editions to make it a string quartet.

Quartet in F major, Op. 2, No. 4

I *Presto.* II *Menuetto I.* III *Adagio non troppo.* IV *Menuetto II.* V *Allegro.*

The *fourth movement* minuet exhibits Haydn's musical sense of humor in an especially conspicuous way.

Quartet in D major, Op. 2, No. 5

I *Presto.* II *Menuetto.* III *Largo cantabile, alla breve.* IV *Menuetto.* V *Finale. Presto.*

Like No. 3, this work was first written and published as a sextet. Publishers simply dropped the two horn parts in later editions to make it a string quartet.

Quartet in B-flat major, Op. 2, No. 6

I *Adagio (Andante).* II *Menuetto.* III *Presto.* IV *Menuetto.* V. *Presto*

The *first movement* adagio constitutes an extended theme with four variations. The bass and the harmonic structure remain constant, the variations consisting of decoration of the melody.

The *third movement,* like that of Op. 1, No. 3, is built of two lines (two voices to each line) presented in opposition.

The *fifth movement* presto is an early example of Haydn's use of the sonata form.

Quartet in E major, Op. 3, No. 1

I *Allegro molto.* II *Menuetto.* III *Andantino grazioso.* IV *Presto.*

The minuet of this quartet is comparable to the bagpipe minuet of Op. 3, No. 3. The andantino movement is particularly fine.

Quartet in C major, Op. 3, No. 2

I *Fantasia con Variazione. Andante.* II *Menuetto.* III *Presto.*

Experts have little to say about Haydn's use here of only three movements.

Quartet in G major, Op. 3, No. 3

I *Presto.* II *Largo.* III *Menuetto.* IV *Presto.*

This is the work with the famous bagpipe minuet.

Quartet in B-flat major, Op. 3, No. 4

I *Allegro moderato.* II *Adagio. Presto.*

This is a strange work, two sonata-form movements in unrelated keys. There is no generally accepted explanation for this deviance from the standard arrangement.

Quartet in F major, Op. 3, No. 5

I *Presto.* II *Andante cantabile (Die sogenannte Serenade).*
III *Menuetto.* IV *Scherzando.*

Tovey singled out this work as particularly notable. The serenade movement has become famous.

Quartet in A major, Op. 3, No. 6

I Presto. II *Adagio.* III *Menuetto.* IV *Scherzando.*

The menuetto movement is notable.

Commentary on Opp. 1–3. For avocational players, these eighteen quartets can be a source of great joy. Their beauty comes in part from their purity and simplicity. Scholars study these as a means to discover Haydn's maturation as a composer. We can enjoy them as a means to discover Haydn's character and genius at the outset.

In general, the six quartets in Op. 3 give players more to work with than the earlier ones. Those for which specific notes exist above can be taken as somewhat more suitable than the others for casual study, but everyone must have somewhat different tastes and opinions. Pleasure—2; Effort—1.

HAYDN, Op. 9

The six quartets in Op. 9 were written sometime between 1768 and 1791, some say in 1769 when Haydn was thirty-seven. Nearly ten years had elapsed since Op. 2. Here, he established the rule of four movements with the minuet in second place. The development sections in the sonata movements are expanded in comparison to those of the earlier quartets. The first violin parts are more virtuosic with brilliant runs and a greater use of the higher registers. This may reflect the fact that Haydn had a violinist in his orchestra, Luigi Tomasini, who could play such parts. Op. 9 is clearly linked to Op. 17, which was written in 1771.

Op. 9 represents an advance over the earlier sets of quartets in several ways other than in the more complex first violin parts. The opening movements in sonata form are more extended with a broader treatment, a more extended sense of development and more exciting modulations, and they show the beginnings of monothematicism. The minuets are more highly developed and begin to incorporate sonata principles. The slow movements are generally more prominent and extended. The finales, however, remain relatively unchanged from those of the first two opuses.

Quartet in C major, Op 9, No. 1

I *Moderato.* II *Menuetto: Poco Allegretto.* III *Adagio.* IV *Finale: Presto.*

The *first movement* is spacious and soaring with most of the action given to the first violin, but the other voices carry out some lovely dialogue in the development.

The *second movement* is sprightly enough but undistinguished.

The *third movement,* a sicilienne, presents a florid and rather uplifting melody in the first violin, with relatively little action for the other voices.

The *fourth movement* deals with its lively arpeggiated theme in a brief sonata, without much innovation.

Quartet in E-flat major, Op. 9, No. 2

I *Moderato.* II *Menuetto.* III *Adagio: Cantabile.* IV *Allegro molto*

The leaping arpeggiated theme of the *first movement* receives a virtuosic treatment in the first violin part.

The *second movement* minuet is small and simple.

The *third movement* constitutes an Italianate recitative and aria, given out by the first violin over a simple accompaniment. It has elements that suggest the slow movement of a concerto, especially in the two fermatas that incorporate little cadenzas.

The *fourth movement* allocates its spirited action fairly well among the voices.

Quartet in G major, Op. 9, No. 3

I *Allegro moderato.* II *Menuetto: Allegretto* III *Largo.* IV *Finale: Presto.*

Quartet in D minor, Op. 9, No. 4

I *Allegro moderato*. II *Menuetto*. III *Adagio cantabile*. IV *Presto*.

The *first movement*, in sonata form, is dark and somber in mood. The weighty meter and the dramatic echoing theme produce a striking effect.

The *second movement* is a large minuet in the major mode with a tempo rather slower than the one that was then conventional for minuets. The trio is remarkable for its tonic major key and for the three part-harmony used in a duet for the violins, the first violin playing double stops.

The *third movement*, a consistently restful and profound adagio, explores the sustained quietness to be found in the adagios of the later quartets by Haydn and by Beethoven.

The *fourth movement* is a quick and brilliant presto with a virtuosic part in the first violin. The development section is very extensive for the period.

Quartet in B-flat major, Op. 9, No. 5

I *Poco Adagio*. II *Menuetto: Allegretto*. III *Largo cantabile*. IV *Presto*.

Quartet in A major, Op. 9, No. 6

I *Presto*. II *Menuetto*. III *Adagio*. IV *Allegro*.

The finale is shorter and slighter than those of almost any other in the early quartets, indicating that Haydn had not yet come to grips with this element in the form.

Commentary on Op. 9. The quartets in Op. 9 all deserve examination by avocational players, partly because they reveal the mind of Haydn so well as he was developing his art and partly because they have many moments of great beauty and substance. The notes given above point out the elements that have attracted notice over the decades. Op. 9, No. 4 is particularly interesting for its relationship to the Mozart D minor quartet. Keller suggests that Mozart really had this quartet in mind when he wrote his own. Keller considers this work, No. 4, to be a most satisfactory introduction to the Haydn quartets. Pleasure—3; Effort—1.

HAYDN, Op. 17

Op. 17 comes from 1771, two years after Op. 9, when Haydn reached thirty-nine. These six quartets show the influence of the works of C.P.E. Bach, which Haydn studied and admired. They show extensive use of folk music of the period and the locale. They exhibit a major expansion in Haydn's concept of the sonata form. They also represent the start of the liberation of the cello from the role of continuo, a process extended even farther in the quartets of Op. 20, written one year later.

Quartet in E major, Op. 17, No. 1

I *Moderato.* II *Menuetto: Allegretto.* III *Adagio.* IV *Presto.*

The sprightly *first movement* gives the violins most of the action.

The *second movement* minuet reverts to the two-line writing of earlier minuets in part. The trio relies on canonic imitation.

The *third movement* sonata is largely a violin duet.

The busy material of the *fourth movement* passes fairly uniformly among the voices.

Quartet in F major, Op. 17, No. 2

I *Moderato.* II *Menuetto: Allegretto.* III *Adagio.* IV *Allegro di molto.*

The *first movement* is a mature sonata with a declamatory theme.

The diminutive *second movement* minuet exhibits extreme simplicity and clarity.

The *third movement* adagio sonata presents a long and finely wrought aria that gives good parts to all voices.

The *fourth movement* is a substantial and quite mature Haydn finale.

Quartet in E-flat major, Op. 17, No. 3

I *Andante grazioso*. II *Menuetto: Allegretto*. III *Adagio*. IV *Allegro molto*.

The *first movement* constitutes a lovely theme with variations.

The *second movement* minuet is astonishing for its simplicity, its clarity of texture and its irregularity.

The *third movement* adagio is rather brief and uninteresting.

The *fourth movement* is a small frisky finale, of no great distinction.

Quartet in C minor, Op. 17, No. 4

I *Moderato*. II *Menuetto*. III *Adagio cantabile*. IV *Allegro*.

The ardent *first movement* develops its tragic theme in a long and fine sonata form.

The Menuetto in C major precedes a C minor trio in the diminutive *second movement*.

The substantial *third movement* presents a lovely theme with two variations.

The *fourth movement* returns to the minor in a tragic and complete finale.

Quartet in G major, Op. 17, no. 5

I *Moderato*. II *Menuetto*. III *Adagio*. IV *Presto*.

The sunny *first movement* makes use of a resolute theme given mainly to the violins.

The *second movement* minuet is undistinguished.

The long and operatic *third movement* adagio amounts to a recitative with arioso.

The flashing *fourth movement* ends with a hush.

Quartet in D major, Op. 17, No. 6

I *Presto.* II *Menuetto.* III *Largo.* IV *Presto.*

The skipping six-eight presto of the *first movement* seems a little inappropriate for the opening movement in a work of this period.

The purity and simplicity of the *second movement* minuet is a relief after the preceding agitation.

In the largo *third movement*, the first violin sings its florid melody over a constant running commentary in the inner voices.

The flashing *fourth movement* presto gives its material to all the voices in a mature finale.

Commentary on Op. 17. Keller considers the quartets of Op. 17 to be of relatively less current interest than the later works and they certainly seem to get less attention. They are, however truly mature works. The C minor quartet, No. 4, and the F major quartet, No. 2, seem especially notable to me. Pleasure—3; Effort—2.

HAYDN, Op. 20
The Sun Quartets

Op. 20 comes from 1772, only one year after Op. 17. It was dedicated to Prince Nikolaus Zmeskall von Domanovecz. The six quartets show a considerable advance over Op. 17, especially in the new recognition that they give to the lyrical potential of the viola and cello. This new use of the lower voices, suddenly appearing in these quartets, permanently changed the concept of the timbre of the string quartet sound. Not only is the timbre changed in these works, but the quartets are innovative in many other ways, presenting astonishing variety and contrasts in mood and harmony. Haydn was experimenting here, and he apparently considered one experiment, the fugal finale, to be a partial failure. At least he never again used it to the extent that he did here in Op. 20.

The quartets in Op. 20 were called "The Sun Quartets" by contemporaries because an early edition had the image of a rising sun on the cover, and the name is still occasionally used. Some contemporaries also called them the Grossen, or Great, Quartets. They were admired and studied by all of Haydn's followers. Mozart much admired Op. 20, No. 1 (in E-flat) and he may have used it as a model for his own quartet in E-flat. Beethoven made a copy of Op. 20, No. 1. Brahms carefully studied the whole opus and he owned the autographs.

Quartet in E-flat major, Op. 20, No. 1 | (1772)

I *Allegro moderato.* II *Menuetto: Allegretto.* III *Affetuoso e sostenuto.* IV *Finale: Presto.*

The *first movement*, a sonata allegro, is quiet, bright, and rather delicate with an improvisatory character. The cello and viola parts are prominent. The development begins with a statement of the principal theme in the tonic before the development proper begins, a device that requires that the exposition have been repeated as written for the full effect to be appreciated. The movement must not be played too fast.

The *second movement*, a plaintive and restrained minuet, appears here before the slow movement. The three-voiced trio, in the same key, is brief and broken off, returning to the minuet in an unexpected way.

The *third movement* is a grave, flowing and restless andante. The instruction, "mezza voce", prescribes a contained tone and careful attention to blending.

The *fourth movement*, a sonata form with a suggestion of rondo form, glides quickly with lively moments, but it is mainly as restrained and quiet as the rest of the work. It ends softly.

Commentary. This lucid, simple and transparent work is the most conventional of the Op. 20 quartets. Authorities see the *third movement* as pointing to the E-flat major quartet of Mozart (K. 428). This is a small, intimate and charming work, infrequently heard and not often played by amateurs. It presents no great technical obstacles, but it contains rhythmically tricky passages and it requires a good command of the technique of ensemble playing. Pleasure—2; Effort—2.

Quartet in C major, Op. 20, No. 2 | (1772)

I *Allegro moderato.* II *Adagio.* III *Menuetto:Allegretto.* IV *Fuga a quattro soggetti: Allegro.*

The *first movement* opens in an unprecedented scoring with its cantabile tune played by the cello, the viola providing the bass. The development section features the second violin. In mood, the movement is cheerful, declamatory, noble, rich and romantic.

The *second movement* is an operatic fantasia. The first section opens with a noble and tragic unison theme which then moves forward in long sequences, alternately dramatic, declamatory and ruminating. This long recitativo ends in a pause, after which an adagio aria appears as a long, simple and consoling response to the drama of the recitativo. This aria ends the movement, with no return and no formal ending. The end is not a resolution, for it leads directly to the *third movement*, played attacca.

The *third movement* theme is hesitant, syncopated and broken, a gentle awakening from the mood of the adagio. The trio features a soft and shaded solo in the cello. The trio must be kept restrained.

The *fourth movement* is a fugue in four voices. Haydn wrote in the score "Praise to the almighty Lord. Thus one friend runs away from the other." This is a complete and splendid fugue, played sotto voce until a sudden forte occurs at the coda. There the fugal form is more or less abandoned so that the movement ends in homophonic style, in a declamatory flourish. The movement works best if it is played quite fast, though it is more difficult at a quick tempo.

Commentary. This expansive quartet is most remarkable. The prominence given to the cello, the operatic adagio and the fugal finale all represent innovations that forever altered the quartet form, freeing it from some of its earlier formal restrictions. The work is fully accessible to amateur players. Those who do not know it will be astonished. Those who get to know it should play it over and over, for its pleasurable effect increases with acquaintance. Pleasure—3; Effort—2.

Quartet in G minor, Op. 20, No. 3 | (1772)

I *Allegro con spirito.* II *Menuetto: Allegretto.* III *Poco Adagio.*
IV *Finale: Allegro molto.*

The *first movement* theme, seven bars long, is fiery and passionate. The thematic asymmetry is complemented by frequent interruptions of the melodic flow by interjections. These are recitative-like passages or off-stage comments, witty and jocular, which intrude on the dramatic and even tragic forestage action.

The *second movement* menuetto is also asymmetric with a five-bar thematic phrase. The trio, featuring the first violin in a running figure over the other voices, leads back to the minuet in a romantic fashion. The essentially tragic nature of the *first movement* is unrelieved by this minuet.

The *third movement* is a broad fantasia, large in scale, inventive and imaginative. Its length and its character require care to see that it is not made dull. Haydn's instruction, "poco adagio", shows that he knew that it would not bear too slow a tempo. Haydn meant the exposition to be repeated, a repeat which is left out of modern editions.

The *fourth movement* is more lively and jocular with a fragmented tune. It ends quietly, however, in a mood that is closer to tragedy than to comedy.

Commentary. This wonderful work seems to be neglected. Perhaps the long and rather opaque adagio is the reason. This is Haydn's only great quartet in this key. The fine minuet is thought by some to have inspired Mozart in his writing of the minuet in his G minor viola quintet (K. 516). The whole work seems most novel. The part writing is a delight. The overall dark mood of the work does not diminish its attractiveness. It presents no major technical difficulties. Pleasure—3; Effort—2.

Quartet in D major, Op. 20, No. 4 | (1772)

I *Allegro di molto.* II *Un poco Adagio affetuoso.* III *Menuetto:
Allegretto alla Zingarese.* IV *Presto scherzando.*

The *first movement* is a crystalline sonata allegro in 3/4 time built on a quiet six-bar theme. It is comical and witty throughout. Triplet figures abound.

The *second movement* is the only really melancholy movement in the work. A theme that is full of pathos is treated to four variations that feature the different instruments, with the fourth variation being extended. The leading instrumental parts in the variations are virtuosic in style. The movement ends with an extended coda.

The *third movement* is a polyrhythmic and complex Gipsy minuet. The trio is based on a scale-figure in the cello.

The *fourth movement* is a calm and unhurried presto sonata with a Gipsy flavor as well as qualities of folk music. It is comical, playful and witty.

Commentary. This is the most popular of the quartets in Op. 20. It has no important faults and much to recommend it. The overall comic spirit is appealing, and the only melancholy movement, the second, is a gem because the attractiveness of the theme of the variations is enhanced by the simple way in which it is treated. This movement represents Haydn's first theme and variations among the great quartets. Keller seems to have a rather low opinion of this quartet because of the relative deficit of innovation that it contains. It is fully accessible to amateurs, and it is most rewarding to all voices, especially because of the splendid second-movement variations. Pleasure—3; Effort—2.

Quartet in F minor, Op. 20, No. 5 | (1772)

I *Allegro moderato.* II *Menuetto.* III *Adagio.* IV *Finale: Fuga a due soggetti: Allegro.*

The *first movement* is a long and fully developed sonata allegro with a tragic motif. It demonstrates an astonishing depth of thought and feeling. The mood remains tragic throughout. A long coda with its own climax is followed by a collapse in pathos.

The *second movement* minuet, though a dance-form, is not at all dancing. Rather, the mood is tragic, urgent and plaintive. The trio offers the relaxation of the tonic major. Its only amiability is a slight reduction in tension. It has no joyful or comic character.

The *third movement* is a lovely adagio sonata with a restful siciliano rhythm. The second violin often shares the melody with the first violin. The extensive figurations in the first violin part in many passages constitute an obbligato or free-invention commentary on the tune. The major key and the gently rocking rhythm of this movement provide the only important release of the tension of this otherwise tragic work.

The *fourth movement* is a double fugue built on a theme that was a cliché of the time. It survives, among other places, in *Messiah*, in several places in the works of Bach, in the Mozart Requiem and in Mozart's double fugue for string quartet or string orchestra. The familiar theme is used here to power a compelling fugue that begins in the second violin. The fugue is subdued in character, sotto voce, until forty bars from the end where a powerful canon, solemn and somber, drives the movement to a splendid tragic conclusion.

Commentary. This most personal work is among the most tragic quartets in the Haydn literature. Haydn favored F-minor for tragic expression. This is a truly grand quartet, deep, thoughtful and rewarding to play. It is not technically difficult. The *third movement* adagio is especially memorable. The work requires a strong second violinist because of the leadership often given to that voice. Pleasure—4; Effort—2.

Quartet in A major, Op. 20, No. 6 | (1772)

I *Allegro di molto e scherzando.* II *Adagio: Cantabile.* III *Menuetto: Allegretto.* IV *Finale: Fuga a tre soggetti: Allegro.*

The *first movement* is technically difficult, especially for the first violinist who dominates throughout. It is a comic and graceful sonata allegro in 6/8, presenting no major problems in performance or understanding.

The *second movement* is a graceful and highly ornamented adagio written in the then-popular style of C.P.E. Bach. It may tend to become a little tedious or to seem to drag without careful attention to style. The second violin has a difficult part because of the flowing sixteenth notes.

The *third movement* minuet is neither particularly notable nor memorable. The tempo works better if it is a rather fast allegretto. The trio retains the key of the minuet, yet it provides the necessary contrast to the minuet. It is a true trio, involving only three voices.

The *fourth movement* is a fugue in three subjects. Like the other fugues in the opus, this one is masterful. The texture is quiet until four bars from the end where a sudden forte passage ends the fugue abruptly.

Commentary. This quartet is neglected by professionals perhaps because it seems relatively undistinguished and by amateurs perhaps because it is quite difficult. The infelicitous key is part of the problem, for it creates considerable difficulties in intonation. The parts are not technically easy. Finally, it is not a simple matter to make this potentially graceful and comical work sound graceful and comical. The work requires a good deal of practice both for technique and for style. It is not a work to be approached casually by amateurs. Pleasure—3; Effort—3.

HAYDN, Op. 33
Gli Scherzi, or The Russian Quartets

Nearly ten years after the appearance of Op. 20, 1781 found Haydn writing the six string quartets in Op. 33, at the age of forty-nine. They are dedicated to the Grand Duke Paul of Russia, hence their common name, "The Russian Quartets." These are the first works that Haydn himself called "quartets." This opus especially prompted Mozart to write the six string quartets that he dedicated to Haydn.

These works, considered all together, constitute a set of mature light comedies. To support this character, Haydn wrote the minuet movements in quick tempos and called them scherzi or scherzandi. For these reasons, the Op. 33 quartets also bear the common name "Gli Scherzi," which means "the jokes" in Italian.

A major innovation found in Op. 33 is the technique of thematic elaboration. The *first movements* retain the sonata allegro form. The slow movements are ternary (romanza) form with a contrasting middle section rather than a development. The scherzi and scherzandi seem not really far from minuets. The finale movements favor the rondo and variation forms. There is an increased sharing of melodic lines among the voices in these works.

Haydn's own description of these as works written in a new and special style indicates his recognition of their novelty and significance, the fruit of nearly a decade of evolution in the thinking of this musical genius.

Quartet in B minor (or D major), Op. 33, No. 1 | (1781)

I *Allegro moderato.* II *Scherzando: Allegro.* III *Andante.* IV *Presto.*

The *first movement*, a sonata allegro, is so interesting and natural that it is played seemingly without much effort. Though it opens in D major, B minor quickly becomes the home key. The mood is spirited and light-hearted.

The *second movement* is much more a spirited minuet than a scherzo. The trio, in the major key, is soft and sparse in texture, contrasting sharply with the minuet.

The *third movement* andante, in the brilliant relative major, opens rather formally but it quickly develops a real beauty. Using two themes, it develops in modified sonata form. It must be played as a calm piece with the sforzatos in the melody subdued.

The *fourth movement* treats a Gipsy tune energetically in sonata form. This is the only sonata-form finale in the opus. It is full of energy, but it must not be played too fast. The movement ends firmly in B minor.

Commentary. This fine mature quartet, displays no truly notable new inventions. It thus seems more like an earlier work than it is. The ensemble in the *first movement* is difficult. The andante movement is especially memorable. The presto is a most successful Gipsy movement. This rather neglected quartet has a natural feel, and it is fully accessible to accomplished amateurs. Pleasure—2; Effort—2.

Quartet in E-flat major, Op. 33, No. 2 | (1781), *The Joke*

I *Allegro moderato, cantabile.* II *Scherzo: Allegro.* III *Largo sostenuto.* IV *Finale: Presto.*

The *first movement*, a merry and spirited sonata allegro, is straightforward. The violin parts are not quite easy.

The *second movement* is more a spirited scherzo than a minuet. It must be played allegro, not to be allowed to lapse in tempo. The trio offers a more relaxed and graceful atmosphere for contrast. Keller advises the use of tasteful portamentos in the trio, stating that Haydn intended them.

The meditative *third movement* features the viola strongly, opening with a lovely viola-cello duo. The theme is restated in the other voices in various combinations to provide contrasts in texture.

The *fourth movement*, a rondo with a trailing coda, presents a witty format in which the four two-bar clauses of the theme are played with two-bar rests between its clauses. This sets things up for the joke in the coda. Haydn may have meant this coda to be no more than a big joke, for the whole rondo is humorous. On the other hand, Keller believes, he was also presenting a new compositional device, thematic disintegration.

Commentary. This is a pleasing work to play, generally mellow and meditative except for the comical last movement. It is popular with violists for the slow movement, and with everyone for the joke at the end. It is not really easy to play. The violin parts are difficult. The slow movement requires close attention to textures. The work is fully accessible to good players. Pleasure—2; Effort—2.

Quartet in C major, Op. 33, No. 3 | (1781), *The Bird*

I *Allegro moderato.* II *Scherzando: Allegretto.* III *Adagio.*
IV *Finale: Rondo: Presto.*

The *first movement* shows an innovation at the outset in that the rhythm and harmony are introduced for one bar before the tune begins. The entries of the violins and viola come (or should seem to come) out of nowhere. This effect is most difficult to get right. The movement is quiet, relaxed and gentle throughout, despite the forte levels achieved at points.

The *second movement* is more a minuet than a scherzo. It is notable for the lovely violin duet in the trio. The mood is grave in the minuet, witty in the trio.

The *third movement* is one of Haydn's loveliest, most popular and most innovative slow movements, combining rondo, variation and sonata forms. The mood is a cheerful lyricism.

The *fourth movement*, one of Haydn's merriest rondos, has a Hungarian flavor. It must be fast and energetic, yet rhythmically calm and stable.

Commentary. This is the most popular quartet of the opus. It was a favorite of Joachim. The common name might refer to the many grace notes of the principal theme of the *first movement*, to the violin duet of the trio or to the cuckoo calls in the last movement. The work is not difficult technically and it constitutes a delight for all players. The two violins are featured in the work. Pleasure—3; Effort—2.

Quartet in B-flat major, Op. 33, No. 4 | (1781)

I *Allegro moderato.* II *Scherzo: Allegretto.* III *Largo.* IV *Presto.*

The *first movement*, a sonata allegro, follows from a fragmented theme and features repeated trills. The first violin part is virtuosic. The mood is bright throughout.

The *second movement*, a compact scherzo, is made especially sprightly by its dotted rhythm. The trio, marked minore, is similarly brief.

The *third movement*, a largo in 3/4 time, is a brief and rather quiet but expressive aria with an ornamental eight-bar theme.

The *fourth movement* presto rondo seems at first to be a rather ordinary dance. The bland main theme alternates with similar conventional tunes, but varies more and more comically at each return. The ending is a flippant and comical pizzicato coda.

Commentary. This is the least impressive work of the opus. All movements are short, and there is little or nothing here that is innovative. Keller and others seem to consider this work as beneath much comment. Still, its cheerful character and its lack of technical and musical problems make it at least worthy of the attention of those who wish to see the mature Haydn in the full spectrum. The *fourth movement* is the most attractive one. Pleasure—2; Effort—2.

Quartet in G major, Op. 33, No. 5 | (1781), *How Do You Do?*

I *Vivace assai.* II *Largo: Cantabile.* III *Scherzo: Allegro.*
IV *Finale: Allegretto.*

The *first movement* has a pianissimo two-bar cadential introduction in tempo that seems to say "How do you do?" It later becomes a part of the movement structure. The ensuing lively sonata allegro is long and complex. Keller emphasizes the need to play both repeats.

The *second movement* is a lovely aria notable for the use of unison playing. The middle section contains a cliché from Gluck's opera, *Orfeo.* The second violinist has a difficult part.

The *third movement* scherzo is notable for its rhythmic structure and for its unusual chromaticism.

The *fourth movement* is a set of variations on a siciliano theme. It will remind players of the finale of Mozart's D minor quartet (K. 421). Indeed, Mozart may have had this movement in mind when he wrote that finale. This is a smaller movement than Mozart's, consisting of three melodic variations and a presto coda.

Commentary. This is a fine work, not quite easy to play. It features the second violin in the lovely largo movement and that part is difficult. The *fourth movement* is particularly memorable. Pleasure—2; Effort—2.

Quartet in D major, Op. 33, No. 6 | (1781)

I *Vivace assai.* II *Andante.* III *Scherzo: Allegro.* IV *Finale: Allegretto.*

The *first movement* is a straightforward sonata allegro in 6/8 meter, cheerful and sturdy in character.

The *second movement* is a fine arioso, quite polyphonic. The second violin has a difficult part. This is a brief and unpretentious movement.

The *third movement* is an unproblematic scherzo with biting upbeats. It must be played truly allegro. The tempo in the trio should be slightly relaxed.

The *fourth movement* rondo is a set of variations on two themes, double variations. It is notable for contrasting alternate major-mode and minor-mode sections. The minor key variations feature the cello. It is a witty and cheerful set of variations, but always well-mannered and modest.

Commentary. This is the smallest and shortest quartet in the opus, unpretentious and unproblematic. It offers no major technical problems except to the second violin in the *second movement.* The *fourth movement* requires care to make it really interesting. Pleasure—2; Effort—2.

HAYDN, Op. 42 and Op. 50
The Prussian Quartets

The single quartet in Op. 42 (1785) long puzzled the experts. Now, it is thought to be the only one surviving of a set of three works that Haydn intended for someone in Spain. Its technical requirements suggest that he wrote it for beginners. Keller suggests that its composition may have been influenced by Mozart's D-minor quartet (K. 421), written in the same year.

The six quartets in Op. 50 were published in 1787 when Haydn was fifty-five. They are dedicated to the Prussian King Frederick William II, an amateur cellist who had sent Haydn a magnificent diamond ring. The dedication was Haydn's response to the gift. It is said that Haydn always wore the ring thereafter when he was composing. This is the same Prussian King to whom Mozart dedicated his last three quartets and to whom Beethoven dedicated the two piano-cello sonatas in Op. 5. The Op. 50 quartets are sometimes called The Prussian Quartets.

These quartets in Op. 50 are notable for the individual treatments of the four voices and for their sense of unity. No. 4 is considered to be the greatest of the opus. No. 6, "The Frog," is the only jocular work in this generally serious and thoughtful set.

Quartet in B-flat major, Op. 50, No. 1 | (1787)

I *Allegro.* II *Adagio non lento.* III *Menuetto: Poco Allegretto.*
IV *Finale: Vivace.*

The *first movement* opens with an accompaniment in the cello for one bar, reminiscent of the opening of "The Bird," Op. 33, No. 3. The persistent triplet figures over the constant pulse create a light, transparent and lively feeling. The movement is full of innovation.

The *second movement* is a rich and reposeful adagio, a set of variations on a lovely theme set in the dark key of E-minor. The theme is never absent from the variations. All instruments have fine parts. There is a long coda. This movement must not be played too slowly.

The *third movement* is notable for the jocular trio.

The *fourth movement*, a monothematic sonata, is witty and comical. It features a false recapitulation, a little violin cadenza and a false ending.

Commentary. This is a pleasant and thoughtful work. The lovely *second movement* and the witty finale are most memorable. The quartet is neither easy nor difficult. It is not profound, but it is a joyful piece to play. Pleasure—2; effort—2.

Quartet in C major, Op. 50, No. 2 | (1787)

I *Vivace.* II *Adagio: Cantabile.* III *Menuetto: Allegretto.* IV *Finale: Vivace assai.*

The *first movement* is conventional and unproblematic. The theme is asymmetric, but the music flows naturally and effortlessly. The mood is calm and unrushed, despite the vivace.

The *second movement* is a lovely adagio. The instruction, "cantabile", is not Haydn's own instruction, according to Keller. An editor presumably added it. The second violin has the tune at the opening that is then passed to the first violin. Running figures underlie the melody. This is a lyrical and flowing aria movement.

The *third movement* is straightforward. The trio that features running figures in the bass contrasts with the graceful minuet theme.

The *fourth movement* is very witty. It must be played very fast, as a light and lively vivace throughout. There is a frolicking interplay among the voices.

Commentary. Like Op. 50, No. 1, this is an unproblematic work that is readily accessible to amateurs. The *second* and *fourth movements* are memorable. The work requires especially good ensemble technique, for the interplay among the voices is critical to satisfying performance. This is a good quartet, but not a great one. Pleasure—2; Effort—2.

Quartet in E-flat major, Op. 50, No. 3 | (1787)

I *Allegro con brio.* II *Andante piuttosto Allegretto.* III *Menuetto: Allegretto.* IV *Finale: Presto.*

The *first movement* is a quite conventional and unproblematic sonata allegro. The abrupt, fragmented and heavily articulated theme does not accommodate too much brio.

The *second movement* is a set of variations on a broad legato theme. It opens as a notable duet for cello and viola. The variations include considerable harmonic variation. This is a long and splendid romantic movement.

The *third movement* is rather undistinguished. The trio grows out of the minuet material.

The *fourth movement* is a hearty presto sonata arising from a theme that resembles that of the *first movement*. It contains many harmonic surprises. The movement is witty without being jocular or comical.

Commentary. Like the first two quartets in the opus, this is a fine and mature work, but not a particularly distinguished one. It is notable for the harmonic innovation. The *second movement* is very fine and the highlight of the work. The key was a favorite of Haydn. The whole work is readily accessible to amateurs. Pleasure—2; Effort—2.

Quartet in F-sharp minor, Op. 50, No. 4 | (1787)

I *Allegro spirituoso.* II *Andante.* III *Menuetto: Poco Allegretto.*
IV *Finale: Fuga: Allegro moderato.*

The *first movement* is a long and thoroughly worked out sonata, blustering and agitated. The key presents many problems in intonation. Here, Haydn rejects the tragic end to a tragic movement with a recapitulation in the tonic major.

The *second movement* constitutes variations on two themes, double variations. Major and minor modes alternate. There is no coda. The movement is fine, but technically difficult.

The *third movement* is a relaxed minuet in six sharps. Intonation is a problem. The major-mode trio is more contrapuntal and so more intense than the minuet. It is no easier to play.

The *fourth movement* is a magnificent monothematic fugue with overtones of sonata form, melancholy in character. Some see it as Mozart's model for the fugal finale in the first of the six quartets that he dedicated to Haydn, but it is quite different in character from Mozart's fugue. This quiet, deep and tragic fugue strains the quartet form almost to its limits. It ends in a homophonic forte coda.

Commentary. This is a supremely difficult work, both technically and musically. All parts are difficult, but especially the cellist's. It is somewhat reminiscent of the Op. 20 quartets in its innovation. The fugal finale, especially, is immensely satisfying. This tragic work should not be undertaken lightly, but serious players should approach it when they feel ready. Pleasure—4; Effort—3.

Quartet in F major, Op. 50, No. 5 | (1787), with *The Dream*

I *Allegro moderato.* II *Poco adagio.* III *Menuetto: Allegretto.* IV *Finale: Vivace.*

The *first movement* is a light and dancing sonata, notable for its sparkling spiccato passages. These are unlike anything to be found in Haydn up to this time. The spiccato constitutes the principal difficulty in this otherwise wholly natural and exquisitely happy movement.

The *second movement* is reposeful, simple and happy. Its mood is expressed in its common title, "The Dream." The second violin and the viola carry the responsibility for the maintenance of the rhythm.

The *third movement* minuet is a happy movement, straightforward and simple. The violin has fantasy passages in triplets.

The *fourth movement* has a grazioso character. One should not lose the grazioso character in the vivace. The movement maintains its sprightliness, gaiety and good cheer throughout.

Commentary. This quartet is exquisite, happy throughout, and wonderfully proportioned. It presents a stunning contrast to the drama of Op. 50, No. 4, which precedes it. This work is quite easy to play in all respects. It is highly recommended to all amateurs. Pleasure—3; Effort—2.

Quartet in D major, Op. 50, No. 6 | (1787), *The Frog*

I *Allegro.* II *Poco Adagio.* III *Menuetto: Allegretto.* IV *Finale: Allegro con spirito.*

The *first movement* is not unusual or problematic. It opens with an unaccompanied theme that seems to begin in the middle of a sentence. The mood is cheerful and declamatory.

The *second movement*, a set of variations on a theme with an inverted siciliano rhythm, is memorable.

The *third movement* is a heavily accented minuet with a jocular trio.

The *fourth movement* indulges in an exercise of bariolage. Some see this as a joke, hence the common name of the work. Others see this as a serious attempt to produce a new tone color, but perhaps with humorous intent.

Commentary. This is a great and famous quartet, the most jocular work in this otherwise serious and thoughtful opus. The work is not difficult and it is readily accessible to amateur players. Pleasure—3; effort—2..

HAYDN, Opp. 54, 55 and 64
The Tost Quartets

These twelve works are collectively known as The Tost Quartets because of their association with Johann Tost, a wealthy merchant and virtuoso amateur violinist. The six quartets in Op. 64 are dedicated to him, and the three in each of Op. 54 and Op. 55 were apparently written with him in mind as the first violinist.

Tost was a close friend of Haydn. He played in quartet sessions with both Haydn and Mozart who took the second violin and viola parts, both composers reportedly preferring to play the viola. Tost's wife is the dedicatee of Haydn's piano sonata in E-flat major, No. 49. As might be expected from Tost's virtuosity, the first violin parts in these twelve quartets are rather difficult.

These works signal the onset of Haydn's greatest period in the writing of quartets. Opp. 54 and 55 came only a year or so after Op. 50. Op. 64 came two years later when Haydn was fifty-eight.

Quartet in G major, Op. 54, No. 1 | (1788)

I *Allegro con brio.* II *Allegretto.* III *Menuetto: Allegretto.*
IV *Finale: Presto.*

The *first movement*, a brilliant and sprightly sonata allegro, opens with a lively staccato theme followed by a legato syncopated second theme. The first violin part is fairly difficult. The movement contains excellent part writing and is exciting to play.

The *second movement* allegretto is built on an exquisite siciliano theme with profound modulations. Care must be taken to make it retain its quiet dancing character, in piano, rather than to let it assume the character of an adagio. It is very beautiful.

The *third movement* is a bright and heavily accented minuet with a refined rhythmic structure and concealed asymmetries. The trio offers the cello a special opportunity.

The *fourth movement* is a light semi-contrapuntal rondo with sonata-form incursions. It is delicate, very quick and a delight to play.

Commentary. This is a brilliant work throughout. The *second movement* is the most memorable. This is a fine work for amateurs because it contains few problems in interpretation, nor are there outstanding technical difficulties. For good reason, it is one of the most popular of Haydn's quartets. Pleasure—3; effort—1.

Quartet in C major, Op. 54, No. 2 | (1788)

I *Vivace*. II *Adagio*. III *Menuetto: Allegretto*. IV *Finale: Adagio; Presto*.

The *first movement* opens with a vigorous, assertive and asymmetric theme. This is a very large and thoroughly worked out movement, almost symphonic in scope. There are many harmonic surprises and contrasts.

The *second movement* is a profound expression in Gipsy style, rhapsodic and free. A sepulchral melody is overlaid with a wild and florid counterpoint. The movement has suggestions of the passacaglia, with elements of ternary and sonata forms.

The *third movement* is texturally thick because of the unusual amount of four-part writing and the extensive use of octave unisons. Striking dissonances mark the trio.

The *fourth movement* is a lyrical double-theme adagio that encloses a short presto episode in the middle. Such a predominantly adagio finale is an innovation. This is a wonderful movement for the cello.

Commentary. This most strikingly innovative work remains in the memory for the brilliance and scope of the *first movement*, the haunting ornamental *second*, and the astonishing *fourth*. It was a great favorite of Hausmann, the cellist of the Joachim Quartet, for obvious reasons. It is not to be missed by skilled amateurs. Pleasure—3; Effort—2.

Quartet in E major, Op. 54, No. 3 | (1788)

I *Allegro*. II *Largo cantabile*. III *Menuetto: Allegretto*. IV *Finale: Presto*.

The *first movement*, a fast allegro contrasting a duple rhythm with rushing triplets, is most inventive and pleasing. It is difficult for the first violin.

The *second movement* is a major-key largo sonata with elements of variation. The first violin has a difficult improvisatory part with ornate embellishment.

The *third movement* is a heavily accented minuet with a more relaxed trio.

The *fourth movement*, a compressed and exciting presto, contrasts a dominant sotto voce with sudden fortes. It is not so difficult for the first violin as the preceding movements.

Commentary. Tovey considers this an unjustly neglected masterpiece. Keller seems less enthusiastic. Certainly, professionals and amateurs alike currently neglect it. It is not as memorable as the others in the opus except for the *second movement*, which is really splendid. This is a rather difficult work for the first violinist. The second violinist has good parts in many places. Pleasure—2; Effort—2.

Quartet in A major, Op. 55, No. 1 | (1788)

I *Allegro*. II *Adagio cantabile*. III *Menuetto*. IV *Finale: Vivace*.

The *first movement* is a typical sonata allegro of the fully developed Haydn with his characteristic trademarks, monothematicism and asymmetry. The theme is declamatory and expansive. Running triplet figures ornament the development.

The *second movement* is a supreme monothematic adagio fusing rondo and variation forms. The mood is one of peace and repose. The movement opens as a trio with the melody in the second violin. The first violin later has florid figuration to play.

The *third movement* minuet strangely has no tempo indication. It should be allegretto, not too fast. In the trio, The second violin, viola and cello play the melody while figuration in the first violin explores the highest registers.

The merry *fourth movement* starts out as a quick and jolly rondo and ends as a quasi-fugue. The theme is asymmetric. The texture is light and transparent.

Commentary. This is a most attractive and straightforward mature work of Haydn. It is less virtuosic for the first violin than are the other works of this period. None of the parts is really difficult technically. This is a good work for a new quartet, one made up of strangers. It is perfectly clear in texture and interpretation. One wonders why it is neglected. Pleasure—3; Effort—1.

Quartet in F minor, Op. 55, No. 2 | (1788), *The Razor*

I *Andante piuttosto Allegretto.* II *Allegro.* III *Menuetto: Allegretto.* IV *Finale: Presto.*

The *first movement* andante is a long and slow movement, unprecedented as such in the Haydn quartets. It is a profound and inventive variations movement with elements of the sonata form. The double variations contrast a passionate main theme with a consolatory secondary theme.

The *second movement* follows the *first movement*, attacca. It is a sonata allegro with an interesting fugal development.

The *third movement* minuet in the tonic major, with the trio back in the home key, is most interesting for the conversational two-part writing. It opens with a lovely tune in the viola.

The *fourth movement* opens with a chromatic rondo theme and develops as a variations movement. It should be played with no suspicion of roughness. This is a wonderfully complex, quite difficult and rather comical movement.

Commentary. This quartet has an unusual structure. It is more highly personal and serious than many of the other quartets from this period of his writing, but Haydn ends it quite brightly. Haydn is said to have considered this quartet to be his best up to this time. It is an unjustly neglected, unusual, rewarding and difficult quartet. It is extraordinarily intellectual and subtle. All serious players should study this quartet seriously. The *second* and *fourth movements* are more difficult than the others. The common name comes from the apocryphal tale that Haydn, shaving one morning with a dull razor, exclaimed that he would trade his latest quartet for a good razor! Pleasure—3; Effort—3.

Quartet in B-flat major, Op. 55, No. 3 | (1788)

I *Vivace assai*. II *Adagio ma non troppo*. III *Menuetto*.
IV *Finale: Presto*.

The *first movement* is an easy, smooth and flowing sonata, strongly contrasting chromatic and diatonic treatments. The legato spirit persists throughout.

The *second movement* is a graceful theme with two variations. The smooth and flowing theme persists, passacaglia-like, through the variations. There is an extended coda.

The *third movement* is lucid and simple. The minuet is forceful and masculine while the trio is soft and lyrical.

The *fourth movement*, an energetic sonata, exhibits an unusual uniformity in the part writing. All four voices have equal parts. There are no "accompaniments." The movement is quite difficult.

Commentary. This is a typical mature Haydn quartet, thematically symmetrical and lucid. It can be understood readily. It is a fine work in which an amateur quartet can learn balance. Keller considers it to be one of the ten greatest Haydn quartets. The work is quite rarely heard now. It is highly recommended. Pleasure—3; Effort—2.

Quartet in C major, Op. 64, No. 1 | (1790)

I *Allegro moderato*. II *Menuetto: Allegro ma non troppo*.
III *Allegretto scherzando*. IV *Finale: Presto*.

The *first movement* is a fine and characteristic Haydn sonata allegro. It opens as a string trio. A soft, light cheerfulness pervades this long movement.

The *second movement* is the minuet, a curious reversion to the old order in such a late work. It opens with the tune in the cello. The minor trio features imitative exchanges among the voices.

The *third movement* allegretto is not a slow movement, and it must not be allowed to become one. This is a delightful and symmetrical theme and variations.

The *fourth movement* presto is humorous. The drumming motif is used to build a comical fugato. The movement ends in a whisper.

Commentary. This is a delightful, humorous, and mature quartet. It is not technically challenging but it requires expert tone production. It is most remarkable for the last two movements. This is the least known of the six works in Op. 64. Pleasure—2; Effort—2.

Quartet in B minor, Op. 64, No. 2 | (1790)

I *Allegro spirituoso*. II *Adagio ma non troppo*. III *Menuetto: Allegretto*. IV *Finale: Presto*.

The *first movement*, a fiery, passionate and extended sonata allegro, seems to open in D major, despite the key signature. Chromatic and contrapuntal coloration gives this movement great weight.

The B-major *second movement* is a lucid and sweet adagio, contrasting strongly with the stormy *first movement*. It is a double variation in form. There are four variations with a coda. The key creates major intonation problems.

The theme of the minor mode *third movement* exhibits striking asymmetry. The movement is notable for the virtuosic technique required of the first violin in the major mode trio.

The *fourth movement* is an innovative sonata rondo, impish and mischievous, with a fine fugato. A humorous and ethereal B major ending finishes the movement with a bar and a half of silence. The movement is a comic-opera parody.

Commentary. This is another great work, unduly neglected. It is difficult to play, both technically and musically. Amateurs are warned away from it until they feel ready to tackle Haydn at his most difficult. Pleasure—3; Effort—3.

Quartet in B-flat major, Op. 64, No. 3 | (1790)

I *Vivace assai.* II *Adagio.* III *Menuetto: Allegretto.* IV *Finale: Allegro con spirito.*

The *first movement* is a sonata allegro marked by striking contrasts between the two themes. The mood is bright, the texture rather thick and busy.

The *second movement* is a lyrical adagio A-B-A form with a broad theme, a minor middle section and an ornamented recapitulation. The middle section offers a variation of the theme in the tonic minor.

The *third movement* minuet is notable for the difficult trills in the viola part. One cannot overdo the contrast between the syncopation of the scherzo and the stomping 3/4 time of the folk dancing in the trio.

The *fourth movement* is a romp, a spirited chase that pauses here and there to take a breath before the chase resumes.

Commentary. This is another neglected work, but it is "as sublime and perfect a masterpiece as any," says Keller. It is not really difficult to play. Pleasure—2; Effort—2.

Quartet in G major, Op. 64, No. 4 | (1790)

I *Allegro con brio.* II *Menuetto: Allegretto.* III *Adagio: Cantabile sostenuto.* IV *Finale: Presto.*

The *first movement*, in sonata form, is happy, symmetrical, and uncomplicated. The first violin part actually descends below other voices at crucial points.

The *second movement* is a characteristic minuet placed second, in the old order. The minuet is rather calm. The trio presents a running melodic figure in the first violin over pizzicatos in the other lines, a rather old-fashioned kind of writing for the time.

The *third movement* is a broad and lyrical A-B-A adagio with an unusual harmonic lability, a minor middle section and an ornamented recapitulation. In form and character, it strongly resembles the *second movement* of Op. 64, No. 3.

The *fourth movement* is a light and transparent presto. One must not play it too fast so as not to sacrifice the lyrical second subject. The structure of the movement depends critically upon dynamic contrasts.

Commentary. This is yet another neglected masterpiece in the opinion of experts. It is strikingly symmetrical. It contains no special innovations, but it is a pleasing work to play. Pleasure—2; Effort—2.

Quartet in D major, Op. 64, No. 5 | (1790), *The Lark*

I *Allegro moderato.* II *Adagio cantabile.* III *Menuetto: Allegretto.* IV *Finale: Vivace.*

The *first movement* opens with a staccato theme in the lower instruments followed by a warbling counter-melody in the first violin. The latter tune is the origin of the common name. The long movement is polyrhythmic, complex, cheerful, and entertaining, but always relaxed.

The *second movement* is yet another lyrical adagio in ternary form, like those of Op. 64, Nos. 3 and 4. Like them, it features a minor mode B section and an ornamented return of the A section. It has a similar warmth and beauty.

The *third movement* is a jocular and witty minuet. The trio opens as a duo with the tune in the second violin. The minuet is heavy and accented, while the trio is leggiero in spirit.

The *fourth movement* is often called a perpetuum mobile, but it is not really that and it benefits from not being played like one. It has a virtuosic sound, but it does not require truly virtuosic technique. It is mostly quiet, reaching a sudden fortissimo climax before the coda. This movement is sometimes called 'The Hornpipe', although it is not exactly that.

Commentary. This is one of the most popular of Haydn's quartets. It sounds more difficult than it is. It is fully accessible to accomplished amateurs. Pleasure—3; Effort—2.

Quartet in E-flat major, Op. 64, No. 6 | (1790)

I *Allegretto.* II *Andante.* III *Menuetto: Allegretto.* IV *Finale: Presto.*

The *first movement* has a highly reflective mood. Its texture is remarkable in that there is extensive writing for duets among the four voices.

The *second movement* is a flowing andante in A-B-A form with a minor-mode middle section that features a powerful and declamatory fantasia in the first violin part. This seems to be a special tribute to Tost.

The *third movement* is a characteristic minuet, demanding a little virtuosity of the first violinist. It must not be played too fast.

The *fourth movement* is a gay, witty and surprising presto, contrasting sharply with the reflective mood of the preceding movements. Broken phrases, pauses and rushing scales make for a hilarious ending. It has a weighty humor, though, and it must not be allowed to become flippant.

Commentary. This work is quite rarely heard. It is difficult for the key, which, however, enhances the opaque and reflective character of the work as a whole. Otherwise, it is relatively easy, both technically and interpretatively, for experienced players. Pleasure—2; Effort—2.

HAYDN, Opp. 71 and 74
The Apponyi Quartets

Haydn wrote six quartets in 1793 at the age of sixty-one and published them as these two opuses of three works each. They are dedicated to Count Apponyi, who later suggested to Beethoven that he should write the Op. 18 quartets of 1798–1800.

These works, Op. 71 and Op. 74, were written between Haydn's two trips to London. His attention had returned to the symphonic form at this time, and he probably had large halls and large audiences on his mind. Some experts suggest that this may account for the symphonic texture and scope of these two sets and of the quartets that follow them. Op. 71 is relatively neglected. Op. 74 was much favored by Joachim. Each of the three quartets in Op. 74 bears Haydn's special inscription, "In Nomine Domini," which he used often with his larger works, probably as a mark of distinction, to show his special esteem for them.

Quartet in B-flat major, Op. 71, No. 1 | (1793)

I *Allegro.* II *Adagio.* III *Menuetto: Allegretto.* IV *Finale: Vivace.*

The *first movement* opens in an unusual fashion with a call to attention in the form of five chords. These chords do not define the tempo to follow. The chords are not strictly an introduction but integral to the whole movement, appearing again at the end of the exposition. The subsequent allegro is a richly textured and complete sonata form.

The *second movement*, a graceful adagio laden with appoggiaturas, is particularly noteworthy for its passages for the unaccompanied violin.

The *third movement* is a lyrical minuet. The canonical trio is even more dancing.

The *fourth movement* is witty, ironic and funny. Scales, contrapuntal episodes, syncopations and opposing accents give it its humor. Keller sees it as a parody of conventionality.

Commentary. This is a fine, neglected work. It offers no major problems in technique and interpretation. It is recommended warmly. Pleasure—2; Effort—2.

Quartet in D major, Op. 71, No. 2 | (1793)

I *Adagio; Allegro.* II *Adagio Cantabile.* III *Menuetto: Allegro.* IV *Finale: Allegretto; Allegro.*

The *first movement* opening, a four-bar adagio introduction is most unusual for this period in the works of Haydn. The following brilliant and lucid allegro has a rather orchestral texture. It is notable for its many octave leaps.

The *second movement* is an exquisite rondo-variations movement. It is sometimes described as an aria for the first violin. The movement should be played freely, with true cantabile style.

The *third movement*, an allegro minuet, is notable for the triadic theme of the minuet. The trio is legato, almost a waltz, with statements and responses that pass back and forth among the voices. The whole movement is jocular.

The *fourth movement* is especially fine, with a theme that Tovey called "kittenish." The form combines rondo and variations. A fermata after the main body of the movement, in allegretto, announces an allegro coda that terminates in a Rossinian climax at the finish. The complex and richly textured movement is witty and comical.

Commentary. The experts are enthusiastic about this neglected quartet. It has a very brilliant sound. The *second movement* is the most memorable. The work offers no major technical problems for amateurs. Pleasure—2; Effort—2.

Quartet in E-flat major, Op. 71, No. 3 | (1793)

I *Vivace.* II *Andante con moto.* III *Menuetto.* IV *Finale: Vivace.*

The *first movement* features a little introduction, a single chord, followed by a one-bar rest. The following sonata is jocular in mood, with frequent little off-stage comments.

The *second movement* is a rather lively andante, a rondo-variation form. The instruction in the score, "licenza," means "that's correct", says Keller.

The *third movement* is unremarkable.

The *fourth movement*, a rondo with a fugato in 6/8 meter, is witty and playful. It must not be played too fast. The tempo should be that of a quick waltz for the movement to work best.

Commentary. Tovey considers this to be the greatest work in the opus. It is not an easy work and it should not be approached casually. Pleasure—3; Effort—3.

Quartet in C major, Op. 74, No. 1 | (1793)

I *Allegro moderato.* II *Andantino grazioso.* III *Menuetto: Allegretto.* IV *Finale: Vivace.*

The *first movement*, like those in Op. 71, has a slow introduction, here taking the form of a tempo-less cadence. The cadence should have an adagio feeling. The bland, legato and chromatic theme of the subsequent allegro explodes into a rich sonata allegro movement.

The *second movement* is a grazioso dance movement, rather like a slow waltz, tender, delicate and plaintive.

The *third movement* minuet is weighty. It is remarkable for its trio in A major, which springs with no preparation from the C major minuet.

The *fourth movement* features virtuosity and brilliance in all voices, not just in the first violin. The silken opening theme in mezzoforte is developed with syncopation and other rhythmic tricks to make a movement of great ingenuity.

Commentary. Tovey calls this work "glorious." It was a great favorite of Joachim. It is not an easy work, presenting technical problems especially for the first violin in the last movement. It is not to be approached casually. Pleasure—2; Effort—3.

Quartet in F major, Op. 74, No. 2 | (1793), *The Military Quartet*

I *Allegro spirituoso.* II *Andante grazioso.* III *Menuetto: Allegretto.*
IV *Finale: Presto.*

The *first movement*, like the others in this set, opens with an introduction but this one is not slow. It is a unison fanfare in the allegro tempo that hints at the ten-bar theme of the long and splendid allegro that follows.

The *second movement*, an A-B-A form, treats its lyrical theme with variations. The second violin part is featured in the minor mode B section. That part lies in a comfortable register and it presents no major technical problems. The movement works better played as a dance than as a quasi-adagio.

The *third movement* is notable for its harmonic variation. The remote key of the quiet and relaxed trio contrasts with the heavily accented allegro minuet.

The *fourth movement* is a dramatic, agitated and thrusting presto.

Commentary. This is another neglected masterpiece, according to Tovey. The *second movement* should attract all second violinists. This is a fine work for a group with an inexperienced second violinist, for that voice gets good parts that are not difficult. The fanfare at the opening is the origin of the common name. Pleasure—3; Effort—2.

Quartet in G minor, Op. 74, No. 3 | (1793),
The Rider or *The Horseman*

I *Allegro.* II *Largo assai.* III *Menuetto: Allegretto.* IV *Finale: Allegro con brio.*

The *first movement*, like the rest in this set, opens with an introduction. Since this material serves as the basis for the development section, it should be played as a theme in tempo, not as an introduction alone. The movement must retain a grazioso character rather than to be treated as a blustering or tragic movement.

The *second movement* is a solemn largo that is notable especially for its remote key, E major. The questioning theme is developed to a "Miltonic grandeur," says Cobbett.

The *third movement*, another weighty minuet, flows in polyphonic legato in a remote key. The dark trio offers some relaxation through its grazioso character.

The *fourth movement*, blustering and tragic at the outset, ends happily. This famous movement must be kept strictly in tempo.

Commentary. This is a famous and popular work, one of the most familiar of the Haydn quartets. Cobbett considers the *second movement* largo to be one of Haydn's greatest compositions. The common name could refer to both the first and last movements. It is not a difficult work, and it should be known well by all those who play the Haydn quartets. Pleasure—3; Effort—2.

HAYDN, Op. 76
The Erdödy Quartets

The six quartets of Op. 76 date from 1797 and 1798, when Haydn was sixty-five years old. He had returned from London to Vienna two years before to serve the fourth of the Esterhazy Princes who employed him, Nicholas II. It was a period of heavy work for him (he composed *The Creation* at this time), with much responsibility, some troubles (from the Prince), and many honors. The quartets are dedicated to Count Erdödy, a Hungarian nobleman about whom authorities say little. The Count kept these quartets for his exclusive private use until they were published two years later.

These quartets, taken together, seem to be particularly condensed, intensified, direct and personal expressions as compared to those quartets that came before. Haydn's famous wit is here subdued. All these quartets show the further evolution of the minuet to the scherzo and they contain other innovations as well. The opus includes some of Haydn's most famous and gratifying works and amateurs should know them all. Their profundities as well as their rich textures make them all favorites. They constitute the peak of Haydn's art in the form.

Quartet in G major, Op. 76, No. 1 | (1797)

I *Allegro con spirito.* II *Adagio sostenuto.* III *Menuetto: Presto.*
IV *Finale: Allegro ma non troppo.*

The *first movement* opens with three great chords, an introduction to a dancing theme that is stated first by the cello and then taken up by the other voices. The contrapuntal development is brilliant, the mood a robust cheer.

The *second movement* is an intensely dramatic adagio.

The *third movement* is a true scherzo. It is remarkable for the pizzicato accompaniment in the trio, which may have been suggested to Haydn by the similar trio in Mozart's D minor quartet (K. 421). The minuet must be played fast, without much dancing quality, while the trio is much slower, polite and lyrical.

The *fourth movement* opens with the introductory statement of a deeply troubled theme in octaves. Thereafter, this theme is treated in variations. This minor-mode finale is almost without precedent in Haydn, but it is not sustained for the tonic major returns at the midpoint. The movement must not be played too fast.

Commentary. This is a fine work for amateurs to study seriously but it is among the less played of this opus. It has no major technical obstacles and it is completely clear in structure and intent. Pleasure—3; Effort—2.

Quartet in D minor, Op. 76, No. 2 | (1797),
Fifths, Quinten, or *The Bells*

I *Allegro.* II *Andante o più tosto allegretto.* III *Menuetto: Allegro ma non troppo.* IV *Finale: Vivace assai.*

The *first movement* opens, without introduction, with a broad and dramatic tune made of descending fifths, hence the common names. The fifths, sometimes in inversion, form the motival skeleton of the whole movement. The development is complex and profound and there is a splendid coda.

The *second movement*, a variation form with elements of ternary and sonata forms, exhibits ambiguity or indecisiveness of key at many points. The movement is full of joy and surprises.

The exhilarating *third movement* is an uninterrupted canon, pure and unadorned. The minuet is dramatic, the trio, stark. This is sometimes called the 'Witches' Minuet'.

The *fourth movement* is a massive movement, dramatic in the minor mode, ending optimistically in the major mode, much as the final movement of Op. 76, No. 1 ends.

Commentary. Justly celebrated as a masterpiece, this work is lucid, rich, inventive and well within the grasp of experienced amateurs. It is a work all Haydn players should know thoroughly. This seems to be the most commonly performed work of this opus, and so it is familiar to listeners everywhere. Pleasure—4; Effort—2.

Quartet in C major, Op. 76, No. 3 | (1797),
The Emperor or The Kaiser

I *Allegro.* II *Poco Adagio: Cantabile.* III *Menuetto: Allegro.*
IV *Finale: Presto.*

The *first movement* is a bright and cheerful sonata allegro.

The *second movement* constitutes four variations on a theme (probably of Croatian origin) that Haydn had composed earlier for the Austrian national anthem. This lovely tune (said to have been a response to that of 'God Save the Queen', which it resembles slightly) is treated with extraordinary harmonic variation.

The *third movement* minuet is heavy and accented. The trio is light and flowing.

The *fourth movement* is a massive structure. As in the final movements of the two preceding quartets, its complex and tragic character is relieved by a coda in the major mode.

Commentary. Except for the slow movement, this work is less impressive than the others in this opus are. As for that movement, the famous tune became that of the German national anthem and was often heard in that context in World War II. This fact puts off many people (those who are old enough to remember that war). It is a good work to play for those who will, but its neglect by those who won't is not a tragedy. Pleasure—3; Effort—2.

Quartet in B-flat major, Op. 76, No. 4 | (1797), *The Sunrise*

I *Allegro con spirito*. II *Adagio*. III *Menuetto: Allegro*. IV *Finale: Allegro ma non troppo*.

The *first movement* opens directly with a sustained, expanding and rising theme in the first violin, the origin of the common name. The theme is treated with continual expansion, augmentation and evolution. Despite the chirpy character of the rest of the movement, the con spirito tempo must not be too brisk, nor the mood too spirited.

The *second movement* contains extensive dialogues. A strikingly restful opening is contrasted by some complicating and tense events in the center with a return to repose at the end.

The *third movement* is declamatory, like a folk dance in quality, with no sense of urgency or haste. The trio is remarkable for the asymmetry of the tune.

The *fourth movement* is suave. It begins relatively slowly and then quickens progressively to maintain a continual expansion and augmentation.

Commentary. This is the most popular of the quartets in this opus. It is admirable in every way, and it is within the reach of all experienced amateurs. Most amateurs know it, and those who don't should. Pleasure—4; Effort—2.

Quartet in D major, Op. 76, No. 5 | (1797), with the *Churchyard (Graveyard) Largo*

I *Allegretto*. II *Largo cantabile e mesto*. III *Menuetto: Allegro*. IV *Finale: Presto*.

The *first movement* has a broad, joyous, and declamatory theme, a siciliano. The treatment, in a basic ternary form, is expansive with extended variation and much dialogue. Despite a rich texture, the movement is lucid and free of technical problems. It has wonderful parts for all voices.

The *second movement*, called mesto, is not so gloomy as all that at the outset, but it becomes so despite the major mode. The viola has a wonderfully evocative solo passage. The key, F-sharp major, makes intonation difficult. This is a sublime movement, filled with a fervent intensity.

The *third movement* is somewhat more a scherzo than a minuet. The trio works best if it is played a little faster than the minuet.

The *fourth movement*, beginning with a repeated cadence, forte, develops into a rhythmically and structurally complex sonata movement, full of invention, joy and wit.

Commentary. This is the last of Haydn's six great quartets in this key. The last movement seems to some to be not quite up to the quality of the others, but the whole is still a splendid work. The common name comes from the many sharps ("crosses") in the *second movement*. It may also allude to its difficult intonation in F-sharp minor. Pleasure—3; Effort—3.

Quartet in E-flat major, Op. 76, No. 6 | (1797)

I *Allegretto; Allegro*. II *Fantasia: Adagio*. III *Menuetto: Presto*. IV *Finale: Allegro spirituoso*.

The *first movement* is a set of variations on a simple and graceful dancing theme. All variations are in the major mode. A fine little fugue ends the movement.

The *second movement* bears no key signature. It begins in B major and progresses through an unprecedented sequence of keys in such rapid succession that each note is simply notated separately. This intense chromaticism is an attack on conventional notions of tonality. An intensely dramatic movement, this Fantasia is difficult to "hear," and so it is difficult to play without a good deal of study.

The *third movement* is the quintessential Haydn minuet-cum-scherzo. The long trio, labeled "alternativo" to emphasize its non-minuet quality, is starkly simple, based on the E-flat scale that is repeated over and over, up and down. This seems to be a rather pedantically comical reaffirmation of tonality after the slow movement.

The *fourth movement* is a rhythmically complex structure built on an E-flat scale that is fragmented and abrupt. The highly contrapuntal movement is noisily and busily playful.

Commentary. Keller calls this the greatest work of the set because of all its innovations. Others have considered it to be strange and poorly understood. It is truly remarkable. It is fully accessible to experienced amateurs and they all should play it. Pleasure—4; Effort—3.

HAYDN, Op. 77
The Lobkowitz Quartets, and Op. 103,
The Unfinished

The two quartets in Op. 77 were written in 1799, when Haydn was sixty-seven years old. He dedicated them to Prince Lobkowitz who is better remembered now as the dedicatee of Beethoven's Op. 18 quartets, composed about the same time. These are the last full quartets that Haydn wrote. He planned to write six but stopped at two, perhaps in recognition of his failing capacities. They are both massive and detailed works, free of experimentation and pointing ahead to Beethoven.

Op. 103 is a fragment, the central movements of an unfinished quartet. Written in 1803, it was not published until 1806. The first published version contained a reproduction of Haydn's calling card on which was printed a quotation from his favorite four-part song, 'Der Greis' (The Old Man): "Gone forever is my strength, old and weak am I."

Quartet in G major, Op. 77, No. 1 | (1799), *The Compliment*

I *Allegro moderato.* II *Adagio.* III *Menuetto: Presto.* IV *Finale: Presto.*

The *first movement* is a military march, a most original idea for the time. Its dotted rhythm is opposed by triplet passages. The march quality must not be over-emphasized lest it overwhelm the texture. The mood is triumphant and joyful.

The *second movement* uses a passacaglia as the basis for a profound and improvisatory structure. The mood is solemn and meditative. The effect is rich and moving.

The *third movement* is a wild scherzo evolved from the minuet. It is fast, rhythmically interesting, clever, and virile. Experts see it as the immediate antecedent to the Beethoven scherzo.

The *fourth movement* is a witty and monothematic presto, rather relaxed, but concentrated and virtuosic in style.

Commentary. This splendid mature work offers no major obstacles in technique or interpretation. It is highly recommended to those amateur players who seek a mature work to play that is not at the same time too difficult. The origin of the common name is not quite clear to me. Pleasure—3; Effort—2.

Quartet in F major, Op. 77, No. 2 | (1799)

I *Allegro moderato.* II *Menuetto: Presto ma non troppo.* III *Andante.* IV *Finale: Vivace assai.*

The *first movement* is a subtle, expansive and lyrical movement, full of joy. It requires particular attention to balance and to blend. It is gratifying to all voices.

The *second movement* is a scherzo-minuet, placed second here for the first time since Op. 64, No. 4. The principal section superimposes a dominant duple rhythm on a triple rhythm. The legato trio is somewhat relaxed in tempo. There is a witty little coda.

The *third movement* is an easygoing, warm-hearted and playful andante. It opens with a wonderful violin-cello duo. The movement has the character of a relaxed march.

The *fourth movement* opens with an attention-getting introductory chord. The following theme is asymmetric. This playful and rhythmically complex movement, some say, reflects Croatian folk music. The underlying rhythm is that of a polonaise.

Commentary. This quartet has everything, innovation, accessibility and virtuosity. It is a favorite of all Haydn fans, and all amateurs should know it. It is a little more difficult than its opus companion, especially in the last movement. Pleasure—4; Effort—3.

Quartet in B-flat major, Op. 103 | (1803), *The Unfinished*

I *Andante grazioso.* II *Minuet.*

Commentary. Some find these two lovely movements diminished by comparison with Op. 77, but others see them as the equal to the best. Amateurs should play them as Haydn's swan song, in any case. Pleasure—2; Effort—2.

IVES (1874–1954)

Charles Ives was little known in his lifetime but after his death he became famous as a highly original composer and idiosyncratic New England personality. His disdain for traditional musical forms and compositional methods led him to produce many works that are not yet appreciated widely enough to have entered the common repertoire. The classical forms of chamber music, with its strong base in tradition, did not appeal to him as a medium, and so he wrote little music of that sort. The major chamber works currently played are the four sonatas for violin and piano, the piano trio and the two string quartets.

The first string quartet was written in 1896, while Ives was a student at Yale, studying composition with Horatio Parker and playing the organ at New Haven's Centre Church. The *first movement* is an exercise that he wrote for his composition class, and the other movements are modified hymn tunes that he played in church. The pastor there encouraged him in such improvisation. The *first movement* was later rewritten to become the *third movement* of his fourth symphony. This first quartet is subtitled "A Revival Service" and also "From the Salvation Army."

The second string quartet, written thirteen years later after Ives had entered the insurance business in New York, reflects his response to conventional approaches to chamber music. Disappointed in a concert by the Kneisel Quartet, he wrote the second quartet, he said, "half mad, half in fun, and half to try out, practice and have some fun with making those men fiddlers get up and do something like men."

The second quartet is probably not quite suitable for amateurs to try, but the first is.

Quartet No. 1 | (1896), *A Revival Service*

I *Chorale: Andante con moto.* II *Prelude: Allegro.* III *Offertory: Adagio cantabile.* IV *Postlude: Allegro marziale.*

The *first movement* is a scholastic fugue. Both the subject and the counter subjects are phrases from common hymn tunes of the time, still popular in Protestant churches. The most familiar are those known by their opening lines, "From Greenland's icy mountains," and "All hail the pow'r of Jesus' name." The contrast between the austerity usually associated with such melodies and their treatment as a fugue is a source of pleasure to those who grew up knowing the tunes as hymns.

The *second movement* Prelude is a tripartite Brahmsian elaboration on other hymn tunes.

The *third movement* Offertory is another Brahmsian elaboration on hymn tunes, including "Come, Thou Font of Every Blessing."

The *fourth movement* Postlude also in the style of Brahms, uses further familiar hymn tunes, especially "Stand Up, Stand Up for Jesus".

Commentary. This quartet antedates Ives's famous revolt against musical conventions. It is readily playable by amateurs, yet it bears the clear stamp of Ives in the vernacular hymn tunes and in the characteristic harmonic innovation. This is a light and quite trivial work. It is, however, an interesting quartet that should be played by amateurs more than it is. Pleasure—2; Effort—3.

MENDELSSOHN-BARTHOLDY (1809–1847)

Ludwig Felix Mendelssohn-Bartholdy's grandfather, Moses Mendelssohn, was a monumental figure in his generation. The son of a poor Jewish scribe in Dessau, he traveled to Berlin alone at the age of fourteen, following his Talmud teacher who had become Chief Rabbi there. The brilliant boy advanced rapidly as a philosopher and theologian, as well as a banker. He soon reached the highest levels in his professions, being referred to in awe by his contemporaries as the "German Plato," "German Socrates," "Luther of the German Jews," and "The Third Moses" (after the second, Moses Maimonides). Of the six of his eight children who reached maturity, the second, Abraham, became the father of Felix.

Abraham Mendelssohn entered partnership with his brother, Joseph, in a banking house in Hamburg. His marriage to Lea Solomon of Berlin united him to a cultured and intelligent woman of considerable education. Felix, born in 1809, followed Fanny, born in 1805, and two other children, Rebekah and Paul, came later. The family prospered in Hamburg despite the ravages of Napoleon who occupied the city in 1806. With the incorporation of the city into the French Empire, the family fled to Berlin.

Both Fanny and Felix showed musical ability from their earliest years. Taught at first at home, they later studied for a time with Marie Bigot, a distinguished pianist in Paris, and then with the best teachers that their wealthy, wise and devoted parents could find in Berlin. The children were playing in private concerts by 1818.

The Mendelssohn family faced a serious question at this period, that of conversion to Christianity. Such conversion was then a common practice among German Jews who sought full admission to European society, and Lea wanted the children brought up as Lutherans. Two sisters of Abraham Mendelssohn had converted already. Perhaps Moses Mendelssohn's emphasis on the concordance of monotheistic religions influenced those decisions. Finally, both the children and the parents were baptized, engrafting a second family name, Bartholdy, a name that had been adopted by Lea's brother upon his own conversion. Felix Mendelssohn may have felt some ambivalence about conversion, for he consistently resisted his father' emphasis on the inclusion of the engrafted name in his published music and programs.

Felix composed prodigiously from childhood, at first writing small pieces for the family circle alone. In 1821, when he was twelve, he went with his music teacher, Karl Zelter, to Weimar to play for Goethe. In the sixteen-day visit, Goethe was enormously delighted, and his enthusiasm for the young genius led to a visit from the whole Mendelssohn family a year later.

In 1825, Abraham Mendelssohn took the teenaged Felix to Paris to meet Cherubini, the director of the Conservatory there, in order to explore the possibility of a musical career for the boy. Felix was not impressed with Paris and they returned to Berlin after a short stay. The Op. 20 octet and the Op. 13 string quartet were written in this period. Felix, now making occasional public appearances, began to enjoy some celebrity.

Three years later, the nineteen-year-old Felix went to England at the urging of his father who sought to broaden his son's experience in this way. He carried letters of introduction to the circles of the wealthy, made public appearances, and toured Scotland and Wales. The Op. 12 string quartet comes from this period. On his return, he saw his beloved sister, Fanny, married to Wilhelm Hansel after a five-year courtship.

In 1830, Felix, now twenty-one, entered upon another long tour, a leisurely sightseeing trip to Italy, Switzerland, Paris, and

London. When he returned to Berlin two years later he had achieved his maturity.

He now sought a fixed position, and he accepted appointment to the position of Director of the Musical Society in Dusseldorf in 1833. He soon resigned, over various problems, to become Director of the Leipzig Gewandhaus Orchestra in 1835. Leipzig provided him a most satisfactory opportunity and he flourished, receiving an honorary degree from Leipzig University in 1836, at the age of twenty-five.

Robert and Clara Schumann became his friends in Leipzig, and there he met Cecile Jeanrenaud whom he married in 1837. This domestic, pious, pretty, and charming woman brought him great happiness. The Op. 44 string quartets come from the period of their early marriage.

Mendelssohn's fame soon brought him offers of other positions. He accepted an appointment as the musical director of the newly expanded Academy of the Arts in Berlin in 1841, but the job proved to be an unhappy one for several reasons. Though he continued to compose and to tour, he was away from Berlin a great deal, and he finally terminated his relationship with the Berlin Academy in 1844. After a two-year retirement to Frankfurt for a period devoted especially to composition, Mendelssohn returned to Leipzig in 1846.

Here, he resumed his public appearances, but the onset of headaches and fatigue limited his activities. Word of his sister Fanny's sudden death from a stroke in the spring of 1847 produced an emotional crisis from which he never fully recovered. The brother and sister had remained close throughout their short lives together. He went to Switzerland that summer, in an effort to recover his spirits on a holiday, writing the Op. 80 string quartet.

When he returned to Leipzig, he was obviously ill. Although he resumed work, it was with little success. He died suddenly in November 1847, after a series of strokes.

The numbering of the quartets of Mendelssohn does not reflect their order of composition. They are most easily grasped, as a whole, in four groups. The first group contains those quartets of 1823–1829, when Mendelssohn was fourteen to twenty years old. The second group was written in 1837–1838, shortly after his marriage and at the beginning of a particularly happy and productive period. The third phase is represented by the single work, Op. 80, written in 1847 soon after the death of his beloved sister, Fanny, and a few months before his own death. The fourth group is a posthumous publication of miscellany.

The quartets of 1823–29 constitute a quartet in E-flat major, Op. posth. (1823), the quartet in A minor, Op. 13 (1827) and the quartet in E-flat major, Op. 12 (1829). The first of these is an immature work that is virtually unknown today. The second and third are mature works, still often heard.

The quartets of 1837–38 are the three quartets in Op. 44. The quartet in E minor, Op. 44, No. 2, was completed first, in June 1837. The quartet in E-flat major, Op. 44, No. 3, was completed in February 1838. Four months later, Mendelssohn completed the quartet in D major, Op. 44, No. 1. The Ferdinand David Quartet premiered the first two. David was the virtuosic violinist for whom the composer wrote the violin concerto. All three quartets are in the current standard repertoire.

The quartet of 1847, Op. 80 in F minor, reflects his mourning for Fanny and, possibly, a recognition of his own declining health.

The posthumous works, published together as Op. 81, constitute a fugue in E-flat major (1827) from Mendelssohn's youth, a capriccio in E minor (1843), and two movements of an unfinished quartet, an andante in E major and a scherzo in A minor from 1847. Some experts suggest that Mendelssohn may have intended the capriccio in E minor to be the final movement of an uncompleted quartet.

The works described here, in the order of the opus numbers, include only those that are readily available and played currently.

Quartet in E flat major, Op. 12 | (1829)

I *Adagio non troppo; Allegro non tardante*. II *Canzonetta: Allegretto*. III *Andante espressivo*. IV *Molto Allegro e Vivace*.

The *first movement* opens with an adagio introduction that is reminiscent of that found in Beethoven's Op. 74, "The Harp." The theme of this introduction is referred to later in the work, as is also that of the ensuing allegro. The allegro theme is broad and sweeping, and the movement is tranquil and reassuring throughout.

The *second movement* canzonetta theme is a minor-mode folk melody, treated in the first and last segments of an ABA form. The melody is made more effective by the use of pizzicato and staccato. The middle section, in the major mode, is more agitated, a playful dialogue between the violins over a pedal note. The coda ends the movement humorously. The whole movement is dancing, graceful, and simple.

The *third movement* theme is a simple aria, brief and uncomplicated. An opening mood of thanksgiving leads to a passionate recitative that is followed by a return to the main theme and mood.

The *fourth movement* is a running and pleasing movement, exhibiting harmonic complexity and a variety of moods, leading to the introduction of material from the *first movement*. There is a brilliant and radiant coda.

Commentary. This work was written about the time of Mendelssohn's trip to Wales and Scotland, the period of the *Fingal's Cave* overture and the Scottish symphony. It is a fine work to play, making few demands on players and listeners. It is a gem of the literature, highly original, characteristic, and seemingly perfect in form. Pleasure—3; Effort—2.

Quartet in A minor, Op. 13 | (1827)

I *Adagio; Allegro vivace.* II *Adagio non lento.* III *Intermezzo: Allegretto con moto.* IV *Presto.*

The *first movement* opens with a notable adagio introduction expressing a motto theme that is derived from a song Mendelssohn wrote that year, 'Frage', Op. 9, No. 1. The tune reflects the lines, "Is it true that you are always waiting for me in the arbored walk?" This motto theme recurs throughout the whole quartet. The allegro that follows is contrapuntal and harmonically radical, full of storm, strife and energy. It contains especially fine parts for the cello and the viola.

The *second movement* is in ternary form. Two treatments of a lovely *Lied* frame a dark and chromatic central fugal section. This is a strange but exquisite movement.

The *third movement* is a miniature scherzo in three parts. The first and last sections, containing a dancing allegretto con moto, frame a sprightly central section, allegro di molto. Mendelssohn settled on the latter instruction after writing and erasing "più presto" and "un poco più mosso." This simple and charming movement is particularly refreshing after the more complex antecedent movements.

The first violin opens the *fourth movement* with a dramatic recitative played above a tremolando accompaniment, A dramatic and highly contrapuntal presto follows. Some see this movement as owing much to the study of Beethoven's Op. 132. The motto theme of the adagio that opens the *first movement* is referred to again at one point and then restated before the brief coda. Thematic material from the other movements is also recalled.

Commentary. This strenuous and striking work reflects the time that Mendelssohn spent in Paris in 1825, when he greatly broadened his horizons. His choice of A minor may reflect the appearance of Schubert's Op. 29 quartet and Beethoven's Op. 132 quartet, both in A minor, in 1825. A thematic resemblance between the *first movement* of this work and of that Op. 132 further supports the idea of a linkage. This is a massive quartet, virtuosic in all parts, but one that is fully accessible to amateurs of advanced abilities. Some players find it to be a superior work to Op. 12, which it preceded by two years, while others prefer the other. It is a matter of taste more than objective assessment, perhaps. One thinks of them as a pair. Pleasure—3; Effort—3.

Quartet in D major, Op. 44, No. 1 | (1838)

I *Molto allegro vivace.* II *Menuetto: Un poco allegretto.* III *Andante espressivo con moto.* IV *Presto con brio.*

The *first movement*, opening with an orchestral tremolando, possesses an exuberant first theme and a contrasting second theme. The sonata allegro form contains an unusually elaborate development. This smooth and euphonious movement presents no surprises. The texture is orchestral throughout.

The *second movement* minuet is Haydnesque with much writing in thirds and sixths. It is dainty, transparent, and melodious. The pleasing trio in the minor mode makes use of a drone in the bass, after the common baroque practice. This is a smooth and pleasant movement.

The *third movement*, an exceptionally lovely and lush song, is treated extensively to harmonic variation and counter-melodies. A degree of mournful sentimentality, even superficiality, does not diminish the quality of the writing.

The *fourth movement* is a flashing saltarello, reminiscent of the final movement of the Italian symphony. It is joyful, deft, and witty, if a little unsophisticated. The texture tends to the orchestral.

Commentary. This quartet was written at about the same time as the E minor violin concerto and the cello sonata in B-flat, Op. 45. Mendelssohn is known to have been particularly fond of it. It is more classical in form and less experimental than the others in the opus are. The writing divides the interest evenly among the four voices. The parts lie in comfortable registers and positions, and the work offers no unusual musical or interpretive problems. This quartet is a favorite both with players and with listeners. It requires a high degree of assurance in amateur players, being difficult but not very difficult. Pleasure—3; Effort—3.

Quartet in E minor, Op. 44, No. 2 | (1837)

I *Allegro assai appassionato.* II *Scherzo: Allegro di molto.*
III *Andante.* IV *Presto agitato.*

The *first movement* opens abruptly with a passionate and lofty melody played by the first violin over a restless and syncopated accompaniment. The second theme is like a folk song. The movement is richly inventive with passages of splendid counterpoint and imitative dialogue. The second subject is a derivative of the first, so that the movement possesses a particular unity. This handsome movement reminds one of the violin concerto.

The *second movement* is an elfin, intense, and energetic scherzo in 3/4 time. The four sixteenth-notes that begin the theme recur in various guises throughout the movement to give a sense of unity. The viola has pleasant little contrasting themes to play. This movement is difficult.

The *third movement* is a song without words, rather simply and briefly presented. The character is noble and grand. The score carries the composer's warning that the movement must not be played too slowly. To do so would unduly exaggerate its sentimentality.

The *fourth movement* is a masterful presto, agitated and dramatic. The principal theme is a peasant dance. A second theme is a passionate cantabile.

Commentary. E minor was a favorite key for Mendelssohn and this work meets his best standards. It was a great favorite of Joachim.

This quartet is somewhat more difficult technically than the others in the opus. Amateurs should not undertake it casually. Pleasure—4; Effort—4.

Quartet in E-flat major, Op. 44, No. 3 | (1838)

I *Allegro vivace.* II *Scherzo: Assai leggiero e vivace.* III *Adagio non troppo.* IV *Molto allegro con fuoco.*

The *first movement* opens with a melody whose upbeat is a group of four sixteenth-notes. This figure recurs throughout this movement and in the third and *fourth movements* as a unifying device. The movement is notable for its many easy modulations to surprising keys, a hallmark of the mature Mendelssohn. The movement is powerful, energetic and impassioned.

The *second movement* is charming and romantic, one of Mendelssohn's greatest scherzos. Its woodland or 'hunting' music presages a style found often in the later German romantics. The rondo is interrupted for a time by a contrasting fugue that begins merrily in the viola. This is a fine and imaginative scherzo.

The *third movement* is a warm-hearted and romantic *Lied,* treated expansively.

The *fourth movement* is a furious and humorous allegro. In a brilliant coda, the second violin and viola carry the melody below figures in the first violin. This movement seems to be a little weaker, perhaps, than the rest of the quartet.

Commentary. The least familiar work of the opus, this quartet deserves better. It seems more progressive than the others, richer and more powerful. Good amateurs can play it, but it requires a particularly fine first violinist. Pleasure—4; Effort—4.

Quartet in F minor, Op. 80 | (1847)

I *Allegro vivace assai.* II *Allegro assai.* III *Adagio.* IV *Finale: Allegro molto.*

The *first movement* is reminiscent of that of Beethoven's Op. 95 in its principal theme and in its character, using rhythmic contrasts and syncopation in a dramatic framework. Its extended coda has an intensity that approaches that of Beethoven.

The *second movement* is also reminiscent of Beethoven. Here, the old minuet form is transformed into a bizarre and savage dance, suffused with sorrow. The trio has a passacaglia-like theme in the viola and cello overlaid by a macabre waltz in the first violin.

The *third movement* is a mournful but peaceful song without words, likened by some to the adagio of Beethoven's Op. 59, No. 1. Like the most profound such movements in Beethoven, this one defies description. Its character can be fully appreciated only in the playing.

The *fourth movement* is tempestuous with contrasting themes, restless syncopation and drooping cadences. The text becomes barren and athematic at points. The movement ends in a sense of profound despair. Pleasure—2; Effort—3.

Commentary. This rhythmic and passionate work has an untempered gloom that may partly account for its neglect. Amateurs can play it, but they will find Mendelssohn in an unfamiliar spirit. It leaves a very different impression than do the other quartets of Mendelssohn. It should not be approached as a characteristic work. Nonetheless, it is well worth examination by those who wish to explore the moods of this composer in the full. Pleasure—3; Effort—3.

MOZART (1756–1791)
Biographical Notes

Wolfgang Amadeus Mozart's father, Leopold, a violinist, was the son of an Augsburg family in which the men had generally found careers as bookbinders and artisans. Leopold Mozart had traveled to Salzburg to study theology and the law at first, but his financial circumstances led him to accept a position as a musician at the Salzburg cathedral. There he was encouraged to develop his innate gifts both in performance and in composition. He became a violinist in the orchestra of the archiepiscopal Court and a music teacher. His marriage to Anna Maria Pertl produced seven children. Only two of them survived infancy, the fourth, Anna Maria (Nannerl) and the last, Wolfgang Amadeus, who was born on January 27th, 1756.

Wolfgang and Nannerl both showed musical ability from their earliest years, and Leopold Mozart soon came to devote most of his energy to the development and exploitation of their gifts. He retained his position in the orchestra for many years, though he was absent from Salzburg for long periods touring with his children.

Leopold took Wolfgang on his first tour at the age of six, a visit to the Court of the Elector Maximilian III at Munich, and soon after to the Imperial Court at Vienna and to Hungary. These were not extended tours, but a tour begun in June 1763, when Wolfgang was seven, lasted for over three years. It included visits to many cities in Germany, Belgium, the Netherlands, Switzerland, France, and England. A tour of Italy soon followed, in 1772, which greatly influenced his development. The Italianate three divertimenti were written in Salzburg soon before this Italian tour began and the Milanese quartets, K. 155–160, come from this period. A year later, on a tour to Vienna, he became acquainted with Haydn and studied his Op.17 and Op.20 quartets. His 'Viennese' quartets, K 168–173, come from this period.

In these years, Leopold was Wolfgang's only teacher in general education as well as in music. The boy's musical gifts flourished, but his education in other subjects was poor, coming as much from experience as from formal instruction. He came to adulthood with a character in which gullibility, a poor sense of discipline, and a degree of irresponsibility tended to obscure his basic good nature.

Barely out of his adolescence, the young Mozart became attached to the archiepiscopal Court at Salzburg alongside his father. Meanwhile he sought a position elsewhere as a Court musician. He developed an attachment to a family in Salzburg named Weber (relatives of Carl Maria von Weber) and his obsession with the second Weber daughter, Aloysia, filled his father with despair. Leopold sent his son on a tour to Paris and Mannheim in 1778, when he was twenty-two, accompanied by his mother, in the attempt to separate Wolfgang from the Weber family and to help him to find a career. The trip was a personal disaster both because Mozart failed to find a position and because his mother died while they were in Paris.

The young Mozart returned to Salzburg to a job as organist to the archiepiscopal Court, and he resumed his involvement with the Weber family. He eventually married Constanze, Aloysia's Weber's younger sister, and by 1787 they had settled in Vienna where Mozart had secured an appointment as Royal and Imperial Court composer. His salary here was meager, for the post was largely honorary, and his income from performance and the sale of his compositions was marginally adequate, especially because of the fiscal irresponsibility of the young couple. With the death of the Emperor Joseph II three years later, Mozart applied for reappointment to the Court but the new Emperor took no action on the request.

In his last year, Mozart continued his unsettled life in Vienna and on tour, dying unexpectedly after a brief illness in December 1791, at the age of thirty-six. The cause of his death was possibly renal failure with hypertension, although there are many theories. He left little money and few material possessions aside from his manuscripts. Constanze's sale of his manuscripts in the attempt to raise money is a well-known story. She remarried and survived to old age.

Mozart's quartets fall into two distinct periods of time, those from his youth and those from his maturity. The youthful quartets begin with K. 80 (1770), a work written during his first visit to Italy. He wrote the three Divertimenti, K. 136-138, in 1772 and the autumn of that same year saw the production, in Milan, of the six Italian or Milanese quartets, K. 155–160. The Divertimenti and the Italian quartets all contain three movements only. They exhibit a fresh and naive cheerfulness expressed with a contrapuntal and decorative style. We now know these compositions mainly as works for string orchestral performance. Indeed, Einstein suggested that Mozart wrote these as symphonies in the Italian style, waiting to have the wind parts added. Played as quartets, they have a more intimate feel, more charm and less brilliance.

The next six quartets (K. 168–173) were written in rapid succession in the late summer of 1773 in Vienna. These 'Viennese' quartets demonstrate the seventeen-year-old boy's response to Haydn's Op. 17 and Op. 20 quartets, which had appeared soon before. These six works, all four-movement works, show Mozart's interest in exploring the form, having more experimentation and less of the naive freshness of the Italian quartets. They remained unpublished for fifteen years, appearing only after his mature quartets had become known.

The mature quartets came after Mozart had established a sound friendship with Haydn in Vienna. The period from 1782 through 1785 saw the composition of the six that he dedicated to Haydn, prompted especially by the appearance of the six works in Haydn's Op. 33. The poor reception to the quartets that Mozart dedicated to Haydn may have prompted him to produce a single quartet (K. 499) as a means of achieving a more popular success. This work, written for a publisher, Hoffmeister, appeared one year later, in 1786, the year of *Figaro*. 1788 saw the completion of an adagio and fugue for quartet, Mozart's transcription of a piano duet that he had written four years before. In 1789–90, Mozart wrote the three quartets dedicated to King Frederick William II of Prussia.

The six quartets dedicated to Haydn (K. 387, 421, 428, 458, 464, 465) were written in the order in which they are numbered over a span of twenty-six months, from December 1782 through January 1785. This long working period, uncharacteristic of a composer who was famous for his speed, indicates the effort he put into them. He himself described them as "the fruits of a long and laborious endeavour," and the autographs show indications of much revision. The six works were not well received by contemporaries.

The last three quartets, from 1789-90, are commonly called the 'Cello Quartets' from the prominence given to the cello in these works. They are also sometimes called the 'Prussian' or 'Berlin Quartets' from their dedication to the Prussian King Frederick William II who was an amateur cellist. Prince Lichnowsky had taken Mozart to Berlin in the spring of 1789 where Mozart met the King. That King is also remembered as the dedicatee of the Op. 50 quartets of Haydn and of the piano-cello sonatas of Beethoven, Op. 5. The King had commissioned six quartets but Mozart, upon returning to Vienna, found himself so burdened by his wife's illness and by mounting debt that he was able to complete only three, K. 575, 589 and 590. Other works from this period are the clarinet quintet (K. 581) and *Cosi fan Tutte*.

MOZART
The Divertimentos

Divertimento in D major, K. 136 | (1772)

I *Allegro*. II *Andante*. III *Presto*.

Divertimento in B-flat major, K. 137 | (1772)

I *Andante.* II *Allegro di molto.* III *Allegro assai.*

Divertimento in F major, K. 138 | (1772)

I *Allegro.* II *Andante.* III *Presto.*

Commentary. These three works share essentially the same format except for the reversal of the positions of the *first* and *second movements* in the B-flat divertimento. The fast movements are all energetic and quick while the 3/4 time of the slow movements gives them all a dancing character. So closely do they resemble one another that the mind cannot readily keep them separated. The violins carry most of the action, leaving the lower strings the responsibility for the rhythmic and harmonic structure. Pleasure—3; Effort—1

MOZART
The Italian or Milanese Quartets

Quartet in D major, K. 155 | (1772)

I *Allegro moderato.* II *Andante.* III *Molto Allegro.*

Quartet in G major, K. 156 | (1772)

I *Presto.* II *Adagio.* III *Tempo di Menuetto.*

Quartet in C major, K. 157 | (1772)

I *Allegro.* II *Andante.* III *Presto.*

Quartet in F major, K. 158 | (1772)

I *Allegro.* II *Andante, un poco Allegretto.* III *Tempo di Menuetto.*

Quartet in B-flat major, K. 159 | (1772)

I *Andante grazioso.* II *Allegro.* III *Rondo. Allegro grazioso.*

Quartet in E-flat major, K. 160 | (1772)

I *Allegro.* II *Un poco Adagio.* III *Presto.*

Commentary on the Italian or Milanese Quartets. These six quartets show a little progress in compositional technique beyond the Divertimenti that just preceded them but they show more individuality. K. 155 is noteworthy mainly for the rustic appeal of the thematic material in the last movement. In K. 156, a light-hearted opening presto gives way to a lovely adagio and a rather perfunctory minuet. K. 157 is prim and formal throughout but comparatively unimaginative. K. 158 is even less interesting. K. 159, however, possesses considerable thematic and compositional interest, and K. 160 is similarly engaging.

These six works remain staples for players new to the avocation of chamber music for good reason. They present the essence of the craft without setting up major obstacles or problems for inexperienced players. Beyond that, they are works of the great master. They present the incomparable genius as he was exploring his maturing talents. Pleasure—3: Effort—1.

MOZART
The Viennese Quartets

Quartet in F major, K. 168 | (1773)

I *Allegro.* II *Andante.* III *Menuetto.* IV *Fuga. Allegro.*

The *first movement* provides an early example of the use of fragments from the main theme in the development of a sonata movement (note, for example, the later use made of bar 3).

The *second movement* shows, perhaps for the first time in quartet writing, Mozart's use of mutes. This contrapuntal movement, opening with a four-part canon, treats all four instruments as equals.

In the *third movement*, a slight and charming miniature, a dainty theme in the Menuetto leads to a Trio that features imitative writing through all the parts.

The *fourth movement* is a strictly organized but playful fugue on a vivacious subject.

Commentary. This quartet, though rather small, shows a considerable advance. It is most rewarding to play and the parts are interesting throughout. Pleasure—3; Effort—1.

Quartet in A major, K. 169 | (1773)

I *Molto Allegro.* II *Andante.* III *Menuetto.* IV *Rondo: Allegro.*

In the cheerful *first movement,* Mozart uses fragments from the exposition in subsequent development. This became a favorite device for Mozart, Beethoven and many others.

The *second movement* is a cavatina with a suave melody played by the first violin over an organ-like accompaniment in the other instruments.

The *third movement* minuet features a lovely theme made of delicate rising fragments.

The *fourth movement* rondo develops a comical leaping theme.

Commentary. This work is rather like K. 168 from the point of view of amateur performance, just as much fun and just as rewarding. Pleasure—3; Effort—1.

Quartet in C major, K. 170 | (1773)

I *Andante.* II *Menuetto.* III *Poco Adagio.* IV *Rondo. Allegro.*

The *first movement* represents the first theme and variations form to appear in the Mozart quartets. The Haydnesque theme receives decorative treatments, the last of which is made humorous by the appearance of rumbling interjections before the unadorned main theme receives a final restatement.

The *second movement* minuet is undistinguished.

The Haydnesque *third movement* constitutes mainly a series of solo passages, played successively by the two violins and viola over a simple accompaniment of detached eighth notes.

The *fourth movement* is a small and almost trivial rondo of no distinction.

Commentary. This work has less appeal to many players than the others in the set. Still, the *first movement* is notable. Pleasure—2; Effort—1.

Quartet in E-flat major, K. 171 | (1773)

I *Adagio; Allegro assai.* II *Menuetto.* III *Andante. IV Allegro assai.*

The *first movement*, a sonata allegro, opens with an adagio introduction, an early example of a format that was to become a standard. The subsequent allegro possesses characteristic Mozartean charm and delicacy. The return of the adagio at the end also seems to foretell the cyclic device that was to become so prominent later.

The *second movement* minuet features a departure from the usual four or eight bar structure, giving it a feel of asymmetry.

The *third movement* andante, played with mutes, is extremely contrapuntal, almost a tribute to Bach.

The *fourth movement*, a sonata allegro, deals with merry and uncomplicated themes that suggest the singing of birds.

Commentary. This quartet is fully as interesting as the later mature quartets and deserves the attention of all players. Pleasure—4; Effort—1.

Quartet in B-flat major, K. 172 | (1773)

I *Allegro spiritoso.* II *Adagio.* III *Menuetto.* IV *Allegro assai.*

The *first movement*, in 3/4 time, features two rustic melodies treated with a rather formal elegance.

In the *second movement* adagio, the first violin plays a lovely and expressive melody over a simple rhythmic accompaniment in the other strings.

The *third movement* constitutes a contrapuntal minuet, a three-part accompanied canon, contrasted by a charmingly innocent trio.

The sonata allegro *fourth movement* distributes its melodies fairly uniformly among the four instruments.

Commentary. This is an interesting but not very striking work, most memorable for the *first movement*. Pleasure—2; Effort—1.

Quartet in D minor, K. 173 | (1773)

I *Allegro ma molto moderato.* II *Andantino grazioso.* III *Menuetto.*
IV *Fuga: Allegro.*

The bulk of the comical *first movement* is given over to the waggish
second theme, seemingly an imitation of clucking chickens.

The *second movement* is a tender and graceful song in D major,
treated at some length.

The formal and stately *third movement* minuet is not distinguished.

The *fourth movement* is an austere but quite conventional fugue on an
earnest chromatic subject. It illustrates Mozart's mastery of the form.

Commentary. The comic irresponsibility of the farmyard music in
the *first movement* is so impressive that the formality of the three subsequent movements cannot obliterate its memory. The fugal finale is
also memorable. Pleasure—4; Effort—1

MOZART
The Late Quartets
(The Haydn, Hoffmeister, and Prussian Quartets)

Quartet in G major, K. 387 | (1782)

I *Allegro vivace assai.* II *Menuetto: Allegretto.* III *Andante cantabile.*
IV *Molto allegro.*

The *first movement* opens directly with a broad declamatory theme. Its
treatment is chromatic, melodic, inventive and natural in feeling. A
sense of sturdy cheerfulness prevails throughout this long and complex movement.

The *second movement* is certainly not a minuet, despite its title. Bold
accents, alternating pianos and fortes in an ascending chromatic scale,
create a cheerful and declamatory scherzo. The trio is gloomy and dramatic, in contrast.

The *third movement* is an intense, mysterious and subtle andante. This
long, complex and inventive slow movement seems to have established the standard for Mozart in all his subsequent quartets.

The *fourth movement* is a great sonata form, full of joy and triumphal spirit. Its fugal nature is probably a tribute to the fugal finales employed by Haydn in Op. 20 and in Op. 50, No. 4. The counterpoint produces startling contrasts in texture. The movement ends in a thrilling soft cadence.

Commentary. All amateurs should know this long and outstanding work. The last movement sounds more difficult than it is, though it certainly requires a fine first violinist. The work is completely natural in feeling so that it is easy to understand. It contains fine parts for all voices. Pleasure—4; Effort—2.

Quartet in D minor, K. 421 | (1783)

I Allegro moderato. II Andante. III Menuetto: Allegretto. IV Allegretto ma non troppo.

The *first movement* has a somber, morose and dramatic character with sinister moments. Its adherence to the key of D minor throughout supports the constancy of its gloomy character.

The *second movement* is a lyrical and simple major-mode melody, singing and restful, though the rhythm maintains a degree of tension. The middle section is highly romantic in character.

The *third movement* minuet begins not as a dance but as a dramatic and somber statement in the minor mode. The trio, in the major mode, treats a rather agitated folk song tune with crude gaiety.

The *fourth movement* has a restless 6/8 siciliano theme in the minor mode that is treated in four variations, only one being in the major. The last movement of Haydn's Op. 33, No. 5, may have suggested the movement. These splendid variations lead to a più allegro section that ends the movement in a spirit of tragedy. Triplet figures and a falling octave in the final phrase seem to refer back to the *first movement*. This is a most interesting and satisfying movement.

Commentary. This largely tragic work is ferociously earnest and it seems deeply personal. This unique character remains unexplained. Mozart's wife was in confinement and labor at the time and this may have something to do with the mood. The last movement is said to have been written in one night. The work is readily accessible to amateurs who must, however, be prepared for its serious mood. There are fine parts for all voices. Pleasure—4; Effort—2.

Quartet in E-flat major, K. 428 | (1783)

I *Allegro ma non troppo.* II *Andante con moto.* III *Menuetto: Allegretto.* IV *Allegro vivace.*

The *first movement* opens in unison with strong octaves in a sinuous and dramatic melody. The exposition is long, and the development is complex and highly innovative. The character is thoughtful and composed, but buoyantly optimistic.

The serene *second movement* is based on a yearning melody with an undulating accompaniment in 6/8 time. The bass has the feel of an Alberti bass. Some experts allude to the '*Tristan*' tone of this romantic movement.

The *third movement* minuet, beginning on an offbeat, is nearly devoid of dancing qualities. The trio, opening in C minor, presents a somber contrast to the brightness of the minuet. A mournful drone appears in the bass of the trio.

The *fourth movement* is a boisterous rondo, its sturdy and rather abrupt themes being treated with vigor and enthusiasm. The movement is reminiscent of the rondos of similar character in the Haydn quartets. It may well be an especially pointed tribute to Haydn.

Commentary. This quartet is perhaps less memorable than the others in the set, and seems rather less often played. It is a fine work, presenting no major problems. It is fully accessible to good amateurs. Pleasure—2; Effort—2.

Quartet in B-flat major, K. 458 | (1784), *The Hunt*

I *Allegro vivace assai.* II *Menuetto: Moderato.* III *Adagio.* IV *Allegro assai.*

The *first movement* opens abruptly with a tune that mimics the call of a hunting horn, hence the common name. Another horn call opens the development. The movement is devoid of a second theme, the first being treated capriciously in fragments. This is a bubbling, spirited and gay movement, strongly reminiscent of Haydn in character and in technique.

The *second movement* minuet is serious, but gallant and cheerful.

The *third movement* has a romantic, hesitant and sad opening theme that is contrasted by an exquisitely lyrical second theme. The mood remains brooding and sad, despite the major mode. The spirit is adagio though the tempo must not be. This is a most memorable movement.

The *fourth movement* returns to the roguish impetuosity of the first. Its theme is taken from a folk song. This contrapuntal movement is reminiscent of Haydn's humorous finale movements.

Commentary. This quartet is famous for the *first movement*, but also memorable for the *third*, perhaps the greatest slow movement in this set of six. The quartet is much loved and much played by amateurs. It offers no major technical or interpretive problems. Pleasure—4; Effort—2.

Quartet in A major, K. 464 | (1785), *The Drum*

I *Allegro.* II *Menuetto.* III *Andante.* IV *Allegro non troppo.*

The *first movement* opens with a graceful theme in the dominant, E. The chromatic treatment is full of enthusiasm, involving much contrapuntal writing. There are happy dialogues among the voices and many innovations.

The *second movement* has the same grace, cheer and enthusiasm as the *first.* The theme is remarkable for its contrasting piano and forte statements.

The *third movement* is a theme with six variations and an extended coda. It is a long movement in the major mode, fervent, lyrical and noble, presaging Beethoven in the ingenuity and freshness of the variations. The timpani sounds produced by the cello in the last variation give the quartet a nickname, The Drum.

The *fourth movement* is based on a chromatic theme that is developed contrapuntally. There is much part-writing in duos. This splendid movement is rich, cheerful and noble in character.

Commentary. This quartet is remarkable for its sturdy cheerfulness and robust character, supported by the persistence of the major mode throughout. Beethoven, who made a copy of the finale for study, greatly admired it. This great work, rather neglected by professionals and amateurs alike, is accessible to accomplished amateurs, offering no major problems in technique and interpretation. It deserves to be known better than it is. Pleasure—3; Effort—3.

Quartet in C major, K. 465 | (1785), *The Dissonance*

I *Adagio; Allegro.* II *Andante cantabile.* III *Menuetto: Allegretto.*
IV *Allegro molto.*

The *first movement* opens with a famous long adagio whose novel chromatic harmony gives the quartet it common name. These twenty-two introductory bars establish a mood of oppression or mystery that is abruptly dispelled by the elementary diatonic theme of the subsequent allegro. The adagio makes even fresher the C major tune when it bursts forth. The theme is fully developed and then treated further in an extensive and expressive coda that comes to a soft and whispered ending.

The *second movement* is in simple binary form, each section having three themes. The part writing involves extensive dialogues among the voices, especially in the first violin and cello parts. This very romantic movement ends softly and secretly.

The *third movement* minuet is brisk, fine and polished. The trio is dark, in the minor mode, with sharp dynamic contrasts.

The *fourth movement* is generally serene and bright, and often witty and incisive. The development section is particularly ingenious with some recall of darker moods. There are virtuosic passages for the first violin.

Commentary. This quartet achieves a singular unity in style and character. The long adagio introduction is another tribute to Haydn who invented the idea and used it especially in his quartets in Op. 71 and 74. Overall, this is a real masterpiece. One should not compare it to the others in the set, perhaps, but many players consider this to be the outstanding work of this set of masterpieces. Pleasure—4; Effort—2.

Quartet in D major, K. 499 | (1786), *The Hoffmeister*

I *Allegretto.* II *Menuetto: Allegretto.* III *Adagio.* IV *Allegro.*

The *first movement* opens directly with a diatonic theme that is subsequently treated in a playful and highly original manner. The mood is bright and optimistic.

The *second movement* is a sober and yet graceful dance. The trio, in the minor mode, anticipates the finale in its witty theme.

The *third movement* is broad, bright, vigorous and serene, with memorable dialogues among the voices.

The *fourth movement* is based on a short and rather casual first theme, with a more jolly and complete second theme. This work has the character of a scherzo and an incisiveness and thrust that make it difficult to play up to speed. The two subjects are treated in conflict and contrast. A wonderful coda ends the movement.

Commentary. Some experts consider this to be an inferior work, written to pander to popular taste. Others see it as Mozart's first step into the independence of musical thought that he found in *Figaro*, written in the same year. In any case, it has a different feel from that of the Haydn-dedicated quartets, seeming to be less imitative and more personal than they are (except for the D minor quartet). No one knows whether it was a commission from Hoffmeister, a tribute to him or the payment of a debt owed to him. It is fully accessible to prepared amateurs. Pleasure—3; Effort—2.

Quartet in C minor, K. 546 | (1788)

I *Adagio; Fuga.*

The double fugue is a transcription of one written originally for two pianos, probably for a patron, Baron von Sweiten, in imitation of J.S. Bach. The tune is an eighteenth-century cliché, one that also appears in other such familiar works as *Messiah*, several choral works of J.S. Bach, the Mozart *Requiem*, and Haydn's finale to the quartet in Op. 20, No. 5. The introductory adagio was written when the transcription for string quartet was made. This is a splendid piece to play. Amateurs, who could get much pleasure from it, unfortunately neglect it. Pleasure—3; Effort—2.

Quartet in D major, K. 575 | (1789)

I *Allegretto.* II *Andante.* III *Menuetto: Allegretto.* IV *Allegretto.*

The *first movement* opens with a delicate and chaste cantabile. The character of the whole movement is restrained, quiet and cheerful. The cello has much responsibility throughout.

The *second movement* is similarly restrained, a peaceful and lyrical andante with a dancing character.

The *third movement* is cheerful, sturdy and rather plain. The cello has a particularly lovely melody in the major-mode trio.

The *fourth movement* is a rondo. The abrupt opening presents a difficult theme for the cello to play over a moving bass in the viola. The theme is derived from that of the *first movement*. The rondo episodes become progressively more complex with triplet figures that give the movement a joyful and celebratory ending. The texture is highly contrapuntal.

Commentary. This work is a favorite of all quartet cellists. The cello part is not at all easy, for it lies in an awkward register. The quartet is highly unified thematically and spiritually, being genial and joyful throughout. The last movement is most memorable. The difficulties lie especially in the cello part. Pleasure—3; Effort—3.

Quartet in B-flat major, K. 589 | (1790)

I *Allegro*. II *Larghetto*. III *Menuetto: Moderato*. IV *Allegro assai*.

The *first movement*, like that of K. 575, opens with a serene and placid tune. The material is developed with vigor, though a calm atmosphere reigns throughout.

The *second movement* opens with a splendid aria in the cello. The material is treated in wonderful cantilena passages with some rather florid writing but the spirit remains open, joyful and peaceful throughout.

The *third movement* is a sturdy dance in a moderate tempo. The long trio, itself having two sections, is remarkable for its lack of relaxation or simplicity, its drama coming especially from the agitated accompanying figures in the lower voices.

The *fourth movement*, a merry rondo, is the most severe and extended of the movements. The episodes show extraordinary and unconventional treatments with thematic inversions and the use of remote keys. The movement ends quietly.

Commentary. This quartet resembles the first of the cello quartets in its character, structure and beauty, though some find it a little less inspired. It is neither easier nor more difficult than K. 575, and it similarly requires an accomplished cellist. Pleasure—3; Effort—3.

Quartet in F major, K. 590 | (1790)

I *Allegro moderato.* II *Allegretto.* III *Menuetto: Allegretto.*
IV *Allegro.*

The *first movement* opens abruptly with a unison theme that is an
arpeggio and descending scale. The effect is abrupt and comical. The
second theme, stated by the cello, is contrastingly lyrical. The development is complex, and the recapitulation exhibits considerable alter-
ation of the thematic material. A coda alludes to the playful opening
of the development section.

The *second movement* is a set of variations on a rocking, peaceful and
humorous tune. Although this is an allegretto in 6/8 time, the mood is
more like an andante and the tempo tends to move in that direction.
The movement is reminiscent of the siciliano variations in the finale of
the D minor quartet, K. 421. All voices have splendid parts in these
wonderful variations.

The *third movement* has a pronounced dancing quality, a folk dance or
waltz. The trio, in the major mode, is contrastingly gentle and graceful.

The *fourth movement* is a quick and roguish rondo, Haydnesque at the
outset but more characteristically Mozartean in later episodes, especially in those that lie in the minor mode. The frequent fermata pauses
give the movement a feeling of disorder. The ending features a bagpipe drone in the bass.

Commentary. This is the most capricious of the three cello quartets
and the most difficult. It presents major problems in technique, especially for the cellist, both in style and in ensemble playing. Amateurs
should undertake this work with more caution than they do the other
two of this set. Pleasure—3; Effort—4.

PROKOFIEV (1891–1953)

Sergei Sergeyevich Prokofiev left Russia in 1918 and spent the
next fifteen years in self-imposed exile, composing and performing as a pianist both in Europe and in the United States. He was
not drawn to chamber music or works for small groups, preferring the larger musical forms. Indeed, there are only four works
for small groups, the sextet Overture on Jewish Themes, Op. 34
(1919), the quintet in G minor for oboe, clarinet, violin, viola and

bass, Op. 39 (1924), the first string quartet, Op. 50 (1930), and the second string quartet, Op. 92 (1942).

He accepted a commission from the Elizabeth Sprague Coolidge Foundation of the Library of Congress to undertake the writing of the first string quartet while he was on tour in California in 1930. He worked at it for many months. It received its premier performance at the Library of Congress in April, 1931 by the Brosa Quartet and quickly entered the standard repertoire.

The second string quartet was written after Prokofiev had returned to Russia. With the Nazi invasion of Russia in 1941, a group of leading artists including Prokofiev was evacuated to the northern Caucasus, to Nalchik in the Kabarda-Balkar Autonomous Republic. There, quickly drawn to the Kabardinian and Balkar folk music of the region, he was inspired to use the quartet form to "achieve a combination of virtually untouched folk material and the most classical of classical forms, the string quartet," as he said. He wrote the second string quartet in November and December of 1941, and it had its first public performance in Moscow in September 1942. It, too, won immediate acclaim.

Quartet in B minor, Op. 50 | (1930)

I *Allegro.* II *Andante molto; Vivace.* III *Andante.*

The *first movement* opens with a rather gay, saucy and grotesque theme. The second theme is moody and brooding. A march theme appears to end the exposition. The development is brief. The form is a compact sonata allegro.

The *second movement* scherzo opens with a graceful and melancholy introduction. In the vivace that follows, the viola and cello drive forward a bright and catchy tune. The cello sings out a strong second theme in a contrasting mood. The first section is then repeated in shortened and altered form.

The *third movement* is a long and fervent andante. Russian-style melodies receive rhapsodic treatment over a constant throbbing accompaniment. The mood throughout is one of despair.

Commentary. This quartet is remarkable for the way in which it conveys deep feelings without sentimentality. The style is austere, without superficial effects or ornamentation. The composer thought so well of the last movement that he made a piano transcription and included it in a set of six pieces, Op. 52. The work is fully accessible to accomplished amateurs. Pleasure—2; Effort—3.

Quartet in F major, Op. 92 | (1942)

I *Allegro sostenuto.* II *Adagio.* III *Allegro.*

The *first movement* opens with a naive and belligerent principal theme that comes from a Kabardinian folk dance. A second theme follows, a tune from a Kabardinian song. The third theme is cheerful. A shortened reprise of the exposition follows a grotesque development section.

The *second movement,* after a brief introduction, features the melody of a local love-song, first played by the cello and later repeated in the other voices. In a middle section, the melody, now altered, appears over the theme of a local folk dance with figures that seem to imitate folk instruments. A brief return of the opening section ends the movement.

The *third movement* begins with a vigorous dance that slightly resembles that of the *first movement.* Other folk themes follow. A cadenza in the cello introduces an agitated development, after which the themes are repeated.

Commentary. This quartet, considered by many to be outstanding, is the more familiar of the two Prokofiev quartets. It is fully accessible to experienced amateurs, but it is not at all easy. The cellist has an especially challenging part to play. Pleasure—3; Effort—3.

RAVEL (1875–1927)

Maurice Ravel entered the Paris Conservatory at the age of fourteen where he was an average student. His training was broadly based, but he was especially drawn to the work of his French contemporaries, Satie and Debussy, and to that of the Russians, Balakirev, Borodin and Rimsky-Korsakov. His first published work appeared in 1895.

The string quartet was written in 1902–03, when he was twenty-seven to twenty-eight. It was preceded in print only by

some piano works and songs. His other chamber works constitute an introduction and allegro for harp, flute, clarinet and string
quartet (1906), three poems of Mallarmé for female voice, piano,
string quartet, two flutes and two clarinets (1913), the piano trio
(1915), the sonata for violin and cello (1920-22), and the sonata
for piano and violin (1923–27).

The string quartet was revised in 1910, and it is this revision
that is current. Ravel was not satisfied with the finale as first written, but Debussy told him not to change it. The actual extent of
the 1910 revision is unclear. The quartet is dedicated to Fauré,
Ravel's revered teacher in composition. Fauré must have known
the work well, given the close relationship of the two composers
at that time.

Comparison with the Debussy string quartet of ten years earlier is inevitable. Ravel's quartet places harmonic texture above
counterpoint and sweetness above vigor or violence.

Quartet in F major | (1902–03)

I *Allegro moderato—Tres doux.* II *Assez vif—Tres rhythmé.*
III *Tres lent.* IV *Vif et agité.*

The *first movement* opens with a graceful rising theme that recurs
throughout the movement. The atmosphere throughout is sweet and
melodious. The form is a sonata allegro.

The *second movement* scherzo has a vigorous pizzicato opening that
produces a sound like mandolins or guitars. Cross-rhythms are prominent. Several experts liken some of its sounds to those of a Javanese
gamelan orchestra. A broad legato trio, marked "lent," provides contrast.

The *third movement* is a formless rhapsody. It has the aspect of a conversation among the four voices. There are references to thematic
material from the preceding movements. The mood is calm throughout.

The *fourth movement* is alternately stormy and calm. The thematic
material refers extensively to the *first movement.*

Commentary. In description, this seems to be a slim work. In performing it, players learn to see its substance. Players, like listeners,
must not try to subject the work to intellectual analysis. Its joy lies in
its harmonic and rhythmic beauty, not in its form. It is accessible to

really advanced amateurs. A major difficulty lies in the 5/8 meter of the last movement, which can be mastered if all players mentally recite, "Rimsky-Korsakov." Pleasure—3; Effort—4.

RESPIGHI (1879–1936)

Ottorino Respighi was born and raised in Bologna but he traveled abroad to study composition with Max Bruch and Rimsky-Korsakov. Much admired in Italy, he took a position teaching composition at the conservatory in Rome. He later became Director of the Liceo Musicale di Santa Cecilia at Rome.

He was a prolific and eclectic composer, but much of his music is now neglected. Though he wrote in many forms, he is now remembered mainly for such small or occasional orchestral pieces as the *Fountains of Rome, Pines of Rome, Roman Festivals* and the *Ancient Airs and Dances.* Chamber music was a minor occupation for him and he left only two string quartets, of which the second, the Quartetto Dorico (Dorian Quartet), is the one still occasionally heard.

The Quartetto Dorico was written in the summer of 1923 and first performed publicly in October in that year in London by the Lener Quartet, the group to which it is dedicated. Its title, given to it by the composer, refers to the fact that its principal themes are in the Doric mode. This reflects Respighi's interest in ancient forms and harmonies, as expressed in many other works as well. The work never achieved great prominence or popularity, and it remains one of those works that many know about but few know.

Quartet, Quartetto Dorico | (1923)

This work is in one movement, consisting of four sections that flow into one another but correspond to the usual four movements of the quartet structure.

The first section begins with a declamatory principal or motto theme expressed forcefully in unison (energico). After a brief development of this theme, a second theme, a gentle tune derived from the motto theme, appears soon to lead back to another unison statement of the motto theme. A third theme emerges in the cello and then passes to all voices and the motto theme returns as a chorale. The mood of this first section is declamatory and passionate.

The second section (allegro moderato) begins with a preludial melody over an ostinato. This leads to a kind of scherzo (molto animato, 3/4 time) in which the motto theme is treated as a frenzied dance, ending in a fugato.

The third section (moderato) begins with a restatement of the motto theme in the viola followed by a recitativo second theme in the first violin. A new theme with a religious character appears in the viola and second violin (molto lento).

The fourth section (moderato energico) opens with the motto theme as a passacaglia over an ostinato. The theme is then treated as a broad romantic song with full harmonies and the movement ends in a unison flourish.

Commentary. The motto theme is attractive because of its character and mode, and so its constant use throughout the work in various guises does not become tedious. There is a satisfying variety of moods in the work, and the texture of the music is especially pleasing. On the other hand, the work is lacking in profundity and innovation. The result is a pleasing 'color' piece, a good short work for reading. It presents technical obstacles to amateurs. They can gain a sense of satisfaction from it, however, with enough effort. Pleasure— 2; Effort—4.

SCHUBERT (1797–1828)

Vienna, in Franz Peter Schubert's time, was the political and cultural center of an empire, and so the city harbored people from all parts of Europe who had come there to find power, education, or (as in the case of Schubert's parents) work.

Franz Peter Schubert's father, Franz Theodore, was Moravian, his people having been laborers and peasants in that part of what is now Czechoslovakia. The composer's mother, Elizabeth Vietz, came from Silesia, a district mainly inhabited by Germans. Her family, having suffered reverses in Silesia, came to Vienna where the orphaned daughters worked as domestics. Elizabeth's marriage to Franz Theodore Schubert improved her lot, for he was a parish schoolmaster. The couple had ten children, only five surviving childhood, of whom Franz Peter was the youngest. When Franz Peter was sixteen, his mother died and his father remarried. Five more children followed.

Franz Theodore strongly encouraged his son's musical talent and so the boy was writing songs and instrumental pieces even before he went to school. The father selected the best school in Vienna for the boy, the Imperial 'Convict' school, a seminary or boarding school attached to the Court Chapel which provided choirboys to the Temple Church. Here, the boy received a broad education and he made friendships that lasted all his life. Music was important in the curriculum and Franz Peter excelled at that, more so than in other subjects. At sixteen, he left the school to become a pupil of Antonio Salieri, who had recognized the boy's musical talents years before at school. The D. 87 string quartet comes from this early period.

Salieri's tutorship lasted five years, 1813–1817. Franz Peter's father, still intending that his son should become a schoolmaster, had persuaded him to enroll in an appropriate training institution in 1813. After two years, his unsuitability for such a career was apparent to everyone and Franz Peter entered upon a Bohemian life, living with friends, studying with Salieri, and composing prodigiously.

The composer soon formed a large circle of friends within the artistic circles of Vienna. Though he lived through dismal events, the French occupations of 1805 and 1809 and the repressive regime that followed, he seems to have been oblivious to everything except music. He supported himself in the essentials by teaching and by the sale of his compositions, but not by public performances. His abilities continued to be recognized only within his circle of friends. 'Schubertiades', organized musical evenings at which he and his friends performed his works for themselves, became regular events that continued throughout his life.

A summer spent in Hungary in 1818, where he taught the children of Count Johann Eszterhazy, might have led to a permanent position for him but it did not. The next summer, in 1819, he vacationed in the Austrian Alps, where he wrote the Trout Quintet. The Quartet Movement followed in 1820. But these holidays and other interludes did not alter his preoccupation with entertaining his friends in Vienna. He failed to find a permanent professional post, though his reputation slowly grew.

1823 was a dividing point in his life. A series of disappointments over the publication of his works and a serious illness with hospitalization left him depressed. A second summer spent at Count Johann Eszterhazy's castle in Hungary in 1824 did little to restore his spirits, but he was improved a little by a second tour to the Austrian Alps in the summer of 1825. He continued to seek permanent positions but he was repeatedly passed over, thus never achieving any real prominence in Viennese musical society. Even Beethoven seems not to have known of him until, on his deathbed in 1826, he saw some scores from Schubert and possibly met him.

The year 1827 began with life as usual for Schubert. In September he made another visit to the Alps and a great burst of composition followed. In the summer of 1828, he again fell ill and went to the house of his brother, Ferdinand (also a musician), to recuperate. He rallied enough in October to make a walking tour to visit Haydn's grave, but he took to bed again on November 14th, dying in delirium on November 19th. He was buried in the Währing cemetery, very near to Beethoven's grave.

Schubert wrote seventeen string quartets altogether. He produced them every year from 1811 through 1816, from age fourteen through nineteen. After a hiatus of four years, quartets again appeared in 1820 and then in 1824 and in 1826. The earliest quartets are lost. Only the last are now readily available. The opus numbers reflect the order of publication, bearing no relation to the order of composition. Only one, the quartet in A minor, D. 804, was published while the composer was still alive.

Schubert wrote music at first for the family circle alone. His art later matured, and this can be seen especially in the quartets. The last five quartets, those from 1816 and later, were written with the advice of Schuppanzigh, the virtuoso violinist who was so prominently associated with Beethoven, and it is these five that now constitute the popular repertoire. All of the known quartets are listed here in chronological order.

Quartet in C major D. 46 (1813)
Quartet in B-flat major D. 68 (1813)
Quartet in D major D. 74 (1813)
Quartet in E-flat major D. 87 (Op. 125, No. 1) (1813)
Quartet in B-flat major D. 112 (Op. 168) (1814)
Quartet in G minor D. 173 (Op. Posth.) (1815)

Quartet in E major D. 353 (Op. 125, No. 2) (1816)
Quartet in C minor D. 703 (Op. Posth.) (1820) Quartet
    Movement
Quartet in A minor D. 804 (Op. 29) (1824) Rosamunde
Quartet in D minor D. 810 (Op. Posth.) (1824) Death and the
    Maiden
Quartet in G major D. 887 (Op. 161) (1826)

Quartet in E-flat major, D. 87 | (Op. 125, No.1) (1813)

I *Allegro moderato.* II *Scherzo: Prestissimo. III Adagio. IV Allegro.*

The opening theme of the *first movement,* a warm but questioning melody, is a typical Schubertian tune. It develops into a lovely and warm-hearted sonata.

The *second movement* scherzo is a brilliant and impetuous little gem.

The *third movement* is a brief and simple aria.

The *fourth movement* presents a Schubertian romp, full of high spirits and good humor.

Commentary. This is the first string quartet that seems to the hearer to reveal the mature Schubert. Its open texture, its invention and its wonderful melodies make it a work that avocational players can enjoy seemingly with little effort. Pleasure—3; Effort—1.

Quartet in E major, D. 353 | (Op. 125, No. 2) (1816)

I *Allegro con fuoco.* II *Andante.* III *Menuetto: Allegro vivace.*
IV *Rondeau: Allegro vivace.*

The *first movement* is remarkably terse. The thematic material is carefree and Italian in style.

The florid *second movement* is rich and mysterious, Viennese in character, with a soaring coda.

The *third movement* is a compact fast-moving minuet, notable for a terse trio.

The *fourth movement* is a sprightly and joyous rondo with an imaginative development.

Commentary. This is the first quartet that ventures much beyond the simpler house-music of the earlier ones. Schubert later disparaged this work. It is interesting especially because one can see in it the seeds of what was to come. It is fully accessible to amateurs of moderate abilities. Pleasure—2; Effort—1.

Quartet in C minor, D. 703, Op. Posth. | (1820),
Quartet Movement

I *Allegro assai.*

This solitary movement begins with a wild tune played in tremolo. The lyrical second subject contrasts with this dramatic opening theme. The development makes use of a highly unconventional sequence of keys. The movement is dramatic, somber, and highly personal.

Commentary. This is the *first movement* of an uncompleted quartet. Schubert started the andante movement to follow it but he never finished it. Brahms must have studied this movement, for he owned the autograph. The movement is a striking departure from D. 353, written only four years earlier. It is a reasonably severe challenge to the amateur, both technically and musically. It is not the work to use to initiate the player new to Schubert, for it is far too demanding and opaque. The quartet in E-flat, D. 87, or the quartet in A minor, D. 804, is the better one for that purpose. Pleasure—2; Effort—3.

Quartet in A minor, D. 804, Op. 29 | (1824), *Rosamunde*

I *Allegro ma non troppo.* II *Andante.* III *Menuetto: Allegretto.*
IV *Allegro moderato.*

The principal theme of the haunting *first movement* is a plaintive song, played over a running figure that recalls Schubert's song, 'Gretchen at the Spinning Wheel'. The development is extensive and the part writing is masterful. The mood is sweetly sad throughout, occasionally becoming tragic.

The *second movement* uses a theme that Schubert had written previously as a part of some incidental music for a play called *Rosamunde*. The theme originally illustrated a scene depicting the heroine in an idyllic setting with her sheep. Schubert also used it in the *Wanderer Fantasie* for piano and in an Impromptu for piano. The style of this movement is intimate, and the mood is serene and gentle for the most part, with tragic intervals.

The principal section of the *third movement* presents a pensive and melancholy theme that is derived from Schubert's vocal setting of a fragment of Schiller's poem, *Die Götter Greichenlands*. The song text reads, "Lovely world, where art thou? Return once more thou fair and flowered age of Nature!" The trio, a folk dance, contrasts real world optimism with the gloomy dream state of the minuet.

The *fourth movement* has a Hungarian theme. It is exuberant and outwardly cheerful, but it contains moments of drama and mystery.

Commentary. Schubert wrote this lovely work "as a means to pave the way to a grand symphony," he said. Schuppanzigh was enthusiastic about it, and his own string quartet gave the work its first performance. The work offers skilled amateurs no major problems. It is the best work to play as an introduction to the Schubert quartets. Pleasure—3; Effort—2.

Quartet in D minor, D. 810, Op. Posth. | (1824),
Death and the Maiden

I *Allegro.* II *Andante con moto.* III *Scherzo: Allegro molto.* IV *Presto.*

The *first movement* is stark, dramatic, and agitated, with little or no release. Heuss (quoted in Cobbett) and others interpreted it as a struggle with death, death being the victor.

The *second movement* is a set of extraordinarily beautiful variations on the theme of Schubert's song, 'Death and the Maiden'. The variations are distinctly and sharply outlined, all remaining in G minor except for one. The subject, according to Heuss, is death, and the mood is one of resignation.

The *third movement* is a scherzo whose dotted-rhythm continues the feeling of the "march of inevitability" (Einstein). The trio gives a brief repose in D major. The ominous dotted rhythm continues in the trio as well, though it is subdued.

The *fourth movement,* a sonata-rondo in 6/8 time, is a tarantella, a depiction of the dance of Death, said some critics. It moves irresistibly to a savage and prestissimo coda.

Commentary. Some don't like this work in part because they see it as blatantly programmatic. Other authorities, however, reject the programmatic view inasmuch as Schubert himself said nothing about it. Mendelssohn called it "bad music." Others find it superficial. It was written at the same time as the quartet in A minor, D. 804. This work, much more emphatically than D. 804, reflects Schubert's pessimism at the time he wrote them. This is a massive quartet, most demanding in both technical and musical terms. Its length alone is forbidding to many amateurs. It is not to be undertaken casually. Pleasure—3; Effort—3.

Quartet in G major, D. 887, Op. 161 | (1826)

I *Allegro di molto.* II *Andante un poco moto.* III *Scherzo: Allegro vivace.* IV *Allegro assai.*

The *first movement* contrasts major and minor modes strongly, even in the opening chords. There is a striking treatment of thematic fragments, contrasting always in mode. The principal of the double chorus is used extensively. This is "vertical" or chordal music, emphasizing harmony at the expense of melody, with sparse part writing. This movement is long, dramatic and difficult.

The *second movement* is a slightly agitated andante. A plaintive melody in the bass is decorated by embroidery in the upper voices. The agitated alternativo provides contrast. Thematic materials from some of Schubert's later songs ('Winterreise' and 'Einsamkeit') appear in this movement. The spirit of the music is mysterious, melancholy, and moving.

The *third movement* has a playful quality, despite the minor key. The trio is a delicate and happy Ländler in the major mode played over a drone.

The *fourth movement*, a long rondo with a tarantella rhythm, is impetuous, compelling, harmonically adventurous, surprising and exciting.

Commentary. This is the epitome of the Schubert quartets. It was unknown to his contemporaries, for it was not performed in public until 1850, twenty-four years after Schubert's death, and it was not published until 1852. This absolute music owes much to Beethoven, whose late quartets, however, were just appearing at the time it was written. The orchestral texture and the harmonic ingenuity of this quartet are most striking. It is a massive work, both in length and in depth. Amateurs should view it as they view the late Beethoven quartets, something to be undertaken when they feel ready, but certainly not casually. Some call this work 'The Titanic'. Pleasure—4; Effort—4.

SCHUMANN (1810–1856)

Saxony, where Robert Alexander Schumann was born in Zwickau, has a long tradition of importance in German music, but musicians were not prominent among Schumann's ancestors. Schumann's father, August, came from agrarian people in Thuringia. August was a bookish and scholarly man, the author of popular novels, a publisher and a bookseller. The composer's mother, Christine Schnabel, was the daughter of a small-town surgeon. Robert was the last of six children.

The years following 1810 marked a time of disorder in Saxony for Napoleon was abroad with his army. Zwickau lay directly in the path of the French army in 1812, and the town was severely damaged. A typhus epidemic claimed Schumann's mother soon after, and the boy spent two years with a foster family until her recovery from her long illness. He started school at six and he began to study music at seven with a local church organist. His precocity and outgoing personality made for rapid advancement and he was, furthermore, encouraged in his education by his scholarly father. The death of his father and the suicide of his sister, both occurring when Robert was fifteen, were tragedies that greatly affected his personality, as much as had, probably, the foster parentage of his earlier years.

Schumann left home at eighteen to become a student of law at Leipzig. He also continued to pursue the study of music with Friederick Wieck, a noted piano teacher in Leipzig. He went to Heidelberg in 1829 to continue his education in law and music with Anton Justus Thibaut, who was both a professor of law and a distinguished musical scholar. Schumann vacillated between law and music in his career choice, finally settling upon music and he returned to Leipzig in 1830 to resume intensive work with Wieck.

He continued to investigate piano performance with Wieck but he also began to compose more seriously than he had done

before. He could not choose between composing and performing as a career. He slowly gave up the idea of a performance
career after he developed a physical disability (perhaps tendini-
tis) in his right hand, a problem which was aggravated by a
mechanical device that he had designed to strengthen the third
finger of that hand.

Schumann's mental or nervous disorder first became evident
as early as 1828 in the form of episodic musical hallucinations,
manic behavior, and depression. He experienced his first really
serious depression in 1833 after the death of his brother from
tuberculosis and of his sister-in-law from malaria. Such severe
emotional breakdowns recurred throughout his life.

After he recovered from his depression of 1833, he and his
musical colleagues established a musical journal, which had long
been a dream for Schumann. About this time, he also formed his
friendship with Mendelssohn who came to Leipzig in 1833 to
conduct the Gewandhaus Orchestra.

Schumann had known Clara Wieck, daughter of his piano
teacher, from her childhood. Clara, ten years younger than
Robert, possessed a prodigious talent. She was well launched in
her career as a virtuosic pianist by the time Robert had founded
his newspaper and established himself as a composer. Their
friendship ripened into courtship, but this was a long and laborious process owing to their separate careers and to the strong
opposition of her father to her marriage to Robert. The conflict
even involved a lawsuit, but Wieck at last acceded to their marriage in 1840.

The Schumanns had eight children. Despite this, they continued to pursue their careers. The years from 1840 to 1844 were
especially happy and productive ones. Then Robert's manic and
depressive behavior returned to interfere with his busy life. He
sold his musical journal in 1845, and the Schumanns moved to
Dresden, remaining there until 1850. He left to take a job as
musical director for the Musical Society of Düsseldorf, a position
that Mendelssohn had occupied briefly and unhappily several
years before. He found a renewal of energy in Düsseldorf, and
about one-third of his compositions came from the period when
he lived there. Here also he met the young Brahms with whom
he and Clara quickly established a close relationship.

Schumann's emotional illness greatly affected his professional
interactions, and so his responsibilities to the Musical Society of

Düsseldorf were not easily maintained. His position grew increasingly difficult until 1854, when his problems culminated in his attempt at suicide by jumping into the Rhine. He was rescued and taken to a private psychiatric asylum at Endenich, then a suburb of Bonn. Though he made a prompt partial recovery, he remained confined until July 1855, when he experienced a major relapse with depression. He ceased eating and died, probably of starvation, on July 29th, 1856. Clara Schumann survived for many years, continuing to promote Robert Schumann's music in her extensive career and becoming a central figure in the circles of German music.

Schumann devoted 1842 to chamber music, just as he had devoted 1841 to the B-flat major and D minor symphonies and other major orchestral compositions. Schumann had contemplated writing string quartets four years before, in 1838. Early in 1842, Clara and Robert Schumann together studied the quartets of Haydn, Mozart, and Beethoven. By June, Robert had completed the three quartets in Op. 41, apparently composing them in the order in which they are numbered. After they were done, he was exhausted and took a brief holiday, only to return to chamber music again. He wrote the piano quintet in E flat, Op. 44, in September and October, and the piano quartet in E-flat, Op. 47, and the piano trio, Op. 88 ('Fantasiestücke'), before the end of that year. Schumann himself was pleased by the three string quartets, and they were generally well received by German contemporaries including Mendelssohn, at least according to Schumann. Mendelssohn's letters and papers do not mention them. They are dedicated to Mendelssohn "with warm respect." Ferdinand David, the concertmaster of the Gewandhaus orchestra, admired them and played them publicly, but another string quartet, the Muller Quartet, rejected them. The quartets were not well received in England for twenty years. Schumann had to plead to get them published seven years after they were written. Brahms owned the sketches for these quartets, and he willed them to Joachim.

After this burst of composition in 1842, Schumann had an attack of nervous exhaustion and rested for several months. He never wrote any more string quartets, but more piano trios followed after several years. The piano trios of Op. 63 and Op. 80 were written five years later, in 1847, and that in G minor, Op. 110, in 1851.

Quartet in A minor, Op. 41, No. 1 | (1842)

I *Introduzione: Andante espressivo; Allegro.* II *Scherzo: Presto.* III *Adagio.* IV *Presto.*

The *first movement* has a rather long introduction in A minor that is reflective and introspective, with rich contrapuntal imitation. After four bars of transition, a classical sonata allegro appears in F major. The gracious and insinuating first theme in 6/8 meter leads to a similar theme that becomes the basis for a fugato. The development section is short, free, and harmonically novel. A brief coda ends this lyrical, warm, and unitary movement.

The *second movement*, a volatile 6/8 scherzo in A minor, is a light-hearted Mendelssohnian rush. A brief intermezzo substitutes for a trio to provide repose before the scherzo returns.

The *third movement* adagio in F minor, after a brief introduction, presents the violins singing a warmly lyrical melody over arpeggios in the viola. The cello then gets the tune for a time. The movement develops in the form of free variations on elements of the themes. The tranquil mood is interrupted by harmonic and rhythmic variation. Elements of the introduction then return to close this warm and lovely movement.

The *fourth movement*, in A minor, features a series of brisk, lively and related themes, treated in sonata form. A "musette" (a dance) interrupts the action briefly (moderato), after which a truncated reprise ends this sprightly movement in A major.

Commentary. The quartet is very Schumannesque, even in the Mendelssohnian scherzo. It has a pleasing sense of unity and adherence. All parts are rewarding. It is not a really difficult work for experienced amateurs to play. Pleasure—2, Effort—3.

Quartet in F major, Op. 41, No. 2 | (1842)

I *Allegro vivace.* II *Andante, quasi Variazione.* III *Scherzo: Presto.* IV *Allegro molto vivace.*

The *first movement* opens without introduction as a flowing and genial theme that is developed without a second theme into an intense, eloquent and passionate sonata allegro. The development is suave, smooth and rich, with much imitative writing. The ending is crisp.

The rhapsodic *second movement* presents a theme, four variations, a reprise of the theme, and a coda. The theme is dreamy and tender. The first variation is contrapuntal, the second ornamented, the third dreamy, and the fourth rather square-cut. The coda was marked "più lento" rather than "più mosso" in early editions, which was probably a misprint.

The *third movement* is an agile and fantastic 6/8 presto in C minor. In the Mendelssohnian trio, the cello has a burlesque theme and there is some levity. A short coda ends the movement.

The *fourth movement*, a vivace rondo in 2/4 meter, is youthful and spirited. Running passages move among the voices. Some see a resemblance between this last movement and that of the symphony in B-flat major, written a year before.

Commentary. This quartet resembles the first quartet in its youthful and romantic character and in its feeling of unity and coherence. It is not really difficult for accomplished amateurs to read and it is a satisfying and pleasing work to play. Pleasure—2; Effort—3.

Quartet in A major, Op. 41, No. 3 | (1842), *Clara*

I *Andante espressivo: Allegro molto moderato.* II *Assai agitato.*
III *Adagio molto.* IV *Finale: Allegro molto vivace.*

The *first movement* opens with a slow, meditative, and questioning introduction. It features a falling fifth motif that can be perceived as a statement of Clara Schumann's name. This motif generates the principal theme of the following sonata form, an amiable and rather bland tune. A more lyrical and expressive second theme, first played by the cello, then appears, and the two themes are treated freely. A fanfare in the first violin ends the exposition. The development is free and harmonically ingenious. The movement is concise, but warm and romantic.

The *second movement* takes the place of a scherzo. It constitutes three variations on a breathless and agitated theme that is baldly stated only after the variations have begun. A rising fourth, the inversion of the falling fifth that speaks Clara's name in the *first movement*, appears in the first variation and again in the second. The theme returns in a canonic poco adagio, after which the vigorous third variation, again featuring the rising fourth, provides a contrast. The coda introduces a suave new theme. The movement exhibits quick changes of mood in brief and concentrated episodes.

The *third movement* opens with a long, eloquent, and fervent song. Freely flowing part writing underlies the song. The theme is developed extensively to a passionate climax, after which the movement ends peacefully. The character is a stately and sustained romanticism.

The *fourth movement*, a rondo, is simple, long, lively and energetic. A gavotte-like episode enters at two points, reminiscent of the musette in the finale of Op. 41, No. 1. A brilliant rushing coda ends this exciting movement.

Commentary. This quartet is the most romantic of the three in the opus. The *third movement* is the most remarkable, but the whole work has great freedom and a feeling of ease. It is technically more difficult than the others but at least as rewarding for enthusiastic and accomplished amateurs. All voices have good parts. The handling of the second theme in the *first movement* requires the mastery of syncopation. It takes long practice. Pleasure—3; Effort—3.

SHOSTAKOVICH (1906–1975)

Dmitry Dmitryevich Shostakovich, born before the Russian revolution, lived throughout a long period of turmoil and change in Russia. As one of the leading artists of his time, he mirrored in his work the cataclysmic era in which he lived. Since the troubles of Russia partly reflected those of the whole world, his works can be taken as a commentary on the major human problems of the twentieth century—revolution, war, tyranny, and anti-Semitism. We may yet be too close to this history to make a balanced appraisal of its artistic expression by Shostakovich, but it appears likely that his work will come to be seen as the supreme musical expression of the period. Shostakovich himself de-emphasized the political reference or programmatic content of his music, yet such reference seems inescapable to those of us who experienced the same events.

Shostakovich's father, an engineer in Leningrad (now St. Petersburg) and his mother, a piano teacher, were not politically active despite the turmoil in that city both before and after the October Revolution. Amateur music was a principal avocation of the family and it led two of the three children to follow musical careers. Maria, the eldest, became a professional pianist. Dmitri, the second child, entered the St. Petersburg Conservatory at fourteen, where he excelled at piano performance and composition. His political awareness developed early, to judge from the titles of some of his early compositions and from the nature of the first symphony, written while he was still a student. Shostakovich himself characterized the first symphony as depicting a young man "who is really beginning to examine the life around him."

The prompt success of the first symphony freed the young genius from the necessity to support himself as a theater pianist. He thereafter earned his living by composing and by teaching at the Conservatory. This early success also placed him immediately in a central position in Soviet artistic circles.

The 1920s were years of great intellectual ferment in Russia, as in all of Europe, and Shostakovich responded to this by exhibiting flexibility and experimentation in style and in form. The wish to make the art of the time serve to bring the revolution to the people led to his nearly total commitment to theater music, operas, ballets, and film scores.

The spirit of revolution was seated at first in Leningrad, but the ascent of Stalinism late in the 1920s, centered in Moscow, created a rivalry between the two cities in all aspects of the revolution. Composers in Moscow came to view those in Leningrad as elitist, and the Leningrad composers saw those in Moscow as debasing music in the interest of mass appeal. One result of this was the satirical spirit that became so prominent in the works of Shostakovich in this period.

The Muscovite faction gradually achieved dominance and the antipathy to Leningrad composers extended to include political circles. Shostakovich's response was an increased variability in style with a shift from the "formalistic, alien, and bourgeois" methods deplored by the masters of the emerging monolithic society to more acceptable styles. The crisis over political control of the arts became personal for Shostakovich in 1936 with Stalin's public denunciation of *Lady Macbeth of Mtsensk*, an opera that Shostakovich had written two years earlier. His fifth symphony, written soon afterward, satisfied the Stalinist demand that he produce a work celebrating the revolution in acceptable style, standing also as an immense accomplishment in the form. Shostakovich then almost abandoned the writing of theater music altogether and began to turn more to chamber music with the first string quartet.

From about 1939 to 1949, Shostakovich produced great works that satisfied the demands of Soviet realism and brought him political favor and international renown. His failure to produce a great celebratory symphony at the end of World War II, as well as other events, brought on a second personal crisis in 1948–49, with another political attack led by Zhdanov. This time he was attacked by other artists as well as by politicians, and he temporarily lost his position at the Conservatory. His response this time was a humble compliance.

After Stalin's death in 1953, Shostakovich enjoyed a decade of calm and stable productivity. After Khruschev's fall in 1964, he was further spared intrusions because of his professional stature, his age, his diminished health, and his reduced social and political concerns. The compositions of his last decade have a private and inward looking character which probably reflects not only his release from political pressures but also the chronic neurological disease that led to his death in 1975.

The fifteen string quartets can be viewed as a chronicle of Shostakovich's creative life after the great personal crisis of 1936. In this most intimate of forms, he found the freedom to follow his own path relatively free of the demands made upon him because of his prominence. The last five quartets show the composer, now chronically ill, retreating into his private emotional world. They are progressively more personal and gloomy. Four of the last five quartets are dedicated to the members of the Beethoven String Quartet, the group so intimately associated with Shostakovich as he worked in this form. The eleventh quartet is dedicated to the recently deceased second violinist, V. P. Shirinsky, the twelfth to the first violinist, Tziganov, the thirteenth to the violist, Borisovsky, and the fourteenth to the cellist, Sergey Shirinsky.

Quartet No. 1 in C major, Op. 49 | (1938)

I *Moderato*. II *Moderato*. III *Allegro molto*. IV *Allegro*.

The *first movement* has a principal theme that possesses the character of a cradle song. The sonata form treats the simple melodies in an unpretentious, playful and relaxed way.

The *second movement* is a set of variations on a melancholy folk theme that is first stated by the viola. The variations present little diversity except in key. The nearly constant repetition of the tune against various counter-melodies creates a movement that has the character of a passacaglia. A determined simplicity is maintained throughout, broken only by an ecstatic climax in the B flat minor variation.

The *third movement* is a classical and convincing scherzo, played con sordino. The wispy scherzo themes have a consistently playful character.

The *fourth movement* is a spirited, witty and cheerful sonata form. It ends briskly and emphatically.

Commentary. This brief neoclassical work, lasting only about fifteen minutes, has been likened to Prokofiev's Classical Symphony. It is lucid, straightforward, and unpretentious. It comes from the period of its composer's reaction to the condemnation of Lady Macbeth of Mtsensk. This may explain its conformity to the Classical-Romantic mainstream, its clarity, and its lack of storm, drama, and profundity. Shostakovich said that, in writing this quartet, he visualized childhood scenes with the naive and bright moods associated with springtime. Though the work is easy to understand, it is not at all easy to play. The *third movement* is difficult and the *fourth* is also difficult. Still, both movements will respond to practice, and the result is a work that can give amateurs much pleasure. This is the only Shostakovich quartet that most amateurs play much and it is the most suitable introduction to his work in this medium. Pleasure—2; Effort—3.

Quartet No. 2 in A major, Op. 68 | (1944)

I *Overture: Moderato con moto.* II *Recitativo and Romance: Adagio.* III *Waltz: Allegro.* IV *Theme and Variations: Adagio; Allegro non troppo.*

The *first movement* is in sonata form, the heading "overture" being an archaic reference. The movement is strong and vigorous, built on a subject that has a broad declamatory style and a heroic character. A dotted figure motif creates a feeling of anxiety, which is augmented in the development. The recapitulation of the heroic principal subject is delayed until the end.

The *second movement* opens with an extended and dramatic recitativo in the first violin. This may reflect a devotion to opera and theater music that the composer had so recently abandoned. After this long lament, a poignant romance appears, tense and anguished at points, somber and tender at others. The dramatic recitativo reappears to end the movement in a mood of despair.

The *third movement* is a series of macabre waltzes, a restless and swift scherzo played con sordino in the minor mode. It rises to a climax that is full of suppressed tension and then relaxes to the quiet of its beginning.

The *fourth movement* opens with a brief adagio introduction that anticipates a main theme which is to be treated subsequently in variations. This melancholy theme, which appears first in the viola, is strongly Russian in character and resembles that of the *second movement* of the first quartet. The variations of this theme increase progressively in tempo and agitation to reach a frenzy before a return to the adagio. After this melancholy mysterioso passage, a tragic and declamatory version of the basic theme ends the movement.

Commentary. The second quartet, a wartime piece, exhibits the vigorous and dramatic patriotism evoked by a war in progress. Like the first string quartet, this work is traditional in form, but it is a far more powerfully expressive work, filled with tension and melancholy. This is a difficult composition in all respects, and amateurs should not take it up casually. The dedicatee, V. Shebalin, was a composer and longtime friend of Shostakovich. Pleasure—3; Effort—4.

Quartet No. 3 in F major, Op. 73 | (1946)

I *Allegretto.* II *Moderato con moto.* III *Allegro non troppo.*
IV *Adagio. V Moderato.*

The *first movement* is a sonata form with a bright and playful mood from the outset. The simplicity of the theme and of its treatment recalls the opening movement of the first string quartet. The vigorous and joyous dance acquires some urgency and tension in its development and fugal treatment. The ending expresses joyous triumph.

The *second movement* has a declamatory and dramatic character at the outset. Later sections exhibit a sense of some uneasiness and bleakness.

The *third movement* is a march-like scherzo with a character that is grotesque, ungainly and driven. Alternations of 2/4 and 3/4 meters give it a sense of irregularity. Such fierce, frenzied, and angry writing is new to the quartets up to this point, but it appears again in the eighth and tenth quartets.

The *fourth movement* opens with a stark and dramatic declamation in unison, a brief recitativo that is answered with a consoling and lyrical phrase. Both the declamation and the response recur in various forms throughout the movement to produce a passacaglia that expresses dramatic suffering, anguish, and despair.

The *fifth movement* begins in a mysterioso mood with a melodic line that has the quality of a legato fugue. This idea is continued in a contemplative and somber passage. A second section introduces more dancing material that is soon replaced by the legato fugal melody of the opening, now more agitated. The dramatic declamation of the *fourth movement* returns. Subsequent treatments of these subjects lead to a terminal adagio, filled with bleakness and despair.

Commentary. The third quartet, a wartime work like the second quartet, is a more contemplative, graceful, and poignant expression of the sense of suffering. This splendid work is remarkable for its sense of unity, fluency, grace, and sincerity. It is somewhat less difficult in technique than the second quartet. It is well worth the attention of those amateurs who seek a work that is deeper than the first quartet but still within reasonable reach. This work was dedicated to the Beethoven String Quartet. Pleasure—3; Effort—3.

Quartet No. 4 in D major, Op. 83 | (1949)

I *Allegretto.* II *Andantino.* III *Allegretto.* IV *Allegretto.*

The pastoral *first movement* is preludial. An oriental melody is played over a drone to produce a sound like that of Eastern bagpipe music. The mood rises quickly from the mysterioso beginning to reach considerable intensity. This mood then yields to a warm, intense and loosely constructed expressivo. The bagpipes return briefly at the end. This is a compact and taut movement, beautifully proportioned.

The *second movement* is ardent and lyrical. A lovely plaintive song appears in the first violin. This melody is then developed to a passionate climax in an interchange between the first violin and the cello. A short violin recitative leads to the return of the unadorned melody. After some chorale-like phrases, the movement ends peacefully.

The *third movement* is a minor-mode scherzo, mysterious and agitated at the outset, delicate and Haydnesque. As it develops, the mood becomes lyrical and then filled with a galloping excitement. The movement leads directly to the last, attacca.

The *fourth movement* seems like a continuation of the third, for the pizzicato chords that underlie the opening melody are a continuation of those that end the preceding scherzo. This melody is a ruminative recitativo in the viola that serves as an introduction to the main body of the movement. Strong pizzicato chords then introduce an oriental peasant dance tune with a melancholy cast. This and similar materials are iterated and combined in improvisatory fashion. A recitativo passage brings a quiet ending in which only soft pizzicato chords reflect back upon the spirit of the peasant dances.

Commentary. In contrast to the dramatic third quartet, this is a strongly lyrical work, traditional in form, nationalistic in character, economical of means and varied in mood. Now the most popular of the Shostakovich quartets in Russia, it was not publicly performed until 1953. It can be seen as a response to the Zhdanov condemnation in its retreat to a simpler form, to pure lyricism, warmth, sensitivity and subtlety. It is not forbiddingly difficult so that it is within the reach of accomplished amateurs who should get to know this wonderful work. Pleasure—3; Effort—3.

Quartet No. 5 in B-flat major, Op. 92 | (1952)

I *Allegro non troppo.* II *Andante.* III *Moderato.*

The *first movement* opens quietly with the viola playing Shostakovich's signature motif, DSCH (D, E-flat, C, B). This little introduction quickly gives way to a stout declamatory tune. A lyrical second melody appears and the whole exposition is repeated. The development treats these materials fully. After an elaborated recapitulation, the movement ends bleakly. The signature motif recurs throughout the movement as a unifying device.

The *second movement* follows the first, attacca, carrying the bleak mood forward and intensifying it in the first andante. A subsequent andantino is more passionate. The contrasting andante and andantino sections then alternate. The mood throughout is tragic.

The *third movement* at first continues the bleak mood of the ending of the *second movement*, attacca. The long introduction leads to a whimsical dancing allegretto. This is developed freely. A reflective andante passage recalls the signature theme, now transmuted, and the movement ends in a mood of repose.

Commentary. This work differs greatly from its predecessor in the absence of a nationalistic character and in the fusion of the three movements. It is likewise a conservative piece, but more adventurous and personal than its predecessor in its use of the musical signature theme, which was also used in the great tenth symphony, written at about the same time. Like the fourth, this quartet was withheld from public performance until after Stalin's death. It is difficult in musical terms and in the extensive use of unison playing, which requires perfect intonation. Consequently, it is not recommended to amateurs unless they are prepared to work hard. This quartet was written to mark the thirtieth anniversary of the Beethoven String Quartet. Pleasure—2; Effort—4.

Quartet No. 6 in G major, Op. 101 | (1956)

I *Allegretto.* II *Moderato con moto.* III *Lento.* IV *Lento; Allegretto.*

The *first movement*, in sonata form, opens with a playful dance tune that is sweet and light-hearted. After the exposition, the development explores the tune in such a way as to develop a degree of tension that is, however, tightly controlled. After the recapitulation, the movement ends with a rather light-hearted cadence.

The *second movement*, a scherzo-substitute, has a diatonic triadic theme that is dancing and child-like. After a legato second theme, expressed mainly in the lower voices, the triadic theme returns. This is followed by a dream-like and pensive passage, sounding distant and broken. The melodic materials are treated in quasi-rondo form. The same casual or light-hearted cadence that ends the *first movement* also ends this one.

The *third movement* is a lento passacaglia. The overlying melodies are hushed, tender, and melancholy. The brief movement leads directly to the last, attacca.

The *fourth movement* opens with a three-bar lento that is really the twice previously heard casual cadence, now expressed for the *third movement*. The following rondo-sonata allegretto is jaunty and light-hearted, like the opening of the *first movement*. A robust dancing tune soon appears in the cello. Subsequent passages treat the materials of the earlier movements in a free construction. The passacaglia theme reappears and the movement ends in warm good cheer, with the now-familiar light-hearted cadence.

Commentary. The sixth quartet is relaxed, sincere, straightforward, and immaculate, its serenity perhaps reflecting the sense of release that must have followed Stalin's death. This quartet is a return to classical quartet traditions with its conventional form, diatonic harmony and simplicity of melodic materials. This happy work is quite suitable for ambitious amateurs to explore, probably the most suitable after the first quartet. Pleasure—3; Effort—3.

Quartet No. 7 in F-sharp minor, Op. 108 | (1960)

I *Allegretto.* II *Lento.* III *Allegro.*

The three movements are played without a break.

The *first movement* has a wistful, melancholy, oriental, and dancing first theme. A second more agitated and dancing theme appears in the cello. These two ideas are treated simply in a spirit of mystery and rustling agitation.

The muted *second movement,* a simple ternary form, has a long legato theme that is played over a flowing arpeggio. The mood throughout is one of melancholy and repose.

The *third movement* begins with a brief introduction that uses materials from the *first movement.* An agitated and driving fugue follows, after which themes from the *first* and *second movements* return. Their subsequent treatment is cryptic and intricate.

Commentary. The seventh quartet, the shortest of the fifteen works, is pure, uncomplicated, terse, concentrated, and pain-filled. It is dedicated to the memory of the composer's first wife, Nina, who had died in 1954. Its tight construction and cryptic nature make it not rewarding to play this work casually. There are no massive technical difficulties (except for the fugue in the last movement) but amateurs should probably not try this one too readily. Pleasure—1; Effort—3.

Quartet No. 8 in C minor, Op. 110 | (1960),
In Memory of the Victims of Fascism and War

I *Largo.* II *Allegro molto.* III *Allegretto.* IV *Largo.* V *Largo.*

The five movements are played without a break. The *first movement* is brief and has the character of a prologue. The composer's signature theme, DSCH (D, E-flat, C, B), is used fugally to make a freely-constructed introduction to a lament, with dramatic references to the first and fifth symphonies. The mood is one of grief and despair. The terminal cadence forms a crescendo into the next movement.

The *second movement* is a frenzied perpetual motion, referring to the signature theme and introducing a quotation from the second piano trio, a Hebraic lament. The mood of driving despair rushes to an abrupt general pause that introduces the next movement.

The *third movement* opens with a brief harsh introduction to a macabre waltz, formed again on the signature motif, with quotations from the first cello concerto. The mood is that of a dance of death.

The *fourth movement* begins with the appearance of three peremptory interjections, repeated in fortissimo, which introduce a tense largo sostenuto. Thematic material quotes the first cello concerto, Lady Macbeth of Mtsensk, the tenth symphony, and a popular Russian revolutionary song. The three peremptory interjections recur. The stark and gloomy mood is sustained smoothly into the next movement.

The opening of the *fifth movement* is marked by the restatement of the signature theme by the cello. This movement is a postlude, a condensed reprise of the *first movement,* using the same materials and having the same sense of bleak despair.

Commentary. This, the most programmatic of the Shostakovich quartets, is highly autobiographical with its constant restatement of the signature motif and its frequent quotations from previous works. It represents the composer's reflection on his life and times. The inscription, "In Memory of the Victims of Fascism and War," suggested to early commentators that he meant it specifically as an anti-Fascist work, which the composer denied, pointing out its autobiographical nature. It was written in a few days during a visit to Dresden where the composer was surrounded by reminders of World War II. Though this is now the best known of the Shostakovich quartets in the United States, amateur players should hesitate to take it up because of its technical difficulties and the depth of its despair. It can be done, but not quite easily. Pleasure—3; Effort—4.

Quartet No. 9 in E-flat major, Op. 117 | (1964)

I *Moderato con moto.* II *Adagio.* III *Allegretto.* IV *Adagio.* V *Allegro.*

The five movements are played without a break.

The *first movement* starts with a figure of legato oscillating seconds, a pattern that recurs throughout the whole work as a unifying device. Here, that device supports a calm, reflective and bemused theme. A more rhythmic theme of similar character appears in the cello and the two themes then undergo development. The rocking seconds and the stable tonality counter a degree of tension produced by the chromatic harmony. A mood of tranquility prevails. At the end, the viola sustains a pitch that carries directly to the next movement.

The *second movement* opens in a spirit of warmth and rapture. The mood of enchantment persists, the long legato lines shaping a wandering course to find a base only in the last four bars. Here a rhythmic figure in the solo first violin introduces the theme of the next movement, whose beginning is marked only by an abrupt change in tempo.

The *third movement* opens as a subdued and rustic dance, made macabre through the use of mutes. When the mutes come off, the dance continues, first as an agitated perpetual motion and later as an unrestrained, whimsical and comical expression. Then the mutes return and the restraint of the first section is restored with the reappearance of the figure of oscillating seconds, to continue into the next movement.

The *fourth movement* carries forward the figure of oscillating seconds as a melody, punctuated by sharp pizzicato chords. A mood of mystery gives way to a dramatic recitativo outburst in the first violin. This falls away to bring back the figure of mysterious oscillating seconds that carries into the next movement.

The massive *fifth movement* begins as a frenzied dance, jagged and abandoned. Suddenly a stolid peasant dance appears, good-natured at first but later acquiring a more mysterioso character. A free development follows, climaxing in tremolando chords placed against a recitativo passage in the cello. The figure of oscillating seconds returns like a memory, after which increasing agitation drives to an exhilarating unison conclusion.

Commentary. The adventurous ninth quartet exhibits Shostakovich's concern with thematic integration, as in the immediately preceding twelfth and thirteenth symphonies.

Dedicated to his second wife, it marks his return to absolute music away from programmatic writing. It is difficult, very difficult indeed in the last movement. Amateurs are warned away from a casual reading. This one needs much study and practice. Pleasure—3; Effort—4.

Quartet No. 10 in A-flat major, Op. 118 | (1964)

I *Andante.* II *Allegretto furioso.* III *Adagio.* IV *Allegretto.*

The *first movement* has the character of a prologue. A serene expectant tune in the violin leads to a mysterioso response played over hollow fifths. After a little exposition of these materials, a passage of rustling sul ponticello intervenes briefly before the mood of expectant mystery returns.

The *second movement* is a fierce and driving furioso. It uses three motifs, the first slashing, the second agitated, and the third declamatory. These recur, driving the music to a brutal and abrupt ending with no release of the tension.

The *third movement* is a wonderful passacaglia, strictly structured with eight rotations of the sensitive theme. At first ardent and yearning, the mood later becomes more peaceful. A modulation in key leads directly to the next movement.

The *fourth movement* begins with the appearance of a rhythmic dance figure in the viola. This tune moves to the second violin to become whimsical and gay. A lyrical second motif appears over a drone. These materials are developed to a high level of tension when the ardent passacaglia theme returns in forte. The dance theme recurs and the tension diminishes to an andante that brings back the opening motif of the *first movement.* The movement ends in quiet repose.

Commentary. The tenth quartet is an expansive return to the Classical-Romantic tradition in form and style with its four distinct movements and its firm diatonic character. The intentions are clear and the textures are spare. The *second movement* is technically formidable, but the rest are quite feasible. This should be a favorite of amateurs once they master the *second movement*. The dedicatee, Moisei Vainberg, was a fellow-composer. Pleasure—3; Effort—3.

Quartet No. 11 in F minor, Op. 122 | (1966)

I *Introduction: Andantino.* II *Scherzo: Allegretto.* III *Recitative: Adagio.* IV *Etude: Allegro.* V *Humoresque: Allegro.* VI *Elegy: Adagio.* VII *Finale: Moderato.*

The seven movements are played without a break.

The *first movement* opens with a contemplative theme in the first violin. The subsequent cello tune is a unifying motto theme that dominates five of the subsequent movements. Here, the theme is used to create a brief mysterioso.

The *second movement* begins when the first violin plays the motto theme in allegretto. The motto theme then moves fugue-like among the voices. The dry texture, the spare writing, and the punctuating glissandi make this movement into a comical and whimsical dance, although a subdued and gentle one.

The *third movement* is only a brief interlude, opening in a stern and severe mood and subsiding quickly to an anticipatory repose.

The *fourth movement* is a racing perpetuum mobile, its running figure built from the motto theme. A derivative of the motto theme in expansion sounds as a chorale beneath the running figure.

The *fifth movement* is comical, the motto theme appearing in augmentation over a whimsical rhythmic figure. The motto theme here acquires a mocking sternness.

The *sixth movement* presents the augmented motto theme as a dramatic unison in the lower voices. Lyrical and consolatory phrases follow in the first violin. A freely developed dialogue over the tread of a funeral march brings the movement to rest in an attitude of quiet expectation.

The *seventh movement* states the motto theme as a childish staccato line over a rocking lullaby rhythm. The whimsical treatment contrasts comic elements in the melodies with a somber and open harmony.

Commentary. A single experience of this small work, filled with a sense of suffering and desolation, leaves one with little idea of the meaning behind the music. The explanation of the work lies in its dedication to the memory of Vasily Shirinsky, the recently deceased second violinist of the Beethoven String Quartet. The work makes sense as a memorial portrait in the form of a series of miniatures. For amateur players, this small work has the appeal of simplicity except for the Etude, which is formidably difficult. Pleasure—2; Effort—4.

Quartet No. 12 in D-flat major, Op. 133 | (1968)

I *Moderato.* II *Allegretto.*

The *first movement* opens with a statement of the twelve-tone row in a single legato sweep by the cello. This recurring angular motif subsides into the subsequent cantilena. The moderato cantilena and contrasting material in an allegretto are repeated in alternation, short evocations of contrasting character. The cantilena is warm and reassuring, the allegretto hesitant and optimistic.

The *second movement* has four parts. The first part is a long allegretto scherzo that uses an imperative figure of five notes to create a mood of fury and violence. A climax of swirling sextuplets sul ponticello subsides into the second part, an adagio triadic chant, muted and tragic. There is an intense yearning soliloquy in the cello at the beginning of this adagio section. The third part, moderato, begins with a forte pizzicato line in the first violin. This yields to dramatic and violent recitativo-like passages that are punctuated by pizzicato. A brief recall of the adagio precedes the fourth part. This part is a warmly lyrical moderato, becoming an allegretto, in which the five-note motif heard earlier is used to create an optimistic atmosphere. The movement ends in a spirit of triumph.

Commentary. This complex work was explained by the composer himself: The world of high ideals (*first movement*) is challenged by destructive forces (scherzo); after a mood of despair (adagio), the music expresses purity of intention and aspiration (moderato), and then presents a reaffirmation of good over evil (final moderato and allegretto). This explanation may help to understand this complex work but it makes it no easier to play. The unusual form, the angularity and the conflict between tonality and atonality all make this a difficult work to play. Amateur players should pass this one by until they are ready to work hard. Pleasure—3; Effort—4.

Quartet No. 13 in B-flat minor, Op. 138 | (1970)

I *Adagio.*

This single-movement work features the viola, as might be expected from its dedication to the Beethoven String Quartet's violist, Vadim Borisovsky.

The viola opens with a bleak lament that is followed by a freely-constructed passage of stark and dramatic fragments featuring a triplet figure, later to be used as a unifying force. With a change in key, the violin plays the triplet figure to mark the beginning of the middle span of the movement. The triplet figure next appears as a lamentation, and then in a dramatic character. A twittering passage is punctuated by rappings on the wood of the instruments. This tense and stark material builds through a complex dialogue to a passage of somber poise. After a return of the triplet motif, a somber viola soliloquy returns the mood to the bleak atmosphere of the opening. After further soliloquies in the cello and viola, a long viola recitative, punctuated by rappings on the wood of the instruments, brings the movement to an anguished cadence.

Commentary. This is a most pessimistic work. The prominence of the minor second, the rappings on the wood and the terrifying triplet figure all create a mood of despair. Amateur players can manage this work if they want to try. They can readily comprehend it, and it is technically feasible. Those who play mainly for fun, however, should pass this one by. Pleasure—1; Effort—3.

Quartet No. 14 in F-sharp minor, Op. 142 | (1973)

I *Allegretto.* II *Adagio.* III *Allegretto.*

The *first movement* begins innocently with an inconsequential tune whose careless and skipping nature soon yields to a passionate intensity. The cello introduces a related second motif that is more anguished. The movement develops further in sonata form. Recitativo passages lead to a coda that leaves the movement ended in a state of suspended tension.

The *second movement* opens with an unaccompanied theme in the first violin. This theme, at first a lament, is subsequently developed with a spare texture to express more complex sentiments. A middle section featuring the cello is warmer, more radiant and richer in texture. The materials and mood of the first part then return, to lead directly to the next movement, attacca.

The *third movement* opening, a simple and square pizzicato line in the first violin, soon gives way to a solo lyrical phrase. The tension builds quickly to an agonized climax with the use of fragments from earlier melodic materials. A section having a wistful mood follows, with a lamenting soliloquy in the cello. The *second movement* is recalled briefly, and the movement ends in a mood of serene and tender sadness.

Commentary. This largely sorrowful work features the cello, in accordance with its dedication to Sergey Shirinsky, the cellist of the Beethoven String Quartet. It is a challenging piece to play for the cellist. The work is somewhat more diatonic than others of this period in the life of the composer, but the angularity and chromaticism of the later Shostakovich is still much in evidence. Most amateurs should probably pass this one up for its technical difficulty. Pleasure—1; Effort—4.

Quartet No. 15 in E-flat minor, Op. 144 | (1974)

I *Elegy: Adagio.* II *Serenade: Adagio.* III *Intermezzo: Adagio.*
IV *Nocturne: Adagio.* V *Funeral March: Adagio molto.* VI *Epilogue: Adagio.*

The *first movement* opens with a starkly simple theme played in fugue. The sustained piano dynamic and the static modal harmonies create a bleak lamentation or elegy with the purity, gravity and poise of Gregorian chant.

The *second movement* follows attacca. It opens with a series of twelve pianissimo-to-fortissimo crescendos on a single note, the notes of the twelve-tone row. Violent pizzicato interjections lead to a somber soliloquy in the cello and the sequence is repeated. The serenade proper then begins, a slow and melancholy waltz played over a spare rhythmic figure. The violent pizzicato interjections and the single-note crescendos return, and the sad waltz is repeated to end with more of the violent interjections, now arco. The waltz returns in fragments interrupted by the arco interjections, subsiding slowly to a mood of ominous expectation.

The *third movement* begins as an impassioned and violent recitativo played by the violin over a pedal point. This subsides to a brief recall of the bleak mood of the elegy of the *first movement*, which carries directly into the next movement.

The *fourth movement*, a muted nocturne, uses a flowing accompaniment to support a yearning melody in the viola. The bleak elegy of the *first movement* returns for an interlude before the yearning nocturne melody is repeated, now in the cello. Violent pizzicato chords in the violins presage the dotted rhythm of the Funeral March that follows attacca.

The *fifth movement* opens with the ominous dotted rhythm of the Funeral March in thick forte chords. Dramatic soliloquies follow in the viola, cello and first violin, punctuated by repetitions of the dotted rhythm figure. These continue, the mood subsiding to the bleakest despair. The opening of the following Epilogue breaks in with terrifying violence.

The *sixth movement* Epilogue opens with a screaming recitativo outburst in the first violin, followed by a passage of hopelessness. The materials and moods of the preceding movements are reviewed in confused and suffocated fragments. The rhythmic figure of the Funeral March returns softly to bring the movement to a quiet close.

Commentary. This is not a work for amateurs to undertake without much thought and practice, both because of its technical difficulties and because of its character. There is no more completely nihilistic work to be found anywhere. As a supreme statement of the sort, it is best left to the professionals for its interpretation, not to speak of its technical demands. And yet, to play it is to learn to know it, and some amateurs will feel moved to try it. Pleasure—2; Effort—4.

SIBELIUS (1865–1957)

The Finnish national hero, Jean Sibelius, is best known today as a symphonist and writer of songs. He developed an interest in chamber music early in life and he is known then to have written four string quartets, four piano trios, two piano quartets, a piano quintet, and an octet, all currently unavailable or forgotten. These are said to have been superficial salon pieces. The one mature piece of chamber music that has entered the repertoire is the string quartet subtitled "Voces Intimae." It was written during a trip to London in 1908.

The quartet is unusual in structure, constituting five movements, none in sonata form. Each is different from the others in
mood, thematic material, harmonic foundation and texture.
Thus, the quartet is much more like a divertimento or a suite
than a standard string quartet. The texture of the whole work is
orchestral.

Quartet in D minor, Op. 56 | (1909) *Voces Intimae*

I *Andante; Allegro molto moderato.* II *Vivace.* III *Adagio di molto.*
IV *Allegretto (ma pesante).* V *Allegro.*

The *first movement* is opened by a brief andante. This is an introspective duet between the violin and the cello on a theme that then gives
rise to the whole movement. Derivative expressions of the theme
appear in the various voices, often in the form dialogues. The mood
is quiet and introspective throughout.

The *second movement* follows attacca. The music has a fabric of light
tremolos throughout, shimmering at first, more forceful later. The
light theme, once created, is retained without modification, and it
rises to a climax with a subsequent falling away to a quiet and unpro-
longed finish.

The *third movement*, the center of gravity of the quartet, constitutes a
piece full of gloom and foreboding. It may express the mood of the
composer at a time when thought he had cancer of the larynx. The
lyrical and fervent music is free of sentimentality. The movement is
characterized by extreme irregularity in meter and rhythm with time
signatures and tempos changing frequently. All forward motion ceases
at several points. This is the movement over which Sibelius wrote
"Voces Intimae."

The *fourth movement* approximates a classical scherzo. Its texture is
thick and orchestral. A rugged and forceful opening theme is followed
by more lyrical melodies. A contrasting middle section is not really a
trio but only a different treatment of the underlying thematic material.
There is a highly original coda.

The *fifth movement* is like a Finnish epic, full-bodied and heroic. The
thematic material is carried at a vigorous and stable tempo. The mood
is cheerful, lively and triumphant, and the movement ends with a
clean cut.

Commentary. This large work is not to be undertaken casually by amateurs. It requires fine individual technique and a full acquaintance with the idiom of Sibelius. It presents major problems in ensemble playing, especially in the *second movement.* It can be taxing both for players and for listeners. Still, those amateurs who are up to it and who want to get to know this splendid work can do it. Pleasure—2; Effort—4.

SMETANA (1824–1884)

Bedrich Smetana came to maturity in the wave of nationalistic fervor that swept central Europe in the 1840s and Bohemian nationalism colored all his compositions. He established a folk music idiom early in his life and he retained it throughout his career. His nationalistic operas, now generally neglected, established his reputation and he became the major influence in musical developments in the parts of Europe that bridge German and Slavic cultures. His preference for the writing of programmatic music was strong and so he showed little attraction to absolute music like chamber music.

He left only three pieces of chamber music, the piano trio and two string quartets, all autobiographical. The trio expresses his grief on the death of his daughter. The two quartets, both subtitled 'Aus meinem Leben', are the reflections of an old man on his life. Of the two quartets, the first is well known while the second is neglected. The first, Op. 116, was completed in 1876 but not performed for two years. The second was completed in 1883 and first performed in 1884, the year in which he died at the age of sixty. Both quartets were written after he had become deaf. Smetana himself thought poorly of the second quartet.

Quartet in E minor, Op. 116 | (1876), *Aus meinem Leben*

I *Allegro vivo appassionato.* II *Allegro moderato a la Polka.*
III *Largo sostenuto.* IV *Vivace.*

The *first movement* opens with a dramatic tremolando, against which the viola plays the tragic and declamatory first theme, said to be a call of fate. The second theme is consolatory. The two are developed freely in sonata form with an orchestral texture. Smetana said that this movement expresses his youthful leaning to art, his romantic nature and his premonition of the tragedy of his deafness.

The *second movement* opens with a first section that features a romping polka. A slower dance appears in a second section. Smetana said that this movement is a reflection of his carefree youth in the first section and of the aristocratic circles in which he lived for so long in the second part.

The *third movement* opens with a melancholy theme in the cello. A more yearning and nostalgic second theme appears and is developed to a brief climax, after which a new consolatory theme appears. A violin cadenza then leads to a series of chords, after which the chief theme returns to be treated tenderly. The movement ends tranquilly. Smetana said that the movement recalls his first love, apparently for his wife who had died shortly before.

The *fourth movement* is built of dance tunes, rhythmic, exuberant and agitated. After these are explored extensively, the mood of gaiety is sharply interrupted by a sustained high E in the first violin. The following coda recalls the consolatory theme of the *first movement* and contrasts it with the dance tune that opens the finale. The movement ends in a mood of sadness and resignation. Smetana said that the dance tunes celebrate his discovery of the nationalistic musical idiom that he used in composition. The high E in the first violin that interrupts the romp is considered to be an allusion to the onset of his deafness.

Commentary. All those who do not disdain sentimentality and programmatic music will enjoy this masterful and popular work. Violists love the work because it features the viola, though all voices have rewarding parts. Its technical difficulties are not great, although the peculiar rhythm of the second section of the *second movement* is so difficult that a professional quartet in Prague refused to play the work when it first appeared. Amateurs are warned not to make the work over-dramatic. The *second movement*, especially, can easily become maudlin. Pleasure—3; Effort—3.

TCHAIKOVSKY (1840–1893)

Pyotr Ilich Tchaikovsky's father, the son of a minor nobleman in Kazan, was a mining engineer. He managed an important government-owned mine in Votkinsk where he and his second wife, Alexandra, lived in style as prominent persons. She was an educated woman, a linguist, pianist and singer. Pyotr was their second son, preceded in the family by a half-sister and by a brother, and followed by other brothers and a sister. The large household also included an aunt and some cousins.

The early education of the children was private, the responsibility of a governess to whom Pyotr's ability in music became apparent in early childhood. He began to study the piano at six. When he was eight, the family moved, the father taking over the operation of a mine in Alapayev, and the boy was sent to a boarding school where he remained until he entered university in 1850. Here, he studied law, graduating in 1859.

He took a job in the Ministry of Justice in St. Petersburg where he worked for a time with little enthusiasm. Meanwhile, he continued his study of music with a succession of teachers, none of whom remarked on an unusual talent. He entered the St. Petersburg Conservatory where he made steady progress, so that the director of the Conservatory, Anton Rubinstein, recommended him for an opening in the faculty of the new Moscow Conservatory in 1866. Nicolay Rubenstein, the brother of Anton, directed the Moscow Conservatory.

Arriving in Moscow, he set about composing with enthusiasm and his first symphony enjoyed considerable success at that time. The next eleven years saw a steady output of works that brought him increasing fame at home and abroad. He began to travel, meeting Liszt, Saint-Saens, and others on brief holiday trips.

In 1877, he came into correspondence with Madame Nadezhda von Meck, a wealthy widow who admired his work and was soon supporting him with an annual stipend. The two maintained an active correspondence for over fourteen years, though they never met. This patron also helped Claude Debussy to launch his career. Also in 1877, Tchaikovsky entered upon his unfortunate marriage to Antonina Milyukov that ended in dissolution after a few months. Tchaikovsky assuaged the emotional consequences of this crisis by spending a period in Switzerland and Italy, returning to St. Petersburg in 1878.

After 1885, he lived a reclusive life in the country where he could work with little interruption, emerging only to undertake increasingly celebratory tours in Europe. He visited the United States in 1891 and England in 1893, where he received an honorary degree from Cambridge University. He died suddenly in October 1893, a suicide rather than a victim of cholera, as was once believed.

Tchaikovsky's three string quartets antedate those of Borodin. He did not consider himself to be a devotee of chamber music and he wrote, besides the three string quartets, only the piano trio and the string sextet, *Souvenir de Florence*. The three quartets came at the beginning of his artistic maturity, close together in time, shortly after he had become established at the Moscow conservatory. The trio and sextet came much later, in 1882 and in 1892. He had experimented with writing chamber music as a student, writing single movements and even a complete string quartet long before Op. 11 appeared, and so he knew potentials and limitations of the form.

The first string quartet, Op. 11, was completed in February 1872, and it premiered in that same month in Moscow. It was written for a concert from which he hoped to make some money, for he was poor at the time. It was well received and it was the first of Tchaikovsky's works to become popular outside Russia. It was first published almost two years later, in 1873.

The second string quartet, Op. 22, was written at the beginning of 1874, at the same time that Tchaikovsky was working on an opera, *Vakula, the Smith*. He himself commented on the ease of its composition: "I wrote it, so to speak, at one stroke." He remodeled the work when Anton Rubenstein criticized it, and the revision was first performed in Moscow in March 1874.

The third string quartet, Op. 30, was started in January 1875, completed a month later, and premiered in March. It is dedicated to the memory of the recently deceased Ferdinand Laub, the first violinist of the Moscow String Quartet, which had premiered the composer's Op. 11 and Op. 22 quartets. Laub had been Tchaikovsky's close personal friend and his colleague as a professor at the Moscow Conservatory. This dedication explains the elegiac character of the quartet.

Quartet in D major, Op. 11 | (1871), *The Accordion*

I *Moderato e semplice.* II *Andante cantabile.* III *Scherzo: Allegro non tanto.* IV *Finale: Allegro giusto.*

The *first movement*, a sonata allegro, opens with a syncopated theme in sonorous full harmony, followed by a somewhat more gloomy section. The development is long and ingenious and the movement ends with a bright and sonorous allegro giusto. The common name of the quartet refers to the harmonic texture of the opening theme of this movement.

The *second movement* is the famous andante cantabile, better known in its transcription as a work for string orchestra. It is in ternary form with a trio. The major theme is a Russian folk tune. This movement's particular simplicity and beauty did much to make both the whole work and the composer famous.

The *third movement* scherzo, also in ternary form, is whimsical in character.

The *fourth movement* is in sonata form. The first theme is bright and beautiful. The Russian second theme first appears in the viola. The themes are treated with imitation and counterpoint, moving among the instruments. The coda is a brisk and energetic presentation of figured versions of the principal theme.

Commentary. This lively and beautiful work has little of the drama and pathos of the later compositions of Tchaikovsky. It is well worth playing, if only to hear the famous andante cantabile in its original setting. It offers no major technical problems to experienced amateur players. Pleasure—3; Effort—2.

Quartet in F major, Op. 22 | (1874)

I *Adagio; Moderato assai.* II *Scherzo: Allegro giusto.* III *Andante ma non tanto.* IV *Finale: Allegro con moto.*

The *first movement* opens with a rousing and poetic adagio of eighteen bars featuring an ornate cadenza-like passage for the first violin. In the following moderato assai, the Russian first subject is richly melodic as is the second theme. The two themes are treated in broad, powerful, bright and festive episodes. The development section is long. The coda opens with the first subject in a quiet modification followed by a dramatic crescendo and a tranquil ending.

The *second movement* is in combined 6/8 and 9/8 meters, giving it a characteristically limping Russian rhythm. The trio is a loping sort of waltz. The coda is energetic and impetuous.

The *third movement* andante is a rondo, with a fifteen-bar poetic introduction. The principal subject is worked out contrapuntally. The second subject is more strenuous. The principal theme and that of the introduction return and the themes are made to work together in the coda. This is a simple movement, autumnal and dreamy throughout.

The *fourth movement*, also in rondo form, begins with a spirited unison introduction. Three contrasting themes make up the following rondo. The first is graceful, the second sonorous and dignified and the third restless. These are treated variously. A fugue appears on a fragment of the first theme. The character of the movement is bright and triumphant, and the technique is chromatic and energetic.

Commentary. This is a fine and satisfying work for amateurs to play, but it is generally more difficult and less pleasing than its predecessor, Op. 11. The final movement is especially difficult. This is a long work and one that should be studied movement by movement rather than all at once. Pleasure—2; Effort—3.

Quartet in E-flat minor, Op. 30 | (1875)

I *Andante sostenuto: Allegro moderato.* II *Allegro vivo e scherzando.* III *Andante funebre e doloroso ma con moto.* IV *Finale: Allegro non troppo e risoluto.*

The *first movement* opens with a long funereal andante with two motifs. The following allegro moderato also has two themes, the first impetuous, the second soft and delicate. The restless development, depending heavily on a triplet figure, reaches a great climax, to be followed by a lullaby episode. An abridged version of the andante introduction closes this long and varied movement.

The *second movement* is comparatively short with a dramatic agitated scherzo and a restrained melodic subject in the trio.

The *third movement* opens on muted strings with gloomy chords. A dirge theme follows. The second subject is elegiac and somber. The themes are treated variously and the movement ends with a bridge theme heard earlier.

The *fourth movement* is a brisk and bold work in the major mode, providing a sharp relief after the melancholy of the first three movements. The themes are Russian in character. A brief mournful episode precedes the brisk and lively coda.

Commentary. The intense melancholy of this quartet, its drama, and its long and complex *first movement* serve to make it the least attractive of the three quartets for amateurs to play. Furthermore, the keys throughout are such as to make intonation difficult. It is not a work to play for fun but it is interesting as an example of a major and serious effort to explore the capacities of the string quartet to express deep and dark moods. The gloom is that of the late symphonies. In playing this work, one thinks also of the last string quartet of Mendelssohn (Op. 80). Pleasure—1; Effort—4.

VERDI (1813–1901)

The string quartet in E minor, Verdi's only published non-vocal composition, was written in March 1873, when Verdi was sixty. He had completed *Aida* a little over a year before and it had had a heroic reception at its Milan premiere in January 1872. Verdi had gone to Naples in the autumn of that year where Aida was to be produced again. The soprano who had sung the part of Aida in the Milan production, and who was also to do so in Naples, fell ill. Rehearsals were postponed and so Verdi was idle. He wrote the string quartet to pass the time. He had been a long-time student of string quartets, examining the great works of the classical period repeatedly as models of economical and lucid writing. This string quartet was first played at his hotel in Naples soon after the Naples production of *Aida*. Verdi was reticent to see the quartet become anything other than a private undertaking and so he resisted its dissemination until his publisher persuaded him to allow its publication five years later in 1877. He later assented to its performance by a string orchestra.

Quartet in E minor | (1873)

I *Allegro*. II *Andantino*. III *Prestissimo*. IV *Scherzo Fuga: Allegro assai mosso*.

The *first movement* opens with a dramatic and foreboding first theme in the second violin, a theme related to one in *Aida* that is associated with Amneris. The second theme is more subdued and contemplative. The development is conventional. The movement is operatic in style and it possesses dramatic vitality.

The highly chromatic *second movement* is in rondo form, to be played "with elegance." The development of the rather cool and simple thematic material over a mazurka rhythm involves a degree of variation.

The brio *third movement* is wholly operatic in character. It is a prestissimo treated in the form of a classical scherzo. The trio constitutes a romantic aria for the cello with an accompanying pizzicato.

The *fourth movement* is an energetic and joyful scherzo. The cheerful theme is treated with ingenuity in a freely constructed fugue. Commentators consider this to be the finest movement of the work.

Commentary. This is certainly an interesting work, and it is good fun to play. This operatic quartet is not a masterpiece, but it is a fine Italian contrast to the German romanticism that dominated quartet writing in the nineteenth century. This work is fully accessible to experienced amateurs. Pleasure—2; Effort—3.

PART II

Works for Three, Five, and More Strings

BEETHOVEN (1770–1827)

Beethoven wrote five works for string trio (violin, viola, and cello) in his earliest years in Vienna, from 1796 to 1798, the same period as the three piano trios that he used to introduce himself to the Viennese audience. The string trio, of course, presents a much different challenge to the composer, though it seems likely that Beethoven was just as eager to make an impression with these string trios as he was with the piano trios.

String trios certainly existed before Beethoven, but he greatly advanced the form in this brief excursion, just as he did in so many other musical structures. Thus, Op. 3 is really an eighteenth-century divertimento containing six movements, two of them minuets. It was probably first sketched in Bonn and completed soon after his arrival in Vienna. The Op. 8 Serenade retains the divertimento, or cassation, style and format, but it constitutes a considerable advance in that it unifies the movements through the use of derivative themes and through the return, at the end, of the little march that opens the piece. The three trios in Op. 9, going even further, exhibit a mastery that approaches that of the Op. 18 string quartets that were already germinating in his mind. It is said that Beethoven himself considered Op. 9 to be the best of his works to that time. If he wrote Op. 9 as a preparatory exercise to the Op. 18 quartets, as some experts say, one should look at Op. 9 as his embarkation on a journey that leads all the way to the *Grosse Fuge*.

Beethoven's fondness for the form of the string quartet did not apparently extend to the string quintet. Although he must have known the viola quintets of Mozart, he himself used the form only once as an original conception (Op. 29). Two other such quintets (Op. 4 and Op. 104) represent his own modifications of works he wrote originally for a different medium. A Fugue in D major for viola quintet (Op. 137), published posthumously, is apparently not Beethoven's doing.

Op. 4 was written in 1796. Wegeler reported it to have been the consequence of a request by Count Apponyi to write a string quartet. Although it is commonly described as a transcription of a wind quintet, that was published later as Op. 103, it differs considerably in ways that make it justifiably called a separate work, and it was presented as such when it was published.

Op. 29 was written in 1801 and published the next year. No special circumstances surrounded its appearance.

Op. 104 arose in 1817, according to some, when Beethoven saw an arrangement for quintet of the Piano Trio Op. 1, No. 3 made by an unknown musician. The idea interested the composer enough that he produced his own version for this instrumentation. It was first performed in 1818 and published as Op. 104 in 1819.

String Trio in E-flat major, Op. 3 | (1796)

I *Allegro con brio.* II *Andante.* III *Menuetto: Allegretto.* IV *Adagio.* V *Menuetto: Moderato.* VI *Finale: Allegro.*

The *First movement* is a vigorous sonata with an impressively accomplished development and a particularly original coda.

The genteel *second movement* andante, in three-eight time, has a wonderful scherzoso quality.

The *third movement* minuet is cheerful, graceful and well behaved.

The long *fourth movement* adagio, the center of gravity of the work, opens seriously and soon becomes dramatic.

The *fifth movement* is another minuet, just as cheerful as the first, but a little friskier.

The lively rondo of the *sixth movement* provides a playful romp of considerable complexity.

Commentary. This work is already well beyond the string trios of Haydn and quite comparable to the great E-flat Divertimento of Mozart. Those who haven't played it may not be prepared for something so advanced. It is really wonderful to experience. Pleasure—4; Effort—3.

Serenade (string trio) in D major, Op. 8 | (1797)

I *Marcia: Allegro.* II *Adagio.* III *Menuetto: Allegretto.* IV *Adagio; Scherzo: Allegro molto.* V *Allegretto alla Polacca.* VI *Andante quasi allegretto.* VII *Marcia: Allegro.*

The *first movement* is a march, rather serious in character but brief and unpretentious.

The *second movement* is a highly ornamented adagio that is connected to the opening movement.

The *third movement* minuet is an airy dance with a vaporous trio.

The *fourth movement*, as the typical center of gravity in a divertimento, is complex, alternating brief passages of an adagio with brief passages of a scherzo in ABABA form. The funereal tune of the adagio, in D minor, contrasts strongly with the sparkling D major Scherzo.

The long *fifth movement* allegretto features off-beat accents and syncopation, as the term polacca implies.

The *sixth movement* andante treats a Mozartean theme to five variations.

After a bridge, the *seventh movement* repeats, literally, the little march that opens the work.

Commentary. This wonderful and complex work seems to be unduly neglected. Because of its form, it seems a bit artificial, an entertainment rather than profound or "serious" music. That, of course, is the intention of a divertimento, and it probably accounts for Beethoven's appellation, 'Serenade'. But this piece contains many clear elements of the 'serious' Beethoven. Pleasure—4; Effort—3.

String Trio in G major, Op. 9, No. 1 | (1798)

I *Adagio; Allegro con brio.* II *Adagio, ma non tanto, e cantabile.*
III *Scherzo: Allegro.* IV *Presto.*

The *first movement* opens with a graceful and engaging adagio that prepares the way for a spirited allegro sonata movement, fully worked out.

The lovely *second movement* uses triplets and sextuplets throughout to exploit a pastoral theme.

The *third movement* is graceful and well mannered throughout, like an 18th century minuet in spirit, but full of energy.

The *fourth movement* presto is one of those scampering pieces of a sort that a later generation came to call Mendelssohnian.

Commentary. This is just as mature as the Op. 18 quartets, but somewhat harder to play because of the fact that it is a trio. The slow movement is truly memorable. Pleasure—4; Effort—3.

String Trio in D major, Op. 9, No. 2 | (1798)

I *Allegretto*. II *Andante quasi allegretto*. III *Menuetto: Allegro*.
IV *Rondo: Allegro*.

The *first movement* is a gentle and rather square-cut sonata movement that seems a bit episodic or fragmented in character.

The graceful *second movement* passes its gentle theme back and forth between violin and cello.

The *third movement* minuet is undistinguished.

The long and complex *fourth movement* announces the theme in the cello, thus anticipating the composer's later quartets.

Commentary. This is a much less impressive work that the other two in the opus. Pleasure—2; Effort—3.

String Trio in C minor, Op. 9, No. 3 | (1798)

I *Allegro con spirito*. II *Adagio con espressione*. III *Scherzo: Allegro molto e vivace*. IV *Finale: Presto*.

The dark and energetic *first movement*, filled with chromaticism, possesses all the drama we have come to expect of Beethoven in this key.

The warm and emotional *second movement*, in C major, is just as dramatic.

The *third movement* returns to C minor with an angry and abrupt force.

The *fourth movement* rondo remains in a serious C minor mood, but presents an agitated triplet theme in cut time.

Commentary. This is just as impressive, and as difficult, as the first in the opus. Some musicologists see it as the more important because of the way in which it presages the quartets of the middle period. Pleasure—4; Effort—4.

Viola Quintet in E-flat major, Op. 4 | (1796)

I *Allegro con brio*. II *Andante*. III *Menuetto:Allegretto*. IV *Finale: Presto*.

The *first movement* is a sonata allegro typical of the sort Beethoven wrote at this period. The nature of its melodies strongly suggests the origin of this work as a piece written for winds.

The *second movement* is a pleasing andante in six-eight meter.

The *third movement* menuet is memorable for the thin texture of the two trios, and for the imitative technique in the second one.

The theme of the long *fourth movement,* like that of the first, hints at the origin of the piece as a work meant for winds.

Commentary. The body of avocational players, so far as I know, has scant knowledge of this work. Only musicologists seem to be familiar with it. Its virtues are those of all the works of the early Beethoven canon. Its shortcomings arise from the company it keeps, the cadre of viola quintets that it came to occupy. It lacks the character we have come to associate with this instrumentation—the deep feelings, the richness, the darkness, and the depths. Instead, it is cheerful and light-hearted. Pleasure—3; Effort—3.

Viola Quintet in C major, Op. 29 | (1801) *The Storm Quintet*

I *Allegro moderato.* II *Adagio molto espressivo.* III *Scherzo: Allegro.* IV *Presto; Andante con moto e scherzo.*

The *first movement* presents a warm-hearted legato theme over a rolling accompaniment, extensively developed in this lucid and satisfying sonata.

The *second movement* is a rather florid aria.

The little arpeggiated theme of the *third movement* is used to produce a lively and humorous dance.

The unusual *fourth movement* features, in the presto sections, a unison rumbling in the lower strings, a thunderous murmur that gives the quintet its common name. The subsequent rushing scalar fragments that make up the theme add to the feeling of a storm. The form is unusual, with two interposed andante episodes.

Commentary. In this product of the composer's experimentation with the quartet form, he was inquiring into the possibilities of the quintet. At the same time, he was developing his musical thought. The result is an interesting work with a remarkable texture, provided by the presence of second viola. The *first movement* seems to the player to be the most natural. The last movement seems just a little odd at first. It needs repetition to get it to feel right. This is a quintet to work on, study, and think about as a matter of education and self-improvement, not one to be taken up just for the pleasure. Pleasure—3; Effort—3.

Viola Quintet in C minor, Op. 104 | (composed in 1795, transcribed in 1817)

I *Allegro con brio.* II *Andante cantabile con variazione.*
III *Menuetto: Quasi Allegro.* IV *Finale: Prestissimo*

The *first movement* opens directly with the soft and mysterious principal theme stated in union. The mood of mystery is maintained throughout the movement. The style is always restrained and graceful.

The *second movement* presents a calm and cantabile theme in the major mode. Five variations follow. These are rich and ingenious, the last variation being especially chromatic. This movement is a fine example of the form.

The *third movement* is a rather conventional scherzo-minuet. The minor mode scherzo is contrasted by the major mode of the trio. The mood is somber and restrained throughout.

The *fourth movement* is a bright and lively rondo in the minor mode. It can certainly be played prestissimo, as marked, but too quick a tempo robs the movement of some of its brightness and charm. Its strict adherence to piano and pianissimo dynamics is unexpected and a bit difficult to manage sometimes.

Commentary. As Beethoven's own transcription of the third Piano Trio, Op. 1, No. 3, this can be taken as evidence of his own particular esteem for the third trio. The dark sound of the viola quintet suits the sense of gravity and seriousness of purpose of the work. This transcription has been sadly neglected. Its neglect served as the focus for the popular novel, *A Certain Music*, published in 1999 by Seth Vikram. All amateurs should get to know this version. Pleasure—4; Effort—2

BRAHMS (1833–1897)

Brahms wrote in many musical forms, and chamber music is an important part of his legacy. He worked at writing string quartets through much of his life, but the fact that he finally released only three suggests that he was not wholly comfortable with the restrictions of that form. He wrote apparently more easily for the extended quartet (quintet or sextet). The literature is greatly enriched by his two viola quintets and his two string sextets.

The form of the string quintet attracted him early. He wrote his first in 1862 (when he was twenty-nine), a work with two cellos in F minor. Dissatisfied with the sound of the work, he revised it as a sonata for two pianos (Op. 34b), and still later as the great piano quintet, Op. 34. The string quintet version does not survive.

Twenty years later, he produced the first viola quintet, Op. 88. It was begun in the spring and completed in the following summer at Ischl, an alpine resort, where Brahms spent a happy holiday. The piano trio, Op. 87, was written at the same time. The cheerful character of both these works probably reflects Brahm's happiness at Ischl as well as the warm friendship of Ignaz Brull, a young and virtuosic Moravian pianist and composer with whom he was working at that time. Dr. Theodor Billroth, the eminent Viennese surgeon, greatly admired the Op. 88 viola quintet. He was an amateur musician to whom Brahms confided much of his music as soon as it was finished.

Eight years later, also during a summer holiday at Ischl, Brahms completed the second viola quintet, Op. 111. It was not quite so warmly admired by contemporaries as the first one had been. Billroth, Joachim, and others found the instrumentation at the beginning of the *first movement* to be troublesome, but Brahms, after some experimentation, refused to change it. It became popular immediately after its first public performance in November, 1890. At its completion, Brahms thought to give up composing and he actually did so for about a year, only to resume writing in his "late period," which saw the writing of the clarinet trio, Op. 114, the clarinet quintet, Op. 115, and the two clarinet (or viola) sonatas, Op. 120. A performance of the Op. 111 viola quintet by the Joachim ensemble was the occasion for one of Brahms' last public appearances, in January, 1897, during his final illness.

The first string sextet, Op. 18, was written at Detmold in 1859–60 where the young Brahms had taken his first official post as a musician to the princely Court. He was employed there as a choral conductor, teacher and pianist, being surrounded by young people. There he had time to study the works of the classical masters. The youthful spirit and the classical form of this work reflect these opportunities. He consulted Joachim in its composition, and he took many of Joachim's suggestions.

The second string sextet, Op. 36, was begun in 1864 when Brahms was on a summer holiday at Lichtental, a resort near Baden-Baden, where he was surrounded by a circle of close friends, including Clara Schumann. He started it in September and completed it in the following May. Brahms was still troubled by his broken engagement to Agathe von Siebold five years before. He dedicated the work to her and he inserted an allusion to her name into the fabric of the *first movement*.

Viola Quintet in F major, Op. 88 | (1882)

I *Allegro non troppo, ma con brio*. II *Grave ed appassionato; Allegro vivace; Presto*. III *Allegro energico; Presto*.

The genial *first movement* sonata has a tuneful, square and rather terse theme. The second subject is bright, partly because it is in A major. The exploitation of these themes is highly manipulative, and the movement is consequently more impressive for its compositional technique than for its profundity. The mood throughout is carefree and amiable.

The *second movement* is an imaginative quasi-rondo form that telescopes the conventional slow and scherzo movements into one. Its grave, passionate and declamatory subject was taken from a sarabande for piano that Brahms had written twenty-seven years earlier as an exercise in Baroque style. In the first section, the theme is worked out in a nearly complete little cavatina with an unusual scoring. A binary scherzo with a dotted rhythm follows. The grave returns to be followed again by the light and energetic scherzo, but now in presto. The movement ends in harmonic ambiguity.

The *third movement* is an ebullient and jolly sonata, fugal in style, having the feel of a perpetuum mobile. A dashing presto coda ends the movement with a flourish. The fugal sonata finale of Beethoven's string quartet, Op. 59, No. 3, may have inspired this movement.

Commentary. Some critics find the *first movement* a little less imaginative than the others. The whole work has a most satisfying sonority. Some authorities consider the frequent shifts from F major to A major and back to F major to be an allusion to Brahms's personal motto, "Frei aber froh." This is the easier and the more familiar of the two viola quintets. The work is not really easy, musically as well as technically, but prepared amateurs will very much enjoy playing it. Pleasure—3; Effort—3.

Viola Quintet in G major, Op. 111 | (1891)

I *Allegro non troppo, ma con brio.* II *Adagio.* III *Un poco allegretto.* IV *Vivace, ma non troppo presto.*

The *first movement* opens abruptly with an ardent leaping theme from the cello that is threatened with eclipse by the rich harmonic superstructure in the higher voices. The Viennese secondary themes are similarly richly scored, and the whole movement has a luxurious sonority. The mood throughout is one of immense joy and high spirits.

The *second movement* is a march in the minor mode, lyrical, subtle and brief. Its eighty bars contain a broad range of feelings and textures within the essentially tragic character of the music. The first viola has a splendid soaring cadenza-like passage near the end.

The *third movement* is an exquisite, plaintive and relaxed scherzo with a trio. The rather complex polyphony does not obscure the simplicity of the structure. The scherzo expresses sadness, while the trio conveys a mood of tenderness.

The *fourth movement* sonata opens with witticisms, but it later develops a dashing Hungarian or Gipsy style. This is a vigorous and forceful movement, containing so much variety that it seems to be a much bigger work than its actual temporal length would seem to allow.

Commentary. In overall character this work is more vigorous and cheerful than Op. 88, but it is considerably more difficult to play. The thickness of the texture is a major problem. Still, it can be a great joy to play, and it is highly recommended to those who can practice it enough to manage it. Most amateurs I know favor the first viola quintet, which is a pity. Pleasure—3; Effort—4.

String Sextet in B-flat major, Op. 18 | (1859–60)

I *Allegro ma non troppo.* II *Andante, ma moderato.* III *Scherzo: Allegro molto.* IV *Rondo: Poco allegretto e grazioso.*

The Schubertian *first movement* sonata, in Viennese 3/4 time, opens abruptly with a broad, suave and lyrical melody in the three lower voices that is then restated by five voices before all six finally play it together. Both this wonderful melody and the equally lovely second subject are manipulated masterfully to explore the wide range of textures allowed by the sextet form. The character throughout is serene and pastoral. A pizzicato waltz ends this lush movement.

The *second movement* is a set of variations on a noble marching theme. The minor key and the throbbing accompaniment of this theme make it seem a bit like a mock funeral march. The variations are quite traditional. They explore a broad range of orchestral colors. One is like a music box, for example, and another recalls bagpipes. The march returns at the end, in a truly funereal character.

The *third movement* is a succinct, sprightly and vigorous scherzo. The trio offers only a little contrast to the character of the scherzo.

The *fourth movement*, a cheerful and witty rondo, uses Haydnesque themes. To some, this seems to be the weakest movement of the four.

Commentary. This work is especially memorable for the first two movements. The mock somber character of the andante movement does not dampen its overall sunny spirit. This work is not profound but it is most refreshing and relaxing. It is a favorite with amateurs and good amateurs can handle it easily. Pleasure—4; Effort—3.

String Sextet in G major, Op. 36 | (1864–65)

I *Allegro non troppo.* II *Scherzo: Allegro non troppo.* III *Poco Adagio.* IV *Poco allegro.*

The *first movement* sonata opens with an unfolding main subject, rising fifths over a bariolage accompaniment. Its air of mystery is broken by an ecstatic second theme. The two contrasting subjects are then treated with some agitation. Agathe von Siebold's name is spelled out [A-G-A-H(B)-E] near the end of the exposition and again before the coda. The mood, despite the rather mysterious and ecstatic themes, remains mostly cool, genial and relaxed.

The *second movement* scherzo in the minor mode is plaintive and grave. The middle section provides a rousing dance in the major mode, after which the grave scherzo returns in altered form.

The *third movement* presents a subtle and vague minor-mode theme. This theme then proceeds through six variations, their moods progressing from quiet oppression through wrath to peace.

The *fourth movement* is a brilliant and subtle sonata-rondo, presenting a broad range of impressions. The overall spirit is suave and relaxed. The principal theme is a sublime cantabile. A fugal development and an animato coda do not distort the underlying geniality of the movement.

Commentary. This sextet has more substance than Op. 18 and it is correspondingly more difficult. The difficulties encompass instrumental technique, ensemble playing, and interpretation. All movements are masterful, and all voices have splendid parts. It is well worthy of careful study by those amateurs who are prepared for its difficulties. Pleasure—4; Effort—3.

BRUCKNER (1824–1896)

Anton Bruckner is famous for his symphonies and other large works. He wrote only one important piece of chamber music, the viola quintet from 1879. His precedents were those of Mozart, Mendelssohn, and others, for the viola quintets of Brahms were written later, in 1882 and 1891, and that of Dvořák is from 1893. This quintet was not published until 1884.

Its composition was suggested by Josef Hellmesberger (1829–1893), the virtuosic violinist whose professional quartet did so much to advance the chamber music of Brahms. He asked for a quartet but got a quintet instead. Hellmesberger found the scherzo movement to be unplayable in rehearsal and so Bruckner substituted a Ländler intermezzo. That intermezzo did not, however, ultimately supplant the scherzo. The rejected intermezzo was separately published posthumously, in 1913.

Viola Quintet in F major | (1879)

I *Gemässigt: Moderato.* II *Scherzo: Schnell.* III *Adagio.* IV *Finale: Lebhaft bewegt.*

The *first movement* is a melodious sonata allegro in 3/4 time. It has the feel of a slow movement, as is often the case in Bruckner's allegro movements, with characteristic frequent shifts in harmony. The character is deeply religious, beginning with uncertainty and ending in joyful triumph.

The *second movement* is a chunky and cheerless scherzo in D minor. The graceful nature of the slower trio in E-flat major provides some contrast.

The *third movement* adagio is the centerpiece of the work. Its quasi-variation form presents music of a highly religious or devotional character with special scoring for the viola.

The *fourth movement* is orchestral in scope, sonority and character. Its themes, successively peaceful, bold and traditional, are treated contrapuntally to produce a massive structure, ending in a pompous coda.

Commentary. Those who like the Bruckner idiom will appreciate this work. Those who are bored by Bruckner will not. Its orchestral feel and its sense of religious devotion make it a unique piece of chamber music. It is difficult to play, and amateurs who undertake it for the first time must be prepared for some tough reading. It is not for everyone. Pleasure—2; Effort—4.

DVORÁK (1841–1904)

Dvorák wrote three works for the extended string quartet: the double bass quintet, Op. 77 (or Op. 18) from 1875, the viola quintet, Op. 97 from 1893, and the string sextet, Op. 48 from 1878.

The double bass quintet comes from the time when Dvorák had just abandoned his youthful pursuit of neo-romanticism (following Wagner and Liszt) and had returned to classical forms and a nationalistic style, as prompted by his admiration for Smetana. This quintet was his second chamber-music effort in this new direction, after the 1874 string quartet in A minor (B. 45, Op. 16). The quintet won a prize from the Bohemian Society of Artists in a competition, but it did not make him famous. The string sextet did that three years later. When this quintet was published thirteen years later, in 1888, the publisher, Simrock, gave it a late opus number, 77, rather than Dvořák's choice, 18, to the dismay of Dvořák at this deception by Simrock for commercial purposes.

The viola quintet is a much more mature work than the Op. 77 (or 18) quintet. It was started three days after the completion of the American Quartet, Op. 96, and finished in about a month. American Indian music is often said to have influenced this work even more than the *American Quartet*, although Dvořák denied that influence for both works, claiming that folk music has the same character everywhere. This quintet was published in the following year, 1894.

The string sextet was written in 1878, at the period of Dvořák's earliest maturity and spreading fame. It was his first work to become widely known outside Bohemia, having been promoted in Germany especially by Joachim. It won an immediate warm reception in Germany and elsewhere because of its fresh nationalistic flavor, and it was instrumental in making Dvořák's reputation international.

Double Bass Quintet in G major, Op. 77 | (1875)

I *Allegro con fuoco.* II *Scherzo: Allegro vivace.* III *Poco andante.* IV *Finale: Allegro assai.*

The *first movement* is written in a light style. Critics comment that it could serve as an operatic overture, an observation that suggests its superficiality. The scoring is a bit thick.

The deft *second movement* scherzo is a more fully developed piece, but the thematic material is undistinguished.

The *third movement* andante, like the scherzo, is interesting mainly for the suggestion that it gives of things to come from Dvořák. Rather mundane thematic material is treated with real depth of spirit.

The *fourth movement*, like the first, is lightweight and operatic in nature.

Commentary. This work has no profundity and it lacks the characteristic nationalistic spirit of Dvořák but there are still two reasons to play it. One is to see the budding genius of Dvorák and the other is to get the feel of the unique instrumentation. The special texture of the voicing seems to have attracted no imitators, for this is the only work I know of for this combination. If there are others, they are either neglected or forgotten. Pleasure—2; Effort—1.

Viola Quintet in E-flat major, Op. 97 | (1893)

I *Allegro non tanto.* II *Allegro vivo.* III *Larghetto.* IV *Allegro giusto.*

The *first movement* has themes that seem to be American Indian in character from their pentatonic tunes and their drumming spiccato figures. The mood is uneasy at first, then sad and finally peaceful.

The *second movement* scherzo has first and third sections that also have an American Indian character, with a dry texture and drumming rhythms. The middle minor-mode trio is remarkable for a long and lovely viola solo, a song as fine as any to be found anywhere in Dvorák.

The *third movement* larghetto is a set of five variations on a devotional theme. The variations are quite formal, maintaining the religious feeling and the tonality of the theme, although the fifth variation is rather frolicsome.

The *fourth movement* is a rushing rondo with a high-spirited and slightly frivolous main theme. Two secondary themes appear, one rugged and primitive and the other lyrical. These are treated with splendid craftsmanship in this pleasing finale.

Commentary. The highly exotic character of this superb work seems to have put off critics a little more than the exotic character of the *American Quartet,* Op. 96, to which it can be compared. The compositional technique and polyphony in this quintet are more complex than they are in that companion string quartet. This work is just as pleasing to play as the American Quartet, but considerably more difficult. Its problems are not insuperable for skilled amateurs. Pleasure—4; Effort—3.

String Sextet in A major, Op. 48 | (1878)

I *Allegro moderato*. II *Dumka (Elegie): Poco Allegretto*. III *Furiant: Presto*. IV *Finale: Thema mit Variationen: Allegretto grazioso, quasi andantino*.

The *first movement* sonata has a delicate and placid main theme. The second theme is agitated and the third is again placid. The themes have been characterized as both Slavonic and Schubertian. They are developed with splendid ease to create a most pleasing nationalistic movement.

The *second movement* is a dumka. Both the first and the last sections present a melancholy and dreamy polka with a five-bar theme. A Gipsy song makes up one of the central sections and the other is a poetic lullaby. The Gipsies return in the coda.

The *third movement*, called a furiant, is a vigorous peasant dance with an echo of the first Slavonic Dance.

The *fourth movement* uses a dreamy melancholy theme (announced by the viola) as the basis for a set of six variations. The variations present delicate figurations and witty imitations. A stretto in the last variation dispels the melancholy mood, and the movement ends in a presto rush.

Commentary. This is one of the most. highly Slavonic works of Dvořák. It is enormously attractive, and that fact makes its current neglect hard to understand. It is fully as pleasing as either one of Brahms's sextets, though it is not so profound as his Op. 36. It offers no major problems to experienced amateurs. It is warmly recommended. Pleasure—4; Effort—3.

MENDELSSOHN-BARTHOLDY (1809–1847)

Beyond the string quartets, Mendelssohn wrote only three chamber works for small groups of strings alone, the octet, Op. 20, and the two viola quintets, Op. 18 and Op. 87.

He started the first viola quintet, Op. 18, in Berlin in 1826 when he was only fifteen. He revised it six years later for its publication in 1833. The revision seems to have been extensive. In the original version, the scherzo was in second place and the *third movement* was a minuet. Mendelssohn wrote a new *second movement*, an intermezzo, moved the scherzo to third place, and discarded the minuet. The new intermezzo movement was meant as a memorial to his boyhood friend, Eduard Reitz, who had died in January 1832.

The second viola quintet is much later than the first, having been completed in Frankfurt in 1845, two years before Mendelssohn's death and seven years after the Op. 44 string quartets. It was published posthumously in 1851.

The Octet, Op. 20 was first written in 1825, just before the first viola quintet and well before the Op. 12 and 13 string quartets. Mendelssohn made extensive revisions before its publication in parts seven years later, in 1832, and in score in 1848. The idea of an octet in 1825 was not a new one. Many octets for wind instruments came from the eighteenth century, and both Andreas Romberg and Spohr had written double quartets in which one quartet was subordinate to the other. Mendelssohn's deployment of the eight voices as near equals was unprecedented and the magnificence of his accomplishment seems to have prevented much emulation.

Viola Quintet in A major, Op. 18 | (1826–32)

I *Allegro con moto.* II *Intermezzo: Andante sostenuto.* III *Scherzo: Allegro di molto.* IV *Allegro vivace.*

The graceful *first movement* presents cantabile themes that are subjected to a lucid sonata treatment. There is splendid contrapuntal writing. The atmosphere is brilliant and radiant.

The *second movement* opens with a fervent and rapturous melody that is not wholly consistent with the idea that this movement is a memorial to a deceased childhood friend. The middle section is more dramatic. The mood of the first section reappears gradually and the movement ends simply and quietly.

The *third movement* scherzo is cheerful. A lovely cantabile theme and a happy fugato motif are prominent. A comical third theme is also delightful. The coda unites the three themes skillfully.

The *fourth movement* is a showy rondo, possibly modeled on Beethoven's finale movement in Op. 18, No. 1. The rather sensitive cantabile theme tends to be overwhelmed by the joyous vitality of the compositional technique.

Commentary. The lack of profundity of this fine work reflects Mendelssohn's youth when he first wrote it. The inner movements are most memorable. The splendid technique may partly reflect the later revision, but perhaps not. The work is not difficult and it can be a source of great joy to amateur readers. Pleasure—3; Effort—2.

Viola Quintet in B-flat major, Op. 87 | (1845)

I *Allegro vivace.* II *Andante scherzando.* III *Adagio e lento.* IV *Allegro molto vivace.*

The *first movement* has a dashing and impetuous first subject, fresh and inventive, if not quite outstanding. A subsidiary cantabile theme makes a fine contrast. Prominent triplet figures persist throughout the movement. The first violin has virtuosic arpeggio passages.

The *second movement* is a rather melancholy andante scherzando that recalls the canzonetta of the Op. 12 string quartet. A major-mode middle section provides a contrasting atmosphere.

The *third movement*, an adagio with the scope of a symphonic essay, is elaborately elegiac, resigned but hopeful in mood. It has been described as reaching heights like those in Beethoven.

The *fourth movement* is based on rather unimaginative thematic materials. Their manipulation, however, is so skillful that one's interest never flags.

Commentary. The outer movements of this work seem a little less satisfying than the inner movements. Still, the techniques of composition are so good that they more than make up for deficiencies in thematic materials and profundity. The work is certainly accessible to good amateur players, but it requires a fine first violinist. Pleasure—2; Effort—3.

Octet in E-flat major, Op. 20 | (1825–32)

I *Allegro moderato ma con fuoco.* II *Andante.* III *Scherzo: Allegro leggierissimo.* IV *Presto.*

The *first movement* opens with a triumphant principal theme followed by little fanfares, while the second subject is rather dreamy. The treatment of these subjects in the development is masterful. The recapitulation presents subtle variants of the themes. A brilliant coda ends this magnificent movement.

The *second movement* is an ornamented andante that has a melancholy cast at the outset. A lively middle section provides contrast.

The *third movement* is a clever phantom scherzo, staccato and pianissimo throughout. The Walpurgis-Nacht of Goethe's Faust is said to have inspired the music. A contrasting trio section returns as the coda. The trio section recalls the corresponding part of the scherzo movement of the Op. 13 quartet. The composer himself later arranged this fine scherzo for orchestra.

The *fourth movement* opens with a magnificent, bustling and romping fugue. The scherzo theme enters into the contrapuntal texture. The mood is one of triumph. A melodious coda ends the movement with a flourish.

Commentary. Youthful enthusiasm dominates this whole work, converting even the middle movements into stage-pieces rather than deeply felt expressions. The irrepressible good humor and the impeccable compositional technique make this an enduring popular masterpiece. The fugal opening of the last movement is a bugbear for the cellists, but it is mercifully brief. The work requires fine technique in all parts, but that should not put off amateurs. It can provide a jolly good time at any level of performance, but one should not expect profound thoughts to emerge from a casual reading. Pleasure—4; Effort—3.

MOZART (1756–1791)

Mozart wrote one great string trio, the Divertimento, K. 563. Although he had experimented in his youth with the special problems presented in writing for three stringed instruments, following the lead of Haydn and others, he seems to have given the form little attention throughout his maturity. At least we have no major examples surviving. Thus, this great work from 1888 seems to have emerged almost without preparation. The apocryphal idea that it represents the response to a request from his friend Michael Puchberg has linked Puchberg's name to the work. Whatever its provenance, it is one of the great monuments of chamber music for strings.

Mozart's works for five or more strings constitute only viola
quintets. He probably learned of the possibilities of the form
from the study of the examples of Sammartini and of Michael
Haydn (the brother of Franz Joseph). The Michael Haydn viola
quintets, described as "elementary" in Cobbett, were long attributed to his more famous brother.

Mozart's viola quintets, in total, are not so homogeneous as
his string quartets. Some are transcriptions he made of works
written originally for other instrumentation, while others are pri-
mary, written directly for the viola quintet ensemble.

The transcriptions include K. 46, K. 179, and K. 406. K. 46 is
an arrangement of four movements from a serenade for wind
instruments, K. 361. K. 179 is a transcription partly of a serenade,
K. 361, and partly of a divertimento, K. 228. K. 406 is a transcription of a serenade for wind instruments, K. 388. The other
smaller works by Mozart for viola quintet are transcriptions as
well.

Though all these transcriptions may hold a good deal of interest for amateurs, it is the five works that Mozart originally conceived in this form that are the more interesting. These constitute
K. 174, K. 515, K. 516, K. 593 and K. 614.

K. 174 (1773) is Mozart's first such work, written when he was
seventeen. Thus, it comes from the period of his early Viennese
string quartets. Experts suggest that he conceived it first as a
divertimento, a later revision bringing it to the form that we now
know. That would explain why it seems so much more mature
than the K. number would suggest.

The other four viola quintets come from 1787–91, the last five
years of Mozart's life. His renewed interest in the form after a
lapse of fourteen years may have arisen from the popularity of
the Boccherini cello quintets at that time.

K. 515 and K. 516 appear to have been written as a means to
earn some money at a period of particular financial stress. Mozart
interrupted work on *Don Giovanni* to write them. He offered
them to patrons on a subscription basis through his friend,
Michael Puchberg, in April 1788, but no one took them up, and
he was never compensated for his efforts. Their unusual character may reflect the fact that Mozart met Beethoven for the first
time in May 1787 and his father died in the same month.

The circumstances of the writing of K. 593 and K. 614 are not
known. The fact that they came so late (December 1790 and

April 1791) show that Mozart remained interested in the possibilities of the form right up to his last months. He died in December 1791. Other works written in this period include the piano concerto in B-flat major, K. 595, the *Orgelstücke für eine Uhr*, K. 608, and *The Magic Flute*, K. 620 (begun in May 1791).

Divertimento in E-flat major for String Trio, K. 563 | (1788)

I *Allegro.* II *Adagio.* III *Minuet.* IV *Andante.* V *Minuet.* VI *Rondo.*

The joyful and triumphant themes of the *first movement* sonata wander romantically into remote keys in the development. There is much contrapuntal writing.

The adagio *second movement* is a meditation on a simple motif that the cello presents first. Its constant expansion produces a grand soaring spirit as the movement develops.

The *third movement* minuet presents a somewhat florid descending melodic line. Its form is the conventional one for the period. Editors subtitle this movement as an allegretto.

The *fourth movement* is the center of gravity of the work, an andante theme with variations. The theme is simple but the variations are fantastic in their invention and complexity. The theme returns in its pure form in the coda.

The *fifth movement* is an innovative minuet, also designated by editors as an allegretto. The use of the minuet theme, in horn-like fifths, follows traditional lines. There are, however, two trios. In the first, the viola gives out a charming but pathetic dance. The second trio is also mixed in character, pensive though happy.

The *sixth movement* is an extensive and innovative rondo, full of variation in the recurrences of the rondo tune with abundant grace and good humor.

Commentary. This is one of those real Mozart monuments, but one that seems less known among amateurs than the others are. The challenge of playing with only two other players may put off some people. Certainly, it is much more like playing alone. Everyone should know this work. Pleasure—4; Effort—4.

Viola Quintet in B-flat major, K. 174 | (1773, revised later)

I *Allegro moderato.* II *Adagio.* III *Menuetto: Allegretto.* IV *Allegretto.*

The *first movement* sonata opens with a first theme that is cheerful, declamatory and questioning. It is treated in a dialogue between the first violin and the first viola. The second theme resembles the first. A graceful, sprightly, and cantabile dialogue among the voices marks the whole movement.

The *second movement* has a broad unison opening, con sordino. The more figured second theme is treated in echo effects. This adagio sonata is fully as lovely as the great adagios of the string quartets.

The *third movement* is graceful and swaying. The theme is treated in echo effects. This memorable minuet is full-bodied, warm and expansive.

The *fourth movement*, a sonata, has two contrasting themes that are treated in dialogue in the exposition, in counterpoint in the development and in contrast in the coda. This vigorous and dramatic movement is the center of gravity of the work.

Commentary. The ease, geniality, and charm of the early Mozart are here supported by the brilliant technique of the mature composer. The result is a striking work, quite uniform in mood with a climax in the finale. There is a little profundity here, a little wit, and much warmth and good humor. This is not a difficult work to play, and it is rewarding to all voices. Pleasure—3; Effort—2.

Viola Quintet in C major, K. 515 | (1787)

I *Allegro.* II *Menuetto: Allegretto.* III *Andante.* IV *Allegro.*

The *first movement* opens with a vigorous and striding upward theme, a C major arpeggio, played by the cello beneath a rustling in the middle voices. This thematic statement is answered plaintively by the first violin. The contrast given by the appearance of the legato second theme is quite delayed. A long development follows the long exposition. A long coda provides a further development before a whispered end. This romantic movement develops intense drama from a pair of simple melodies.

The *second movement* minuet is metrical, flowing, and calm. The trio takes a long time to establish its tonality. This hesitation and the questioning motif of the trio give the required contrast to the firm assurance of the minuet.

The *third movement* is an inspired andante. The first viola takes the leadership, cautiously at first but more securely later. The cantabile theme is treated in complexity to produce a long, warm and romantic andante, as fine as any to be found in the chamber music of Mozart anywhere.

The *fourth movement* presents vigorous and humorous themes, treated in a combined rondo and sonata form. Developmental passages occur at intervals between contrasting thoughtful and dreamy passages. A festive coda ends this incomparable movement.

Commentary. No verbal description can do justice to this magnificent work. It is to be fully understood only in the playing of it. It is not difficult technically, and it is lucid musically. All amateurs should know it. Pleasure—4; Effort—3.

Viola Quintet in G minor, K. 516 | (1787)

I *Allegro*. II *Menuetto: Allegretto*. III *Adagio ma non troppo*. IV *Adagio: Allegro*.

The *first movement* opens directly with a fragmented main theme that is gloomy and questioning. The more declamatory second theme in the same key maintains a spirit of despair. The long exposition and the abbreviated development add only agitation to the somber atmosphere. The recapitulation with variants and the brief coda offer no relief from the melancholy.

The theme of the *second movement*, like that of the *first movement*, is jagged in form, irregular in meter and still tragic. The major-mode trio achieves tranquillity without joy.

The *third movement*, an adagio con sordino, presents a fragmented main theme that is treated in echos. The sad and questioning atmosphere is not changed by the more declamatory second theme. Many different effects take place in subsequent developments but the mood remains sad.

The *fourth movement* opens with an extended adagio introduction, a rather rare event in Mozart. This introduction with its ostinato bass is dramatic and operatic. A happy G major rondo in 6/8 then bursts forth. The themes reflect those of the antecedent movements. The mood is one of untempered joy.

Commentary. Like K. 515, K. 516 defies adequate verbal description. This is the best known of the Mozart viola quintets for good reason. This work and K. 515 represent the apex of Mozart's chamber music, many would say. It is not really difficult to play in the technical sense or to understand. All amateurs must get to know it. Pleasure—4; Effort—3.

Viola Quintet in D major, K. 593 | (1790)

I *Larghetto: Allegro.* II *Adagio.* III *Menuetto: Allegretto.* IV *Finale: Allegro.*

The *first movement* has a pensive larghetto introduction with an elegiac and chromatic melody. It is a foil for the declamatory theme of the following allegro. The spirited atmosphere of the main body of the movement is interrupted by the return of the pensive larghetto before a truncated coda.

The *second movement* is pensive in its principal theme and more melancholy in its second. The two themes are treated in contrast in this natural and appealing adagio.

The *third movement* is a healthy and forceful minuet, full of counterpoint. The trio, in the same key, offers more contrast in texture than in mood.

The *fourth movement* rondo-sonata is a virile, spirited and willful romp. Both the rather plain principal theme and the livelier second theme are treated in ingenious counterpoint. A powerful, capricious and brief coda ends this marvelous movement.

Commentary. This work overall is strong, vigorous, spirited, and forthright. The lack of drama in its thematic material is compensated by splendid contrapuntal treatment of the tunes. The difficulties of this work lie mainly in the last movement. It is warmly recommended to amateurs. Pleasure—3; Effort—3.

Viola Quintet in E-flat major, K. 614 | (1791)

I *Allegro di molto.* II *Andante.* III *Menuetto: Allegretto.*
IV *Finale: Allegro.*

The *first movement* sonata opens with a twittering theme in the inner
voices that is answered by the first violin. A bantering dialogue flits
through the movement. The mood is one of graceful amiability.

The *second movement* andante is like a French romanza. The formal
and ornamented theme recurs in continuously novel variants. The
spirit is a solemn graciousness throughout.

The *third movement* is also gracious and elegant in the minuet. The
trio, in contrast, is Haydnesque, like a depiction of a Viennese street-
scene.

The *fourth movement,* a rondo-sonata, is Haydnesque. Wit and good
humor persist despite episodes of fierce fugato. Boisterous high spirits dominate this movement.

Commentary. This work may be considered as a last tribute to
Haydn. It is effortless, and it seems to be wholly spontaneous. It lacks
the profundity of K. 515 and K. 516. The technical difficulties lie
mainly in the last movement. This lucid quintet is fully accessible to
amateurs. Pleasure—3; Effort—3.

SCHUBERT (1797–1828)

Between his early quartets and the later ones, Schubert got interested in the string trio but only briefly. In 1816, he completed
one movement of a String Trio in B-flat (D. 471) and wrote a few
bars of the *second movement,* which was the germ for some elements of the later great piano trios. One year later, he wrote a
complete work of this sort, the String Trio of D. 581.

When Schubert sought larger chamber music forms than the
string quartet, he commonly turned to works with piano. The
major exception is the cello quintet from the year of his death,
1828. The quintet was written at the suggestion of the publisher,
Probst, but it was not actually published until twenty-six years
later, in 1853, by another publisher, Spina.

In August 1828 Schubert had moved to the house of his
brother, Ferdinand, in following his physician's advice to move to

live nearer the country. Soon after, he developed a serious illness from which he recovered only temporarily in October. Besides this illness, difficulties with his publisher plagued him in his final months. Despite that, he wrote the cello quintet as well as the three piano sonatas, D. 958-60, in these final months of his life.

The cello quintet has long been considered to be a nearly perfect example of chamber music for strings alone, from the lyrical and dramatic point of view. The reverence held for it by performers is not entirely shared by audiences, and so it remains a rather private joy of players. Its great length may tend to put off audiences, a problem that also characterizes the two piano trios and the last two string quartets.

Schubert's choice of the cello as the fifth voice may well have been prompted by the popularity then of the cello quintets of Boccherini, who wrote ninety-one, according to Aulich and Heimeran. Very few composers after Schubert attempted the form, perhaps out of awe. Aulich and Heimeran mention only three others, one by Bax (a 'Lyrical Interlude'), one by Dame Ethyl Smythe (Op. 1), and one by Sir Charles Stanford (Op. 85). They fail to mention one by Taneiev (Op. 14) from 1904 and one by Borodin, a youthful work. Access to these latter quintets is so limited that only connoisseurs must know them.

String Trio in B-flat major, D.471 | (1816)

I *Allegro*

This amiable and mannered sonata movement combines clarity of thought with economy of texture. Though one may see the spirit of Mozart, it is undeniable Schubertian in style.

Commentary. This work is well worth investigation by all amateurs. Pleasure—2; Effort—2.

String Trio in B-flat major, D. 581 | (1817)

I *Allegro moderato*. II *Andante*. III *Menuetto: Allegretto*. IV *Rondo: Allegretto*.

The short *first movement* is full of rococo ornamentation on a spare structure.

The *second movement* constitutes wit and surprise with ornamentation.

The *third movement* is suave and subdued. The trio gives the tune to the viola.

The modest little rondo that opens in the *fourth movement* leads to adventures and escapades that recall the teasing tone of so much of the music by Haydn.

Commentary. This is a considerable work, one that seems to have inspired no further progress in the form by Schubert but itself clearly reflects the composer's study of its antecedents in Haydn. Pleasure—2; Effort—2.

Cello Quintet in C major, D. 956, Op. 163 | (1828)

I *Allegro ma non troppo.* II *Adagio.* III *Scherzo: Presto.*
IV *Allegretto.*

The *first movement* opens with a powerless and resigned theme that is then restated. An agitated bridge leads to the immensely romantic second theme. The development is strenuous and agitated, vacillating between major and minor. A soaring and passionate exploitation of the second theme comes to dominate the scene, but the movement ends peacefully.

The *second movement* has a long first section of expectant and contemplative character. Sustained chords with periodic enharmonic changes and little interjections in the first violin over a pizzicato skeleton in the bass constitute this nearly minimalist music. A terrifying and stormy section follows. The idyll of the first section returns, now with running passages in the second cello. A memory of the stormy middle section recurs before the peaceful close.

The *third movement* scherzo begins with feverish energy. The theme reflects the call of a hunting-horn for which reason the movement has been called "La Chasse." This masculine scherzo is followed by a trio which is no mere foil but an expression of "the most terrifying requiem mood in the whole literature of chamber music," said Moser (quoted in Cobbett). The scherzo returns, da capo.

The *fourth movement* rondo blends joy and sadness with a minor-mode Gipsy tune that is set to a dance rhythm. Joy comes to dominate, tempered by the persistent minor key and rhythmic agitation.

Filigree ornamentation and rhythmic intricacies carry the movement to a stretto that ends the movement in triumph.

Commentary. Descriptions and comments seem fatuous in the face of the grandeur of this quintet. Amateurs new to the work will find it difficult because of its profundity and its technical demands. The second cello part is more difficult than the first and it requires much study and practice. All serious amateur players must study this piece at some time. Its difficulties should not dissuade those who feel ready to undertake it. At the beginning, it is probably best to study this massive work one movement at a time. Pleasure—4; Effort—4.

TCHAIKOVSKY (1840–1893)

In 1890, Tchaikovsky went to Florence to work on his opera, *The Queen of Spades.* On leaving Italy later that year, he wrote the string sextet, *Souvenir de Florence.* It was played privately in December 1890, but its first public performance did not occur until two years later. This delay was the result of his visit to the United States and of other commitments that slowed the revision that he wished to make before its publication. He wrote the sextet quickly, although he said that he found writing for six strings to be difficult. His death came less than a year after the first public performance.

String Sextet in D minor, Op. 70 | (1890), *Souvenir de Florence*

I *Allegro con spirito.* II *Adagio Cantabile e con moto.* III *Allegretto moderato.* IV *Allegro vivace.*

The *first movement* opens directly with a jaunty and rather heroic dance tune in triple rhythm. It soon gives way to a more lyrical second melody that is derived from the first. A third theme is in the style of a serenade. The three themes receive contrapuntal treatment in a quasi-rondo form. Guitar-like pizzicato accompaniments provide a Mediterranean character. The mood is cheerful and optimistic throughout.

The *second movement* opens with an introduction of legato chords presented in dense harmony to produce a sound like that of an organ. The following adagio uses an elegant cantilena melody over a pizzicato accompaniment, treated in dialogue between violin and viola. A short central section is agitated with a rustling motif in triplets. The elegant cantilena returns with elaboration. After a recurrence of the organ-like chords, a coda is formed from the cantilena melody to end this lovely movement.

The *third movement* opens with a whimsical dance tune that has more a Russian than an Italian character. Its expression becomes more dramatic and agitated as the scherzo proceeds. A humorous and frisky trio with a spiccato melody contrasts sharply with the scherzo. The reprise of the scherzo has a more dramatic or emphatic character. A diminutive coda ends the vigorous movement.

The *fourth movement* begins with a tune that has the character of a Russian folk dance. A lyrical and optimistic second theme also has a Russian character. The two themes are treated in alternation in various derivatives with an extensive fugal treatment of the first theme. The optimistic second theme ends the movement in ebullient good spirits.

Commentary. This work is remarkable for its freedom from the drama and pessimism of Tchaikovsky's other late works. Lucid, optimistic and triumphant, it is easier to grasp than the later two string quartets but it is at least as difficult technically. It is well worth the effort of study and practice. Amateurs who can handle the technical difficulties can get much pleasure from this work. Pleasure—3; Effort—4.

PART III

Strings with Piano: Piano Trios, Quartets, and Quintets

ARENSKY (1806–1826)

Anton Arensky, a Russian composer, pianist and conductor, occupied a central place in the circle of Russian musicians of his time but he is little remembered today. He studied with Rimsky-Korsakov in St. Petersburg, he was the teacher of Rachmaninov, Scriabin and Gliere at the Moscow Conservatory and he was in close touch with Tchaikovsky and Tanayev. His short life was ended by tuberculosis, said to have been a consequence of his dissipation.

His chamber music, like his more extended works, is now much neglected, only the Op. 32 piano trio in D minor being much heard. His works for piano with strings constitute only two, that piano trio and a piano quintet in D major, Op. 51. There are also two string quartets, Op. 11 and Op. 35.

The piano trio in D minor, written in 1894, was composed in memory of the great cellist, Davidov. Experts see the influence both of Mendelssohn and of Tchaikovsky in this work.

Piano Trio in D minor, Op. 32 | (1894)

I *Allegro moderato.* II *Scherzo: Allegro molto.* III *Elegia: Adagio.* IV *Finale: Allegro non troppo.*

The *first movement* opens with an impassioned melody that resembles that of the Mendelssohn piano trio in D minor. A more abrupt and agitated theme (più mosso) soon appears and a third theme, expressive and legato, follows. These three themes are treated brilliantly, if conventionally, in the brief development. There is a full recapitulation with an adagio coda.

The *second movement* scherzo has a Mendelssohnian rush in the outer parts but it is made dramatic by contrasting pianos and fortes. A central trio section (meno mosso) provides contrast in its warm legato melody.

The haunting *third movement* opens with an elegiac and melancholy tune played in the cello that is soon handed to the violin to be played with a countermelody. A central più mosso section provides a somewhat more dramatic theme from the piano over triplet figures in the strings. After this idea is extended, the melancholy first part returns.

The *fourth movement* opens directly with an intensely agitated theme. A second theme, derived from one in the *first movement,* is slightly more relaxed. After some exposition, an andante section elaborates the relaxed second theme, after which an adagio recalls the opening melody of the *first movement.* The agitated allegro theme returns to end the movement with bravura.

Commentary. This is a pleasing work, but no masterpiece. It is highly melodic and fluent and the piano part is brilliant. It offers no real technical or musical problems to experienced players. One tires of it easily because of its superficiality. Still, it is a pleasing Romantic work, and one much favored by those amateurs who have discovered it. Pleasure—3; Effort—3.

BEETHOVEN (1770–1827)

Although there are a few works of Beethoven for piano with strings beyond the piano trios, those trios are the ones most commonly considered by amateur players. The piano trios arose only from the early and middle periods of Beethoven's career, for they end with Op. 97.

The three piano trios in Op. 1, dedicated to Prince Lichnowsky, are the first works that Beethoven chose to publish. They brought him immediate fame, helping him to launch his career in Vienna in 1795 when he was twenty-four. He certainly began writing them well before that. He may well have started them when he was still in Bonn before he moved to Vienna in 1792, for they were played for Haydn in 1793. Haydn, then at the peak of his career at sixty, admired the first two piano trios but he advised Beethoven not to publish the third. Beethoven, favoring the third trio, concluded that Haydn was jealous. His opinion, Haydn later said, meant only that he thought the third trio would not be well-received by the public, perhaps because of its more personal and dramatic nature. These three trios are certainly not Beethoven's first compositions. Several songs and other small works published much later are now considered to have been composed in Bonn and in Vienna before Op. 1 was brought forth.

The piano trio in Op. 11 was written for the piano, clarinet, and cello, but it is at least as familiar in Beethoven's alternate instrumentation for the work in which a violin replaces the clarinet. It was published in 1798, probably soon after its composition. Countess Thun, to whom the work is inscribed, was the wife of a Viennese philanthropist and the mother of Beethoven's patron, Prince Lichnowsky. The trio may well have been written with a specific clarinettist in mind. The theme of the final variations movement is that of an aria from an opera by Weigl. That opera had been first performed in 1797, and the aria theme was then popular. Czerny (a pupil of Beethoven) said that Beethoven later considered substituting another final movement, letting the variations stand as a separate work, but he never did so.

Thirteen years after Op. 1, Beethoven again undertook piano trios in writing the two works in Op. 70. They were written in 1808, first performed that same year and published in 1809. Evidence suggests that they were first conceived as solo piano sonatas. They were dedicated to Countess Erdody in whose house Beethoven lived at that time. Before their publication, Beethoven thought to change the dedication to honor his patron, the Archduke Rudolph, because he had quarreled with the Countess, but he never did so. Other works from the same year include the sixth symphony (The *Pastoral*) and the cello sonata in A major, Op. 69.

The piano trio of Op. 97 (The *Archduke*) was begun in 1809, soon after the Op. 70 piano trios were finished, but it was not published until 1811. Its dedicatee, the Archduke Rudolph, was Beethoven's most sympathetic patron. Other works from this time include the Op. 74 and Op. 95 string quartets, the *Egmont* overture, and the seventh and eighth symphonies. Op. 97 became popular immediately and it remains so to this day.

There are other published works of Beethoven for the piano trio. Some are single movements and others are transcriptions of works written for other instrumentation. These smaller works are more important historically than esthetically and they are not of so much interest to amateur players.

Beethoven's seven great piano trios, as a whole, are not equal to his string quartets in artistic or historical terms. Beethoven appears to have found the form of the piano trio to be less attractive than the string quartet. Still, the Op. 1 piano trios and the *Archduke* are firmly established in the repertoire. The two trios in Op. 70 are rewarding as well. Op. 11 is great fun to play, even if it is less inventive than the others.

Piano Trio in E flat major, Op. 1, No. 1 | (1792–95)

I *Allegro.* II *Adagio cantabile.* III *Scherzo: Allegro assai.*
IV *Finale: Presto.*

The *first movement* opens with a bright theme that modulates immediately into the subdominant, giving the impression that the listener
has been introduced into the middle of something already begun. The
spirit is cheerful and sparkling throughout.

The *second movement* is a bland and sweet Mozartean adagio, fine but
exhibiting little of the characteristic Beethoven idiom that was to
come.

The *third movement* scherzo is emphatically not a minuet, showing
immediately in this first work how firmly Beethoven had embraced the
evolution in the form. The movement is filled with harmonic surprises
and instrumental innovations that give it a comic and frisky character.
The brief trio is similarly comical.

The *fourth movement* is also light-hearted. Three preparatory bars
played by the piano introduce the frisky theme that follows in the
strings. The style is more that of Haydn than that of Mozart, with more
rhythmic than harmonic invention.

Commentary. This cheerful and comical masterpiece offers no major
technical or musical problems, yet it is not really easy to play. It
requires good technique, especially in the piano part. It is a fine work
with which to begin the serious study of piano trios. It remains a
source of great pleasure even after repeated study and a favorite of
amateurs. Pleasure—3; Effort—2.

Piano Trio in G major, Op. 1, No. 2 | (1793–95)

I *Adagio; Allegro vivace.* II *Largo con expressione.* III *Scherzo.*
IV *Presto.*

The *first movement* opens with a brief adagio introduction. The subsequent sonata allegro is Mozartean, cheerful, and good-humored
throughout.

The *second movement* is a meditative and calm largo. It exhibits some
passages that are quite characteristic of the Beethoven style as it later
developed.

The *third movement* is another true scherzo, but one lacking the freshness and originality of that in Op. 1, No. 1. The trio also seems rather conventional.

The *fourth movement* is a most vivacious and sparkling rondo, but showing little that is really innovative.

Commentary. This work is overall less impressive than Op. 1, No. 1. It is neither more nor less difficult than the first trio and it can be considered as a companion-piece. It is much less often played than No. 1, probably because it seems somewhat less inspired. It is just as good a work to take up for those players who are beginning to study the art of the piano trio seriously. Pleasure—3; Effort—2.

Piano Trio in C minor, Op. 1, No. 3 | (1793–95)

I *Allegro con brio.* II *Andante cantabile con variazione.*
III *Minuet: Quasi Allegro.* IV *Prestissimo.*

The *first movement* opens directly with the soft and mysterious principal theme stated in union. The mood of mystery is maintained throughout the movement. The style is always restrained and graceful.

The *second movement* presents a calm and cantabile theme in the major mode. Five variations follow. These are rich and ingenious, the last variation being especially chromatic. This movement is a fine example of the form.

The *third movement* is a rather conventional scherzo-minuet, not so emphatically a non-minuet as the corresponding movement of Op. 1, No. 1. The minor-mode scherzo is contrasted by the major mode of the trio. The mood is somber and restrained throughout.

The *fourth movement* is a bright and lively rondo in the minor mode. It can certainly be played prestissimo, as marked, but too quick a tempo robs the movement of some of its brightness and charm. Its adherence to piano and pianissimo dynamics is startling and difficult to manage sometimes.

Commentary. This is the most interesting of the three works in Op. 1. It possesses a sense of gravity and seriousness of purpose that is deficient in the other two. It is not different from the others in the technical and musical skills required. Amateur players should study this work carefully. It is a most satisfying and rewarding piece to know. Pleasure—4; Effort—2.

Piano Trio in B-flat major, Op. 11 | (1798)

I *Allegro con brio*. II *Adagio*. III *Theme with Variations on an Italian Air, "Pria ch'io l'impegno."*

The *first movement* is a conventional and rather uninteresting sonata allegro. It is pleasant without being cheerful. Players who are new to the work should not stop with this movement!

The *second movement* is a gem. The cello first states an expressive cantabile melody before it is passed to the violin with echoes in the piano. The mood is soulful, introspective, and optimistic throughout the brief movement. One wishes it were extended.

The *third movement* is a real curiosity. The opera aria theme has the character of a drinking song, lilting and rather silly (it resembles the tune of "You Are My Sunshine"). The nine variations that follow are rather contrived and pedantic, maintaining a frivolity or mock serious-ness throughout. The first variation is a virtuosic piano solo treatment, the second a string duet and so on, with great variety. The last varia-tion leads to an allegro in 6/8 meter that ends with a brief four-bar coda in the common time of the opening.

Commentary. Critics tend to disparage this trio. The lovely adagio is not to be missed. The last movement is good too, if one takes it as a frivolous and mocking piece, without looking for any profundity at all. The work is not really easy, especially for the pianist in the last move-ment. It is a trio that good amateurs can enjoy very much if they take it in the right spirit. Pleasure—3; Effort—2.

Piano Trio in D major, Op. 70, No. 1 | (1808–09), *The Ghost*

I *Allegro vivace e con brio*. II *Largo assai ed expressivo*. III *Presto*.

The *first movement* sonata allegro opens with a short and agitated theme played in unison, after which the cello plays an ardent lyrical theme that is then imitated by the violin. This lovely melody comes to form the crux of the whole movement so that the movement maintains a striking unity in content as well as in its rapturous mood.

The *second movement*, in the minor mode, is a difficult one both for listeners and for players. Its dramatic mysterioso character gives the trio its common name. A simple one-bar theme that is first stated in the piano forms the text for the whole movement. The theme is treated over and over in increasingly complex ways. Minor dramatic climaxes recur, with a last tremendous climax that gives way to a brief dying coda.

The *third movement* is, appropriately, a small piece after the drama of the second. It is a lively and gay presto, attractive, ingenious and full of high spirits with no profundity or even seriousness at all. The movement ends briskly.

Commentary. This work is most striking for its variety of moods, rapturous joy in the *first movement*, hair-raising drama in the second, and frivolity in the third. The memorable *second movement* is difficult both in technique and in understanding. It needs a great deal of study and practice. This work should not be undertaken casually. Pleasure—2; Effort—3.

Piano Trio in E-flat major, Op. 70, No. 2 | (1808–09)

I *Poco sostenuto; Allegro ma non troppo.* II *Allegretto.* III *Allegretto ma non troppo.* IV *Finale: Allegro.*

The idyllic *first movement* opens with a long and lovely sostenuto introduction. This sostenuto passage recurs again in altered and curtailed form at the end of the movement. The long intervening sonata allegro has a most meditative and pleasant spirit, characteristic of Beethoven in this period when he was not in a dramatic mood.

The *second movement* is a rather small movement, the scherzo-substitute of the work. It has a remarkably quaint and skipping figure as its theme.

The *third movement* is the center of gravity of the work. One of Beethoven's greatest cantabile melodies is here treated at length with the most profound inspiration. The effect is one of quiet, refined and simple charm.

The energetic *fourth movement* opens with its principal theme expressed as a forte peremptory statement. This is answered immediately by a soft, lyrical and reassuring reply. The two themes are then treated in contrast in a long sonata form.

Commentary. This agreeable work is neglected, possibly because the idiosyncratic *Ghost* trio and the monumental *Archduke* trio frame it. It lacks the passion and high drama of those trios. This is as weighty a composition as the *Ghost* trio, but not so massive as the *Archduke*. It requires as fine instrumental, ensemble and interpretive skills as do its companions without being so forbidding. This is a fine piece for those amateurs who feel that they are not up to the challenge of the *Archduke*. Pleasure—2; Effort—3.

Piano Trio in B-flat major, Op. 97 | (1809–11), *The Archduke*

I *Allegro moderato*. II *Scherzo: Allegro*. III *Andante cantabile, ma pero con moto*. IV *Allegro moderato*.

The *first movement* sonata allegro opens abruptly with a majestic and noble legato theme. After a contrasting second theme is introduced, the two themes are treated to an extended development that is characterized by the alternation of agitation and repose. An emphatic coda follows after a nearly full recapitulation. The mood overall is one of calm and noble joy.

The *second movement* scherzo is also joyful but this is a free and frisky joy. The trio provides contrast mainly in its extreme chromaticism. The scherzo section is repeated three times, and the long movement finally ends on the trio.

The *third movement* is a long and peaceful theme with variations. Four variations follow after the statement of the lovely cantabile theme. The first three variations present increasing agitation and motion while the fourth is peaceful once more. A long coda, really a terminal development, ends in an extended cadence that leads directly to the finale, attacca.

The *fourth movement* is a rollicking rondo formed from a tune that is a joyful, stomping and slightly rude peasant dance. The refrain recurs five times. The long movement ends in brilliance.

Commentary. This is one of those works that defies adequate description. It is massive in scope and profoundly expressive in all its many moods. It is long and taxing to play and all the parts are difficult. Amateurs may tend to approach it with too much enthusiasm. Its performance benefits from delicacy and restraint. Like the late string quartets, this is a work that all serious amateurs should strive to study when they feel prepared to do so. Pleasure—4; Effort—4.

BRAHMS (1833–1897)

In writing chamber music, Brahms devoted a great deal of effort to works that combine the piano with strings. Aside from the sonatas for one stringed instrument with piano, these works constitute five piano trios, three piano quartets and one piano quintet.

Brahms followed the practice of destroying the manuscripts of works that he did not finally approve of, even though he may have committed much effort to their composition. Breitkopf and Hartel claimed a piano trio in A major that they published in 1938 to be one such work by Brahms that had survived destruction. This manuscript was not authenticated, being written in the hand of an unknown copyist, but the publisher presented it as a work of Brahms written in 1853, just before the Op. 8 piano trio. Most current authorities do not accept the claim for this long and rather uncharacteristic work. This trio is not summarized here.

The piano trio in B major, Op. 8, was completed in its first version in 1854. The requirement for a new edition in 1890 prompted Brahms to revise the work completely, and this version is the one that we now know as the Op. 8 trio. In the extensive revision, Brahms shortened the work by more than one-third, and he greatly increased its vigor and intensity. The first version is occasionally heard today. The work was begun in 1853, a year of optimism, when Brahms first traveled extensively and first came to know Joachim, von Bulow, and others who were to become his life-long friends and colleagues. Schumann's disastrous collapse, which so affected Brahms, occurred in the following year, 1854, just after Op. 8 was finished. When this trio was reissued in 1890, the fifty-seven year-old composer was an international celebrity. The Op. 111 viola quintet (which Brahms then thought would be his final work) was written in that same year. Thus, the Op. 8 trio as we know it reflects both the exuberance of the young genius and the mature compositional techniques of the master's last years.

The piano trio in C major, Op. 87 was not written all at once. The *first movement* dates from March 1880, and the other three come from June 1882. The summer of 1882 was a joyful one that Brahms spent at Ischl, a favorite resort in the Austrian Alps. That same summer saw the completion of the viola quintet, Op. 88 and both these works reflect his cheerful state of mind on that holiday.

The piano trio in C minor, Op. 101 was written in 1886 at Thun, Switzerland, during the first of three successive summer holidays Brahms spent there. He vacationed with many old and close friends—the poet Widmann, the singer Stockhausen, the composer Roentgen, the philologist Wendt, the organist de Lange, and others. Many other great works came from this period, including the second cello sonata, Op. 99, the *Zigeunerlieder,* the Opp. 105–107 songs and the violin sonatas of Op. 100 and Op. 108. Thus, this piano trio arose in company with some of Brahms's greatest chamber works and songs. Note that the revision of the Op. 8 piano trio did not take place until eight years later.

The horn trio, Op. 40, is included here because of its alternate instrumentation with a cello playing the horn part. The year of its composition, 1865, was a year of great change for Brahms. His mother's death in February cemented his decision to abandon his long off-and-on relationship with Hamburg and to settle in Vienna. This work marked Brahms's temporary abandonment of chamber music. The Op. 34 piano quintet, the Op. 36 string sextet and the Op. 38 cello sonata immediately preceded the horn trio, but Brahms wrote no more chamber music until he undertook the string quartets of Op. 51, eight years later. Those eight years were devoted mainly to vocal music, including the *German Requiem.*

The clarinet trio, Op. 114 is included here because of its alternate instrumentation with a violin or viola playing the clarinet part. Written in 1892, it arose from the renewed enthusiasm for composition that came to Brahms after his premature retirement in 1890–91. In late 1890, he began to review his unpublished works, destroying those that he rejected, completing others and disposing of his material possessions in a will, dated in May 1891. In March of that year, he discovered the virtues of the clarinet in hearing a performance by the virtuoso, Richard Mühlfeld, at Meiningen. He soon completed two of his great works that involve the clarinet, this trio and the clarinet quintet. Both were performed in December 1891. The two clarinet sonatas appeared in 1894, after he had written his last piano works.

The three piano quartets have rather complex histories. The Op. 60 piano quartet in C minor originated from two widely separate periods. The *first movement,* originally in C-sharp minor, and the *third movement* andante were first written in 1855, in the period of emotional turmoil that came to Brahms with Robert

Schumann's catastrophic collapse in 1854 and the consequent complexity of Brahms's relationship with Clara Schumann. The *first movement* of the C minor symphony (the first) comes from the same period. Brahms later explained the stark character of the *first movement* of the piano quartet, Op. 60: "Now imagine a man who is just going to shoot himself, because nothing else remains for him to do." Brahms put the work aside uncompleted, only to take it up again twenty years later, in 1874–5. He then revised the two completed movements, replaced an incomplete final movement, and added the scherzo. Certain events of 1873 may have prompted him to take up this work that he had neglected for so long. He had experienced a renewal of interest in chamber music with the Op. 51 string quartets of 1873 and he had participated in a great Schumann festival at Bonn in that same year. Op. 60 was actually completed in a happy summer he spent at Ziegelhausen. The string quartet of Op. 67 was finished at about the same time.

The other two piano quartets, Op. 25 and Op. 26, were mostly written in 1860 (five years after the beginning of Op. 60), a year he spent in Hamburg before his decision to settle finally in Vienna. It was a happy time for him. The troubles surrounding the Schumann relationship had receded, his family and professional relationships in Hamburg were good, and his fame was spreading. Op. 25 was probably started well before 1860, perhaps as early as 1857, but it underwent much revision before its completion. Op. 26 probably had a similar history, for Brahms tended to write two works of similar form and character at the same time, as exemplified by the paired string quartets of Op. 51. Op. 26 figured in the public concert with which Brahms introduced himself to Vienna when he first went there in 1862.

The Piano Quintet, Op. 34, also dates originally from 1860, in the period of calm after the troubles of the Schumann disaster had faded. It was written then in the form of a cello quintet (now lost), then revised as a sonata for two pianos (Op. 34b) and finally reconstructed as the piano quintet in the summer of 1864. That summer was spent at Lichtenthal in the company of Clara Schumann, her family and many other friends. That happy summer also saw the completion of the string sextet, Op. 36.

Piano Trio in B major, Op. 8 | (1854–1890)

I *Allegro con brio.* II *Scherzo: Allegro molto.* III *Adagio.*
IV *Allegro.*

The *first movement* sonata allegro opens abruptly with an ardent main theme in the piano and this lyrical, expansive and joyful declamation goes on for some sixty bars. Triplet figures introduced in the long exposition create complex cross-rhythms which persist throughout the long development. A long and tranquil coda follows the full recapitulation.

The *second movement* scherzo is modeled on the Beethoven scherzo form. This is an ample and weighty movement with dramatic rhythms and bold harmonies. The central trio section is more ardent, expansive and diatonic, reflecting the character of the *first movement.* After a complete recapitulation of the agitated scherzo theme, a striking coda ends in a climax with three F-sharp octaves.

The *third movement* adagio has a picturesque chorale as its main theme, with a Schubertian second theme. A reprise of the chorale follows and the movement ends with the three F-sharp octaves like those that end the *second movement.*

The *fourth movement* reverts to B minor with a quiet and insistent dotted-rhythm theme that is interrupted by three ritenuti before the suave and soaring second theme appears in the cello. This second theme is a reference to the last song in Beethoven's song-cycle, "An die ferne Geliebte," also used by Schumann in the Fantasy for piano, Op. 17. The two themes reappear with intervening developmental episodes.

Commentary. This long, complex and massive work is certainly the most difficult of the Brahms piano trios. The unorthodox keys create serious intonation problems for the strings. The piano part is especially difficult and its brilliance allows the piano easily to overwhelm the sound of the strings. Still, amateurs can come to get much pleasure from this work with much study and practice. It is not a suitable introduction to the Brahms piano trios and it must not be approached casually. Pleasure—3; Effort—4.

Piano Trio in C major, Op. 87 | (1880–1882)

I *Allegro.* II *Andante con moto.* III *Scherzo: Presto.*
IV *Finale: Allegro giocoso.*

The *first movement* is an Olympian sonata form, grand, expansive and mellow. The sweeping main theme is followed by a group of secondary themes that present varied rhythms, textures and harmonies. A full recapitulation and a long coda follow the long development. The piano part is extravagant and there are fine dialogues between the strings.

The *second movement*, in the minor mode, is a tragic and declamatory theme with variations. The five variations differ in dramatic intensity but all of them are exquisite and richly detailed. The last variation, resigned in mood, is protracted into a terminal development that ends the movement in a mood of repose. This movement is one of the most memorable of Brahms's works in chamber music.

The *third movement* is a shadowy, fleeting and agile scherzo in a remote key. The central trio-substitute offers a broad, diatonic and triumphant tune, in high contrast to the scherzo.

The *fourth movement* presents a profuse and varied succession of jocose themes, diverse in rhythm and harmony. They are elaborated in witty and ingenious ways, and the movement ends in a jolly mood.

Commentary. This well-known work is a favorite with both players and audiences. The variations in mood among the four movements (nobility, tragedy, mystery and jollity) present an attractive diversity. The keys are all friendly ones, and the musical language is not at all subtle. Its performance does not require great technical virtuosity. As a result, this is the standard work with which amateurs start to examine the Brahms piano trios. The slow movement is never to be forgotten. Pleasure—4; Effort—3.

Piano Trio in C minor, Op. 101 | (1886)

I *Allegro energico.* II *Presto non assai.* III *Andante grazioso.*
IV *Allegro molto.*

The *first movement* is a sonata form with fiercely tragic and heroic themes. These are explored in a short development section in which the subjects are ingeniously combined, with prominent triplet figures.

Dependent material rather than the first theme introduces the recapitulation, but the first theme returns to end the movement passionately. The mood throughout is one of anger, impatience and tragedy.

The *second movement* is a shadowy minor-mode scherzo, succinct and straightforward. With its hurrying, dark, and mysterious mood, it is impressive for its remarkable and constant tone color.

The *third movement* is a relaxed and rather whimsical slow movement with an irregular meter. The central section of the ABA form provides more animation than the outer sections. The little coda is rather playful.

The *fourth movement* sonata presents grim and energetic themes in minor keys. The themes are explored in a busy and tempestuous manner. A coda suddenly transfigures the mood, giving forth the main theme in the major mode to end the work in solemn triumph.

Commentary. This work is shorter, more concise, and less immediately appealing than Op. 87. It is also more difficult in interpretation, requiring much thought and study for effective performance. It is a powerfully dramatic masterpiece, however, and the effort to get to know it is amply rewarded. Its relative neglect at the hands of amateurs is a pity. Pleasure—4; Effort—3.

Piano Trio in E-flat major, Op. 40 | (1865), *The Horn Trio*

I *Andante; Poco più animato.* II *Scherzo: Allegro.* III *Adagio mesto.* IV *Finale: Allegro con brio.*

The *first movement* is unusual in form in that an andante theme alternates with a more lively second theme, the two recurring in ABABA form. The last section reaches a climax followed by a solemn dying coda. The mood throughout is pastoral and contemplative.

The *second movement* is a spacious scherzo, lively and energetic, built on constant quarter notes. The slower middle section, in A-flat minor, provides a high degree of contrast with its gloomy and mysterious mood.

The *third movement* is also a dramatic and gloomy mysterioso but not an expansive or protracted one. It puts the violin and cello (horn) in a prolonged duet.

The *fourth movement* is a sonata form. Hunting music is presented, full of vigor and enthusiasm. The tunes are fully developed and the spirit of the chase is maintained throughout.

Commentary. The work fits the horn so well and is so familiar in that instrumentation that it sounds a little odd with a cello playing that part. But the alternate instrumentation, Brahms's own transcription, makes this pleasing work far more accessible to amateurs. The dramatic and pastoral spirit of the work, its technical ease, and its lucidity should make it appeal to all amateur piano trios but many amateurs seem not to know that. It can be a fine introduction for novices and it is a great work for those who want to play another good solid work of the master. Pleasure—4; Effort—3.

Piano Trio in A minor, Op. 114 | (1892), *The Clarinet Trio*

I *Allegro.* II *Adagio.* III *Andante grazioso.* IV *Allegro.*

The *first movement* sonata allegro opens abruptly with a broadly soaring first theme. The exposition is spacious but the development is concise and thoughtful. The mood throughout is melancholy, the style is declamatory, and the technique is taut and devoid of redundancy and elaboration.

The *second movement* is a passionate major-mode arioso. The lyrical and expressive themes recur as dialogues among the voices. The mood throughout is yearning and passionate.

The *third movement* is a stylish re-creation of the Viennese spirit of the Liebeslieder Waltzes. The gracious waltz tunes are bathed in a melancholy and nostalgic light. The thematic material seems rather thin but it serves to support a movement of considerable dimensions.

The *fourth movement* is a compact but fully developed sonata allegro in the minor mode. The two related themes are full of agitation but they contain little genuine storm or passion. The terse development leads to a reprise with a quick and modest ending.

Commentary. This exquisite trio does not deserve its reputation among some as a minor work. It only seems so from its juxtaposition to the great clarinet quintet. Brahms's alternate scoring with violin or viola substituting for the clarinet works very well and such instrumentation makes this masterpiece far more accessible to amateur players of piano trios. The clarinet part is quite difficult for the clarinet and it seems no easier for a stringed instrument. This wonderful trio deserves to be much more widely played by amateurs than it is. Pleasure—4; Effort—3.

Piano Quartet in G minor, Op. 25 | (1857[?]–1861)

I *Allegro.* II *Intermezzo: Allegro ma non troppo.* III *Andante con moto.* IV *Rondo alla Zingarese: Presto.*

The *first movement,* a grand sonata allegro, is "the most original and impressive tragic composition since the *first movement* of Beethoven's Ninth Symphony," says Tovey. That may be something of an overstatement, but this is certainly a splendid tragic movement. A spacious and dramatic first theme is followed by a more plaintive second theme. These themes are developed in an astonishing way to produce a movement that is symphonic in scope.

The *second movement* is a gigantic lyrical scherzo. The movement has a mysterious and tender character with the strings muted. The animated trio offers some agitation to contrast with the lyricism of the scherzo.

The *third movement* is also a large movement, a grand andante in ABA form. The main theme, broad, warm and noble, is treated expansively. The central section is a military march. The main theme then returns unchanged in character so that the movement ends in a spirit of nobility and grandeur.

The *fourth movement* is a Gipsy rondo, seen by some authorities as inspired by the famous Gipsy rondo in one of Haydn's piano trios (Hoboken xv: 25). Whether or not that is true, this is a highly original movement. It is episodic in structure but it retains its vigorous dance-like quality and its energy throughout. Before the coda, a wonderful cadenza-like passage brings all the themes together in a fantastic polyphony. The coda ends the movement in a headlong rush, molto presto.

Commentary. This is an enormous work. All the movements are constructed on a grand scale and all are magnificent. The work is quite difficult in all respects and it is physically taxing to play. The outer movements are quite orchestral while the inner movements have more of the character of chamber music. The pianist must apply restraint in the outer movements so as not to overwhelm the strings. This work is wonderful to play but it takes a lot of learning and a great deal of energy. Pleasure—4; Effort—4.

Piano Quartet in A major, Op. 26 | (1860)

I *Allegro non troppo.* II *Poco Adagio.* III *Scherzo: Poco Allegro.*
IV *Finale: Allegro.*

The *first movement* is a sonata allegro that is lyrical in character
throughout. The themes are united seamlessly and there is a strikingly
beautiful legato and sostenuto feel throughout the movement. A great
climax occurs just before the coda.

The *second movement* is a rapt nocturne with the strings muted. The
theme, having the character of a song without words, is treated in
rondo form.

The *third movement* is a scherzo with trio. The scherzo theme is amiable, graceful and sinuous, even a little bland. The trio, in contrast, is
stormy, furious and canonic, in the minor mode. The movement is
long, and the thematic material is copiously developed.

The *fourth movement* presents a principal theme that is dance-like
with strongly worked rhythms. A multitude of secondary themes follows. The structure is loose so that the movement sometimes seems a
little undisciplined but the music always retains its cheerful Hungarian
energy. An animato peroration ends the movement in a symphonic
coda.

Commentary. This work is altogether more accessible than Op. 25.
This one is livelier in spirit, simpler in conception and happy where
the other is tragic. It is also much less difficult to play, but it is still not
easy. It is a better work for amateurs to play than Op. 25, in all
respects. Pleasure—4; Effort—3.

Piano Quartet in C minor, Op. 60 | (1855–1875)

I *Allegro non troppo.* II *Scherzo: Allegro.* III *Andante.* IV *Finale:
Allegro comodo.*

The *first movement* opens abruptly with a stormy and tragic subject
played in unison. A second tragic subject soon appears, to be presented further in three free variations with a climactic restatement. The
stormy development section ranges widely. The recapitulation provides some moments of relative tranquillity in the recurrent variations
but the strong and tragic mood returns to dominate the end of this
angry and powerful movement.

The *second movement* continues the stark and ferocious C-minor mood of the first. The scherzo is compact and brutal. A lyrical and legato theme adorns the central section of the movement as a trio equivalent before the violent material of the opening section returns.

The *third movement* andante abruptly interferes with all the anger. The sixteen-bar theme, one of Brahms's greatest lyric melodies, appears at once in the cello, in the remote key of E major, and then it continues in the violin and viola. A glorious development follows and the movement ends with a coda-like summary. A mood of rapturous serenity is maintained throughout.

The *fourth movement* opens with a plaintive theme over a perpetual rustling accompaniment. This evolves into a long and complex movement, moving and filled with a sense of overwhelming pathos and tragedy. A tranquillo section in C major at the end provides only a little release from the tragic character of the movement.

Commentary. This is one of the most profound, personal and deeply felt works in the chamber music literature. Its profoundly tragic character gives it rather little appeal to amateurs who are interested in an evening of casual reading. Furthermore, it is not quickly comprehended or learned. It is difficult enough in all respects that it requires considerable familiarity to be fully appreciated. It should not be approached casually, therefore, but taken up as a work for serious study. A little serious study soon reveals a profound masterpiece that can never be forgotten. Pleasure—4; Effort—3.

Piano Quintet in F minor, Op. 34 (1860–64)

I *Allegro non troppo.* II *Andante, un poco adagio.* III *Scherzo.*
IV *Finale: Poco sostenuto; Allegro non troppo.*

The *first movement* is almost wholly tragic in character. The dramatic and declamatory first theme is introduced at once in unison, in four bars. After a pause, a small and energetic development occurs that quickly gives way to a new theme, yearning, plaintive, and still in the minor mode. These subjects are treated to an extensive exposition and development., maintaining the minor mode. Near the end, a slow passage in the strings alone promises a release from the tragic mood but the stormy minor mode returns to give a tragic ending to this powerful tragic movement.

The *second movement*, a sharp contrast to the first, is an ABA romanza written in simple four-bar phrases with a harmony that favors thirds and sixths. This creates a wonderful romantic mood, warm and placid.

The *third movement* opens with a restless and shadowy tune over a pizzicato pulse in the cello. After a passage with more agitation, a broad chorale bursts out followed by a series of spectacular passages built on a driving pulse. A trio section then presents a noble diatonic melody that is expanded in a passionate lyricism. The dramatic scherzo returns and the movement ends in a stark and brutal passage with the previously-heard hammering pulse.

The *fourth movement* opens with a long sostenuto introduction that is characterized by a groping chromaticism. It seeks to find a home key, like similar introductory sections in some of Beethoven's string quartets. The rising semitones seem to presage a tragic or noble allegro, but what follows is a tranquillo mood instead, with a whimsical and plaintive march-like tune in the cello. A similarly undramatic second theme appears and the two themes are treated freely as a sort of discussion or dialogue in repeated recapitulations rather than in a formal development. The construction seems loose and undirected. The long coda pulls the pieces together and the coda finally explodes in a presto epigram, full of uninhibited energy.

Commentary. This is a justly celebrated masterpiece with all of the energy, complexity, innovation, and optimism of the young Brahms. The piece is not really difficult in technique or understanding except for the piano part, which is formidable. An overenthusiastic pianist can easily overwhelm the strings and pianists are advised to play with restraint. The string parts are gratifying in all voices. This monumental work can be enjoyed at all levels of effort and skill and it is a great favorite with all amateurs. Pleasure—4; Effort—3.

DVORÁK (1841–1904)

Dvorák was a sound pianist but not a virtuosic one and so it is not surprising that a considerable fraction of his chamber music combines piano with strings. This literature constitutes four piano trios, two piano quartets, one piano quintet and the Bagatelles for harmonium, two violins and cello. In these works, there is a better balance between the piano and the string voices than occurs in the piano-string works of more pianistic composers, like Brahms, Schumann, and Mendelssohn. This may be the consequence of Dvorák's own less virtuosic ability at the keyboard. This good balance makes these works especially suitable to amateur performances yet they seem to be less familiar to amateurs than those piano-string works of the great pianistic composers of the Romantic period.

The piano trios are Op. 21, in B flat, Op. 26, in G minor, Op. 65, in F minor, and Op. 90 (The Dumky) in E minor, spanning the period from 1875 to 1891.

Op. 21, in B flat, was written in 1875 at the beginning of Dvorák's maturity, when he rather abruptly established his characteristic nationalistic idiom. Soon before, his bass quintet in G major (originally Op. 18, published later as Op. 77) won a prize in a competition and that success may have prompted him to proceed immediately to write more chamber music. The Op. 21 piano trio, the Op. 23 piano quartet in D major, and the Op. 22 serenade for strings were all completed by June 1875. Later that year, he was at work on the symphony in F major and an opera, Vanda. The Op. 21 piano trio was revised slightly before its publication in 1880.

The Op. 26 piano trio in G minor was written about eight months later, being completed in January 1876. Late in 1975, Dvorák had lost his second daughter in a sudden and brief illness, and this tragedy affected the character of the works he wrote immediately after that, including this trio, the string quartet in E major (Op. 80), and the Stabat Mater, all finished early in 1876. It was another work from this period, the Moravian Duets, that specifically brought Dvorák to the attention of Brahms and of Simrock, the publisher who later became so important to Dvorák's career.

The Op. 65 piano trio in F minor is a much later work, from 1883. Dvorák had fully achieved his characteristic style by then, and he was gaining international acclaim. This work is the first of a series of works now seen as representing the peak of Dvorák's creative life. Dvorák was greatly affected by his mother's death in 1881, and this fact is reflected in the storm and melancholy of this trio and in the character of the symphony in D minor, Op. 70, which was written soon afterward.

The Dumky Trio, Op. 90, comes from 1890–91, about the time that Dvorák took a professorship at the Prague Conservatory and soon before his journey to America in 1892. This trio is the best known of his works in this form, representing his full artistic power in a period of happiness and honor. Other major works from this period include the *Requiem Mass*, Op. 89 (1890), and the *Te Deum*, Op. 103 (1892).

The piano quartets come from two different periods of Dvorák's career. The first, the piano quartet in D major, Op. 23, was written in 1875, at about the same time as the Op. 21 piano trio and at the beginning of his compositional maturity. Like the Op. 21 piano trio, Op. 23 is a pleasant but undistinguished work.

The second piano quartet, Op. 87, in E flat was written in 1889 at the request of Dvorák's publisher, Simrock. Dvorák was now an acclaimed international celebrity at the height of his career. This work was written just after the piano quintet, Op. 81, and just before the symphony in G major, Op. 88.

The Bagatelles for two violins, cello and harmonium written in 1878 would be a favorite were it not for its unusual instrumentation. It evokes rural Bohemian life in a nostalgic miniature that perfectly suits domestic players, the amateurs for whom it was written, but it does not fit well into a concert hall.

The piano quintet in A major, Op. 81, was written in the autumn of 1887, in the peak period of Dvorák's artistic career. It preceded the Dumky Trio by three years, the American Quartet by six years, and the second piano quartet, Op. 87, by two years. These four works are the best known of Dvorák's chamber music today.

An earlier piano quintet in A major, Op. 5 is now little known and rarely heard. It was written in 1872, before Dvorák had fully conceived his idiom. Its immaturity is made up for by its freshness but it is to be read today mainly for its historical interest.

Piano Trio in B flat major, Op. 21 | (1875)

I *Allegro molto.* II *Adagio molto e mesto.* III *Allegretto scherzando.* IV *Allegro vivace.*

The *first movement* opens without an introduction, the soft lyrical theme being repeated in several keys in the exposition. After an extensive development section, an expansive and soaring coda finally ends the movement gently. The spirit of the movement is pastoral and the mood is one of calm cheerfulness.

The *second movement*, a prayerful adagio, opens softly with an ardent and rather somber theme in G minor, played by the three instruments in succession. A second theme is more passionate and full of longing. These two themes are treated in alternation. The movement ends serenely.

The *third movement* is a tranquil scherzo with a polka rhythm in the major mode. The trio offers only a little contrast, being quieter and graver though still in the major mode.

The *fourth movement* is a sonata allegro with an agitated passionate first theme in the minor mode. The second subject is a vigorous march and the third is tense and chromatic. After these three themes are briefly developed, the first theme of the *second movement* returns. There is a brief recapitulation. The movement ends joyfully.

Commentary. This robust and optimistic work gets rather little respect from critics. Its early origin is the explanation for its deficiency in nationalistic or Slavonic flavor, and for its lack of profundity. Although it is neither a masterpiece nor a characteristic work, it is both sincere and well crafted. It is not difficult and it is immediately accessible, so amateurs can get much pleasure from reading it. This trio deserves to be much better known by all those who love Dvořák. Pleasure—2; Effort—2.

Piano Trio in G minor, Op. 26 | (1876)

I *Allegro moderato.* II *Largo.* III *Scherzo: Presto.* IV *Allegro non tanto.*

The *first movement* sonata allegro has a somber principal subject that is presented first in a terse and simple form, only to recur immediately in a more decorated and rhythmically complex variant. The two forms of the theme then return in alternation, along with a subordinate theme that expands the mood of uneasiness and longing. This spirit prevails throughout the movement.

The *second movement* is a modified rondo largo in three parts. The sole theme is lyrical, yearning and tense. The theme receives treatment in colorful modulations in the middle section of the movement. This creates a climactic passage that contrasts with the somber and melancholy treatments of the same theme at the beginning and ending of the movement.

The *third movement* is an agitated presto. Despite its lively rhythmic subject, the mood is melancholy because of the character of the melodies and the prevailing minor mode. The themes are treated in interesting canonic and moderato passages. The trio offers rather little contrast, providing only the soothing effect of the major mode with a slightly more lyrical subject.

The *fourth movement* sonata allegro rests on two themes. One is decisive and declamatory and the other is a hesitant and fragmented polka. These subjects are treated in alternation. The first subject then bursts forth in a frolicking variant. The development and the recapitulation increase the high spirits and the movement ends in gaiety.

Commentary. This is a far more serious work than is Op. 21, written only eight months before. The work is remarkable for its overall somber mood (which is relieved only in the last part of the *fourth movement*), for its thematic frugality, and for its masterful craftsmanship. This trio is not difficult technically and musically but the depth of feeling it contains requires considerable intensity of effort. It is highly recommended to all amateurs. The cello part is splendid! Pleasure—3; Effort—3.

Piano Trio in F minor, Op. 65 | (1883)

I *Allegro ma non troppo.* II *Allegro grazioso.* III *Poco adagio.* IV *Allegro con brio.*

The *first movement* sonata allegro opens with a somber, declamatory and dramatic subject, full of majesty and pathos. The second subject is angry and defiant but subsequent passages of the exposition are more restrained in their passion and even tranquil at times. The development section is quite truncated. An expansive and dynamic coda ends this powerfully passionate movement.

The *second movement* scherzo presents a whimsical but defiant dance tune in the minor mode, played over a monotonous staccato triplet figure. Variations in the keys provide some relief and even some gaiety in the mood in the first and last sections. In the middle section, a pensive major-mode cantilena rides over a gentle and sinuous accompaniment.

The *third movement* adagio opens with a tranquil and yearning melody that is first stated rather simply by the cello and then repeated in a more ornamented form. The second subject, more resigned in character, is treated in canon. A middle section is built upon a blunt and rhythmically marked theme that then expands freely in a broad and fervent treatment. The third section returns to the themes and character of the first section and the movement ends in a brief and delicate coda.

The *fourth movement* is built upon two stirring and rather angry subjects, treated in a combined rondo-sonata form. Tranquillo passages interrupt the agitation and drama of the main subjects. A broad coda continues the alternation of contrasting moods and the movement ends peacefully.

Commentary. Those who do not know this work will be astonished at it, for it is uncharacteristically profound, complex, personal and passionate. All the movements are massive, full of interest and deep feeling. This work is monumental, far beyond any of the other Dvorák piano trios, and it is not a work to be treated casually. Casual reading is not likely to be much fun, but a little practice and study quickly reveal what there is to be found here. This is a masterpiece of the Romantic tradition, strangely neglected, as fine a work as any in this form from this period. Amateurs are strongly encouraged to study this great trio. It is, however, very difficult. Pleasure—4; Effort—4.

Piano Trio in E minor, Op. 90 | (1890–91), *The Dumky Trio*

I *Dumka: Lento maestoso; Allegro quasi doppio movimento.*
II *Dumka: Poco adagio; Vivace non troppo.* III *Dumka: Andante;*
Vivace non troppo; Andante. IV *Dumka: Andante moderato; Allegro*
scherzando; Allegro. V *Dumka: Allegro.* VI *Dumka: Lento maestoso;*
Vivace.

This trio is unique in form and content. The six movements are stylized examples of an established and classical form in Slavic folk music, the dumka. In this form, pensive or elegiac passages alternate with riotous high-spirited sections. Dvorák was fond of this structure, and he used it occasionally in many other pieces of chamber music. Here, he indulged in an orgy of the dumka, presenting six dumky (the plural) in what appears superficially to be a sort of divertimento.

But this is not a wholly accurate view. Closer inspection shows an approximation to classical form. The first three dumky (played in immediate succession) can be viewed as a connected whole, each equally contrasting lamentation and gaiety. The fourth dumka is mainly melancholy. The fifth is mainly lively, while the sixth is again alternatively somber and lively. Thus, the first three dumky can be seen to constitute a ternary rondo. The fourth is a slow movement, the fifth is a fast movement, and the sixth approximates a rondo finale.

The first dumka presents a yearning and pathetic theme in the lento, with a gay diatonic dance in the subsequent allegro.

The second dumka opens in the major mode with a delicate melancholy tune in the cello, a soothing cantilena. The second section, vivace, is a gay folk dance.

The third dumka is in three-part form with a single fundamental melody. The mood in the outer sections is pastoral and nocturnal. The middle section is agitated.

The fourth dumka andante makes use of a subject that has the character of a Russian folk song. The melancholy mood is briefly dispelled at intervals by a playful tune (Allegretto scherzando) and by an explosive dance subject (Allegro) but the movement ends in the poetic melancholy spirit with which it opens.

The fifth dumka is mainly an allegro movement with an agitated and syncopated theme, dark and passionate. Subsequent treatments of this theme are somewhat more gentle and lyrical. A soft and resolute coda ends this dumka.

The sixth dumka opens in lento with a sorrowful theme. The alternate section is a fiery vivace, and a whirling coda provides a brilliant close.

Commentary. This unique work is justly celebrated as a splendid exposition of Slavic folk music. It is not a profoundly emotional or thoughtful work, but it is fully genuine and sincere as a celebration of the style. There is little or no Germanic intellectualism here, only the heart-on-the-sleeve feelings of folk music. This is a difficult work to play. It requires excellent instrumental technique. Furthermore, the abrupt changes in mood and tempo make casual reading difficult. Players must get to know the whole work quite thoroughly before they can get satisfaction from it. Amateurs who are new to the work will find themselves constantly stopping and starting. Once gotten in hand, this trio is great fun to play. Pleasure—3, Effort—4.

Bagatelles in G minor, Op. 47 | (1878)

I *Allegro scherzando.* II *Tempo di minuetto: Grazioso.* III *Allegretto scherzando.* IV *Canon: Andante con moto.* V *Poco allegro.*

The *first movement* creates a pastoral mood in its elaboration of a melody derived from a Bohemian folk song, 'Hrály Dudy'.

The *second movement*, a simple minuet, retains the Bohemian character. Its unrelenting, sostenuto, dotted-rhythm melody creates a hypnotic, magical, nocturnal mood.

The *third movement* treats the same tune as that of the first in a kittenish way.

The *fourth movement*, a plaintive canon on a theme with the character of a folk song, evokes a dreamy contemplative atmosphere.

The *fifth movement*, a cheerful and comical polka, uses a tune derived from that of the Allegro scherzando movement at the beginning.

Commentary. The unusual instrumentation limits one's appreciation for this nostalgic little wonder, for most players must substitute a piano for the harmonium. The sweet. reedy, fragile drone of a harmonium (a parlor organ using metallic reeds activated by a gentle stream of air), can now be satisfactorily reproduced by some electronic keyboards. Perhaps an accordion could also do it. Once heard or played with the correct instrumentation, this work becomes indelibly implanted, an eternally fresh, seemingly spontaneous depiction of the spirit of the bucolic life we all wish we had once had. Pleasure—4; Effort—2.

Piano Quartet in D major, Op. 23 | (1875)

I *Allegro moderato.* II *Andantino cantabile.* III *Allegretto scherzando; Allegro agitato.*

The *first movement* is striking for its changeable mood. The opening theme is calm and lyrical. Subsequent themes are bustling or strongly rhythmic. These themes are treated conventionally in the development section. A grandioso passage closes the movement, with a quiet chord at the end.

The *second movement* constitutes the presentation of a folk song, with five variations and a coda. The five variations are, successively, rhythmically marked, ornamented, march-like, lyrical and fragmented. A pensive mood is maintained to some degree through all the variations. The coda is warmly lyrical.

The *third movement* combines the functions of a scherzo and a finale. The allegretto scherzando section has a waltz-like melody, first presented in a melancholy cast and then in a gayer style. The following agitato is more cheerful, constituting variations on a happy lyrical tune. The scherzando returns to be followed by a return of the agitato and the movement ends in a restrained upbeat mood.

Commentary. Although this early work is not characteristic of the mature Dvorák, it is an intimate and pleasing product of the period that also produced the first piano trio, Op. 21. No masterwork, this trio is still to be valued for the view that it gives of Dvorák in his first flowering. It is not very difficult to play and amateurs should not hesitate to undertake this neglected piece. Pleasure—2; Effort—2.

Piano Quartet in E-flat major, Op. 87 | (1889)

I *Allegro con fuoco.* II *Lento.* III *Allegretto moderato, grazioso.* IV *Allegro ma non troppo.*

The *first movement* opens with a firm, resolute and virile theme that is played in unison. This theme and its character dominate the whole movement, the soft and lyrical second subject (first delivered by the viola) always remaining subordinate. The development section is lively and imaginative. The coda is bold at first but it suddenly declines to a delicate intermezzo that closes this powerful movement.

The doleful *second movement* is of unusual formal design with its two thematically and structurally similar sections. The two sections are rather like an exposition and a recapitulation without an intervening development section. The two sections are built of five lovely themes. The mood throughout is mainly calm and grave, though there are intervals of some agitation and passion. The movement ends in tranquillity.

The *third movement* is a scherzo in ternary form. The outer sections have a mildly playful character with a quiet and dancing main subject and a legato, slightly oriental second subject. The quicker trio section is much livelier with a jumping theme played over sinuous triplets in the accompaniment.

The *fourth movement* returns to the virile character of the first. An energetic and robust principal theme is contrasted with the warm and lyrical legato of the second subject. A compact development and recapitulation proceed to a brilliant and joyful conclusion.

Commentary. This is a coherent, concentrated and balanced masterpiece. It presents no major problems in technique or understanding, though it is certainly not easy to play. It seems to be a neglected work, and such neglect is hard to understand, for it is one of the great works of the Dvořák canon. Amateurs are strongly encouraged to learn it. Pleasure—3; Effort—3.

Piano Quintet in A major, Op. 81 | (1887)

I *Allegro ma non tanto.* II *Andante con moto.* III *Molto vivace.* IV *Allegro.*

The *first movement* presents two main subjects, both of which are legato and melancholy in character. In the exposition, these two themes are presented again in more energetic and enthusiastic forms. They are further explored in a broad development section. The movement ends with a brief and jubilant coda. This spacious movement is remarkable for its changeability of mood and for its enormously varied and original treatments of the thematic material. It is, overall, a joyful and optimistic movement.

The *second movement* is a dumka, a three-part rondo with a quick middle section, having the form ABCABA. The outer sections use lament themes to create a sadly pensive ballad. The middle section is a whirling dancing furiant, with a theme that is derived from one of those of the outer sections.

The *third movement* is a furiant, a dance with three sections. The first section, gay and bright, is built on three themes, one jumping and the others legato. The middle section is calm and pensive with a Russian-style chorale theme. The third section returns to the bright tunes of the first.

The *fourth movement* is a bustling sonata allegro. The strongly rhythmic themes are treated contrapuntally with great ingenuity. Frisky high spirits prevail throughout with a few brief legato intervals. The movement ends in a wildly joyful outburst.

Commentary. This is a justly celebrated work, wonderfully crafted, and full of Czech high spirits. It is a work that is wholly characteristic of the mature Dvořák. In places, it seems a little aimless because of the seemingly endless succession of new ideas that keep coming up, but one forgives that because the ideas are so imaginative. The work provides a nearly perfect balance among the voices. Really serious problems of technique and interpretation are virtually absent though the work requires good technique. It is a true companion to the Brahms piano quintet. Pleasure—4; Effort—3.

FAURÉ (1845–1924)

Gabriel-Urbain Fauré's long life spanned most of the Romantic period, from Berlioz and Chopin to Bartok and Stravinsky. Throughout his life he maintained a conservative and traditional course expressed in small forms, piano pieces, theater music, songs and chamber music.

After his education in Paris, Fauré supported himself by playing the organ in Parisian churches while composing and teaching privately. He became professor of composition at the Paris Conservatory in 1896, at fifty, and he was its director from 1905 to 1920, when he resigned because of deafness. In that position, he exerted a major influence on French music.

His major chamber works (other than sonatas and other works for one instrument with piano) are only six, spanning his long life:

Piano Quartet, Op. 15 (1879)
Piano Quartet, Op. 45 (1886)
Piano Quintet, Op. 89 (1906)
Piano Quintet, Op. 115 (1921)
Piano Trio, Op. 120 (1923)
String Quartet, Op. 121 (1924)

Fauré was considered to be a master of chamber music, though his actual output of such works was rather small. The whole body of this work is strangely neglected today, despite the celebrity he enjoyed among his contemporaries. The two piano quintets, the piano trio, and the string quartet all currently lie outside the mainstream repertoire and they get scant attention from amateur players. The two piano quartets, however, are more often played and heard. Amateurs can enjoy them as early works by a master whose enduring influence in classical music can be seen in much contemporary music.

Piano Quartet in C minor, Op. 15 | (1879)

I *Allegro molto moderato.* II *Scherzo: Allegro vivo.* III *Adagio.* IV *Allegro molto.*

The intense *first movement* opens with the three strings playing a bold and strongly rhythmic theme in unison over syncopated chords in the piano. A graceful and flexible second theme appears before another episode of the first theme. After an elegant development, the themes are recapitulated in classical fashion. The authoritative rhythm expressed at the outset dominates throughout.

The *second movement* opens with five bars of hurried pizzicato accompaniment in the strings, after which the piano plays a breathless, fragmented and skipping theme. This theme is treated in a dialogue with contrasting 6/8 and 3/4 meters. The trio is a legato song played by the strings con sordino, after which the scherzo is repeated in full.

The *third movement* opens with a solemn theme that is played first by the cello and is then expanded to include the other strings and finally the piano. Then a new more sensuous and yearning theme appears, to be treated in a dialogue in the strings, mounting to a climax. The solemn theme of the opening returns in the coda.

The *fourth movement* opens with a skipping theme that resembles a mazurka. A more lyrical second subject provides contrast. A third theme follows and the three themes are treated complexly in fragments and in contrasts. All this leads to a melodramatic finish.

Commentary. This work is a fully mature work despite its low opus number. The idiom is wholly characteristic of Fauré and the conception is lucid. Furthermore, it is readily accessible. The string parts are only moderately difficult and the piano part is not virtuosic. The principal difficulties are rhythmic but they can be overcome with a little practice. Care must be taken not to make the ending gaudy by giving it too much a sense of triumph. This is a magnificent work for amateurs to play and experienced amateurs should not hesitate to undertake it. Pleasure—3; Effort—2.

Piano Quartet in G minor, Op. 45 | (1886)

I *Allegro molto moderato.* II *Allegro molto.* III *Adagio non troppo.*
IV *Allegro molto.*

The *first movement* opens directly with the first theme, as impulsive, impassioned and grandiose a subject as any to be found anywhere in the works of Fauré. A more tender and graceful melody provides second-theme contrast. A third theme, of peaceful character, is derived from the first subject. These subjects are developed in contrast. After a recapitulation, a peaceful coda ends this large movement.

The *second movement* begins like that of the first piano quartet. The piano plays a rushing syncopated tune, a perpetual motion against pizzicato chords in the strings. The rushing motif persists to form a substructure for a transformation of the second theme of the *first movement* in ternary rhythm and for a lyrical transformation of the principal theme of this movement. There is no trio.

The wonderful *third movement* opens with a bell-like phrase played by the piano alternately with a contemplative melodic phrase in the viola. The viola phrase expands into a full melody, the first subject. A second subject is related to the first. The bell-like motif recurs at intervals as these themes are expanded and transformed. The coda ends on a note of resignation. The mood of the movement is intimate with an ethereal or unreal atmosphere.

The *fourth movement* opens with a brutal and tragic triplet motif that underlies the whole movement. A lyrical subject then appears and a second theme follows, one of more anguished character. The brutal rhythmic motif is treated in contrast and in conflict with the more lyrical melodic material. The work builds to a great climax, ending in an impetuous rush of the triplet motif of the opening.

Commentary. This is the lesser known of the two piano quartets but it is the greater in power. The ideas are more spacious, the harmony is more innovative and the feeling is more intimate and personal. The work is correspondingly considerably more difficult, which is probably why amateurs play it less. Its difficulties are not wholly technical though the piano part is not at all easy. Rather, it is difficult to understand and grasp the sense of the whole. It takes repeated readings to understand this work. Thus, it is not so accessible as the first. Amateurs are advised to leave this one alone until after they are comfortable with its companion. Pleasure—3; Effort—4.

FRANCK (1822–1890)

Franck wrote little chamber music and he wrote very little for the piano with strings. Indeed, there are only five such works, four piano trios and the piano quintet.

Franck's piano trios are not major works. There are three such trios in Op. 1. Written probably in emulation of Beethoven's Op. 1, they were dedicated to King Leopold I of Belgium and presented to him, apparently without reward or compensation. Some time later, Liszt induced Franck to write a new finale for the third piano trio, and the original final movement was published as a single-movement work called the "Fourth Piano Trio, Op. 2," dedicated to Liszt. These are all immature works, written when Franck was a student at the Paris Conservatory.

The piano trio in F-sharp minor, the first, is far superior to the others. The reason for this is not really clear. D'Indy speculates that it was written under inspiration while the others were added at the behest of Franck's ambitious father who wanted his son to have a set of three (like Beethoven's) to present to the King.

After Franck's student days, he entered upon his long career as a performer, during which time he produced mainly liturgical music and music for the keyboard. After he settled into his position at the Paris Conservatory in 1872, he returned to chamber music to produce the string quartet (1889) and the piano quintet (1878–79).

The piano quintet and the piano trio in F-sharp minor remain the only piano-string works of Franck that are currently performed. Saint-Saens disliked the piano quintet when he first heard it, though it was dedicated to him, and the discouraged composer put it away at first, only to resurrect it after a time.

Piano Quintet in F minor | (1878–79)

I *Molto moderato quasi lento; Maestoso; Allegro.* II *Lento con molto sentimento.* III *Allegro non troppo, ma con fuoco.*

The *first movement* is in sonata form. After a long introduction and a statement of the first theme, a cyclic theme appears, first in several exploratory keys and finally in A-flat major. This warmly expressive melody, formally the second subject, recurs throughout the work in the other movements, but the formal first theme dominates the long and vigorous development of this *first movement*. The cyclic or second theme returns in a terminal development. A placid coda that is based on the first theme ends this highly romantic movement.

The *second movement* constitutes three sections. The first section makes use of a lyrical melody that is derived from the first theme of the *first movement*. The second section makes use of the cyclic theme. The third section returns to the theme of the first section. The mood is sorrowful in the first and third sections, with a sense of repose in the second section.

The *third movement* opens with an introduction that makes use of fragments of subsequent melodic material. The first theme is then stated in unison. The second theme is derived from a theme of the *second movement*. A long development section treats these themes with chromatic complexity. The familiar cyclic theme returns in the recapitulation. A quiet coda ends this brilliant and triumphant movement.

Commentary. This masterful example of the cyclic form is one of Franck's greatest works. This quintet and the piano-violin sonata are the two chamber pieces of Franck that are most heard today. This is not at all an easy work, making both technical and musical demands that place it among those monuments to be studied carefully and taken in small doses. Those who love the Franck idiom should study this work. Those who don't will find it tedious. Pleasure—3; Effort—4.

HAYDN (1732–1809)

Haydn wrote many piano trios. There are thirty-one in the Breitkopf and Härtel edition. These mostly come from the period of his maturity, after 1770. Only one, the one most favored by amateurs, is summarized here.

Although these trios generally exhibit the wit, charm and ingenuity of Haydn's mature style, they lack the sense of exploration and innovation that is so prominent in the string quartets. The Haydn piano trios remain quite consistently Classical in form, showing little evolution toward the form of the piano trio that was to become so important to Romantic composers. It was Beethoven who pointed the way with his Op. 1, especially with No. 3.

The Haydn piano trios are all highly pianistic works. The piano parts are brilliant, and they carry much of the action.

The violin parts frequently approach the same level of responsibility, but the cello is, for the most part, treated as a sustaining bass instrument. As a result, the works rarely achieve a uniform voicing and they show comparatively little variety in texture.

This imbalance seems to be an imperfection to modern ears and this may be one reason for the neglect these works suffer from modern amateurs. Another reason may be the requirement for a really skillful chamber music pianist. The brilliant keyboard part easily overwhelms the strings. This is not Haydn's fault, of course, for he was writing for a primitive piano with a timbre quite different from that of the modern piano.

Why should amateurs undertake to play these trios at all? Even with strenuous effort, the result is a product that is little more than witty and clever. In playing them, however, one can quickly come to see what an enormous effort Haydn had devoted to the form of the string quartet.

Piano Trio in G major, Hoboken XV:25 | (1795)

I *Andante.* II *Poco Adagio.* III *Finale: Rondo in the Gipsies' style: Presto.*

The *first movement* is an andante in 2/4 meter, but the feel is that of a poco allegro in 4/4 meter. The placid and flowing theme is treated to four ornamented variations. The mood throughout is calm and cheerful, and the character is rather formal and stylized.

The *second movement* opens with a transparent cantabile theme in the piano, which is later answered in the violin. The single melody is treated freely in this three-part movement, but the delicate character of the theme is maintained throughout.

The *third movement* is the celebrated Gipsy rondo. A perpetuum mobile theme appears first in the piano and then in the violin. Episodes with harmonic and rhythmic contrast occur, but the Hungarian or Gipsy character is retained throughout this long and flashing dance-movement.

Commentary. This is the most interesting and memorable of the Haydn piano trios. It requires a polished pianist throughout. The string parts are quite manageable by experienced players. The last movement is most remarkable and memorable. It has been seen by some as the inspiration for the last movement of Brahms' piano quartet, Op. 25. Pleasure—2; Effort—1.

MENDELSSOHN-BARTHOLDY (1809–1847)

Mendelssohn's major works for piano with strings constitute three piano quartets, two piano trios and a sextet for piano, string quartet and bass. This seems a rather small output for a composer who was noted as a pianist. It is probable that, like Beethoven, he found it difficult to combine virtuosic piano technique with the sound of stringed instruments to produce a satisfactorily varied timbre and texture. Whatever the case, only two of these six piano-string works, the two piano trios, remain much played as enduring masterpieces.

The three piano quartets were produced in 1822–25 when the composer was fourteen to sixteen years old. Op. 1 was written in 1822, Op. 2 in 1823, and Op. 3 in 1824. This indicates that Mendelssohn addressed the problem of the piano-string combination almost from the beginning of his career. Op. 1, in C minor, is modeled on the style of Weber and Beethoven, while Op. 2, in F minor, seems somewhat more characteristic. Op. 3, in B minor, is a broader and more adventurous work, still occasionally performed. For amateurs who play mainly for pleasure, only Op. 3 is really suitable but it is still a minor work.

The sextet for piano and strings is also an early work, published posthumously as Op. 110. The fact that Mendelssohn himself did not have it published suggests that he was not pleased with it, and for good reason. The only reasons it should be heard at all are to see how quickly Mendelssohn developed his gift and to see the kinds of trials that he made.

The two piano trios are both wonderful. Op. 49, in D minor, was written over a seven-month period in 1839, when Mendelssohn was thirty years old. It was immediately acclaimed as a masterpiece and, as Schumann predicted, it has remained a permanent staple of the concert stage. Op. 49 was written soon after the Op. 44 string quartets (1837-38) and essentially at the same time as the Op. 45 cello sonata (1839). The piano part to Op. 49 was revised before its publication, probably at the advice of Ferdinand Hiller, to make it more brilliant.

The other piano trio, Op. 60 in C minor, was written over a four-month period in 1845 and it was published a year later. It is dedicated to the great violinist and composer, Louis Spohr. This work had less immediate success than its predecessor did, perhaps because it is more serious, more dignified and less flashy than Op. 49, and it remains a comparatively neglected work today.

Piano Trio in D minor, Op. 49 | (1839)

I *Molto allegro agitato.* II *Andante con moto tranquillo.* III *Scherzo: Leggiero e vivace.* IV *Finale: Allegro assai appassionato.*

The *first movement* opens directly with the first theme in the cello. This is an Italianate melody, passionate and melancholy. This theme later dominates the movement with ingenious counter-melodies at each return. A second theme of similar character figures in the wonderfully inventive development section. This lyrical movement remains youthful and passionate throughout. The piano part is particularly brilliant.

The *second movement* makes use of a lush melody that is a characteristic Mendelssohnian song without words, introduced by the piano. The central section of this ABA form is dramatic and stormy, in the minor mode. The warm *Lied* theme returns in the final section, ornamented with lovely counter-melodies.

The *third movement* is playful and elfin. This is a typical Mendelssohnian scherzo, quick, light and staccato. The middle section is declamatory without being really dramatic.

The *fourth movement* uses a dancing Schubertian theme to form a long and inventive structure but it remains dark, in the minor mode. A second theme is a broad cantabile, full of warmth and passion. The major-mode coda is a brilliant and flashing display of virtuosity.

Commentary. This masterpiece has a wealth of almost everything, melody, inventiveness, brilliance of display and the sense of spontaneity and ease so characteristic of Mendelssohn at his best. There is little profundity here and good amateurs can readily handle the technical demands. Even the virtuosic piano part is not so difficult as it sounds. This is instantly understandable music. Indeed, it seems so natural to play that amateurs can readily fall victim to an excess of exuberance, which must be tamed to make the piece work most effectively. All serious amateurs should play it. Pleasure—4; Effort—3.

Piano Trio in C minor, Op. 66 | (1845)

I *Allegro energico e con fuoco.* II *Andante expressivo.* III *Scherzo: Molto allegro quasi presto.* IV *Finale: Allegro appassionato.*

The *first movement* opens with an intense and urgently flowing melody played by the violin and piano over a pedal point in the cello. This opening leads to a more lyrical melody in the strings and a more suave subject soon follows. These three themes are worked out with striking ingenuity, and a high degree of sonority and tension is always maintained. This magnificent movement ends in a fiery coda.

The *second movement* makes use of a theme that is a gentle, sad and appealing song without words. This theme is treated freely. A central section provides a contrast that is chiefly melodic and harmonic, the lyrical melancholy spirit of the main sections remaining unrelieved.

The *third movement* is a virtuosic scherzo with a chattering perpetuum mobile theme. The middle section has a pronounced Gipsy character. This is a delicious movement, full of wit and good humor.

The *fourth movement* opens abruptly with a leaping ninth that launches the dramatic, agitated and tragic first theme. Later themes are vigorous and triumphant but there is some gentleness and even a feeling of remorse at intervals. After these themes and moods are explored, a great majestic chorale appears unexpectedly and this is then developed so as to form the climax of the whole work. An orchestral treatment of the chorale theme and of earlier materials follows. The long major-mode coda is full of even more triumph.

Commentary. This is altogether a different sort of work from Op. 49. It seems far more serious in intent, far more varied in character, more sincere and more personal. The scope of the first three movements is so great that the massive finale with its great chorale seems a little misplaced. After all this, the long coda can seem bombastic and even ridiculous if its sense of triumph is overdone. Amateurs are warned not to take this work lightly. Technically and musically it offers no great problems, but it requires a good deal of thought, care and restraint in interpretation to make it work well. It deserves to be better known than it is. Pleasure—3; Effort—3.

MOZART (1756–1791)

Mozart's chamber music for piano with groups of strings constitutes mainly piano trios and piano quartets. Like Haydn, he devoted less effort to such forms than he did to the string quartet.

The Mozart piano trios, like those of Haydn, are pianistic works. The piano is generally the dominant voice, and it often plays in a register between the two string parts. As a result, the string parts often seem mainly to be reinforcing what is otherwise a solo piano sonata. Thus these trios often seem to lack the balance and textural variety of the sound of the piano trio as it was developed later. Mozart, like Haydn, never seemed to manage to make the piano trio work wholly successfully. He had, indeed, previously discovered how to solve the general problem of combining a piano with string groups in the two piano quartets. Why he did not apply this solution more fully to the piano trio is a mystery.

Although there are several early works for piano trio, notably the divertimento in B-flat major, K. 254, the first work that can really be called a piano trio is K. 496 from 1786. K. 502 and K. 542 are more fully developed piano trios. These are late works, K. 542 having been written just before the last three symphonies. The later two piano trios are not on the same level as K. 502 and K. 542. K. 548, in C major, is a fine but somewhat less imaginative work. K. 564, in G major, was first conceived as a piano sonata, probably intended for students, and is of little interest to amateur players.

In the piano quartets, Mozart had solved the problem of balancing the piano with the string voices. There are only two such works, K. 478 in G minor from 1785 and K. 493 in E-flat major from 1786. In these works, he set the piano and strings as antiphonal voices, and he separated the register of the piano from that of the strings. The piano quartet was a novel form at the time. Mozart invented it, and these two works became the models for the great piano quartets of the Romantics.

It is instructive to compare these piano-string works chronologically with the string quartets. The great piano-string works of Mozart were written between 1785 and 1788. All of the six Haydn-dedicated string quartets (the last from 1785) preceded these works. The Hoffmeister quartet came in 1786, early in the period of the piano-string works. The three "Prussian" or "cello" quartets came in 1789-90, after the piano-string works.

The chronology of the major piano-string works is as follows:

Piano Quartet in G major, K. 478 (1785).
Piano Quartet in E-flat major, K. 493 (1786).
Piano Trio in G major, K. 496 (1786).
Piano Trio in B-flat major, K. 502 (1787).
Piano Trio in E major, K. 542 (1788).
Piano Trio in C major, K. 548 (1788).
Piano Trio in G major, K. 564 (1788).

Divertimento (Piano Trio) in B-flat major, K. 254 | (1776)

I *Allegro assai.* II *Adagio.* III *Rondo: Tempo di Menuetto.*

The *first movement*, in 3/4 meter, opens with a spirited and jaunty theme alternating forte and piano bars. Later melodic material is contrastingly gentler, more tentative, and more lyrical. After a brief development, a full recapitulation ends in a brief coda. The mood throughout is optimistic and light-hearted. The piano dominates throughout.

The *second movement*, in 4/4 meter, first gives its simple major-mode theme to the violin to play over a flowing arpeggiated line in the piano. Sudden climaxes in forte introduce drama. The instruments reverse roles and a second tune appears, the two then being developed into a movement that is serious, poised and gracious.

The *third movement* is a minuet played in rondo form. The graceful theme, played by the violin, later becomes more dramatic. The spirit of the music is genial and polite throughout.

Commentary. This work is a typical serious sonata as Mozart employed the form in his youth, not the salon music that the title, divertimento, usually implies. The texture is strongly pianistic, the violin being treated largely as an obbligato voice and the cello only outlining the bass line. The work is not very interesting to play casually but it is instructive to compare it to the later works for this combination. Pleasure—1; Effort—1.

Piano Trio in G major, K. 496 | (1786)

I *Allegro*. II *Andante*. III *Allegretto*.

The *first movement* opens with the solo piano stating a dashing, brilliant, and complex theme. The violin then takes it up. A softer and more graceful second subject appears. The development section, notable for its use of the violin and cello as equal voices in the texture, achieves dramatic force.

The *second movement*, also in the major mode, develops its melodic material almost wholly from that of the opening two bars. This gives this andante the unitary feel of a theme with variations although it is not. It is filled with harmonic surprises and astonishing counterpoint. The mood is a cool optimism.

The *third movement*, a theme with variations, uses a lively and imperative gavotte theme with a prominent turn-figure. Its major-mode simplicity suits it to a series of conventional variation treatments, one in the minor mode, and one in adagio tempo. The final expanded variation leads to the brilliant ending of a movement that began in an unpromising manner.

Commentary. This attractive work is less pianistic than its predecessor of ten years before, because it treats the strings more fully as equal voices in the trio. It is cheerful and high-spirited throughout, always graceful but never profound. It is fun to read casually and rewarding to study seriously. This is the longest of the Mozart piano trios. Pleasure—3; Effort—2.

Piano Trio in B-flat major, K. 502 | (1787)

I *Allegro*. II *Larghetto*. III *Allegretto*.

The *first movement* is a monothematic sonata allegro. The long and complex theme is graceful and pensive. Its treatment exploits a virtuosic piano part in which running arpeggios and scale-figures underlie the lyrical and passionate statements of the violin and cello. New thematic material opens the development section. The character is subdued and gracious throughout. The movement ends quietly.

The *second movement* begins with the solo piano playing a long and complex melody. It comes back in varied ornamented guises in the piano and violin parts. The movement, lyrical, wistful and placid throughout, ends in repose.

The *third movement* begins with a principal theme that contains internal contrast, the three dramatic descending half-notes leading to a lyrical response. Its first statement by solo piano leads to a forte reply by the strings, in the fashion of a concerto solo and tutti sequence. The movement develops as a brilliant rondo, remaining subdued in character, but agitated by the running lines, often in triplets, that dominate the piano part beneath the lyrical statements of the strings. The movement ends firmly in a forte, diatonic declamation.

Commentary. The concerto-like character of this trio may reflect the fact that Mozart was writing piano concertos in this period. This character is the major pitfall for amateurs who choose this trio to play, for it is easy for the pianist to forget that this is chamber music. It has all the invention, variety, and surprise that one hears in the mature works of Mozart, and it can be a delight to play at any level of familiarity, if only the pianist keeps a sense of proportion. Pleasure—4; effort—2.

Piano Trio in E major, K. 542 | (1788)

I *Allegro.* II *Andante grazioso.* III *Allegro.*

The *first movement* begins with the solo piano playing a chromatic, wandering and unsettled melody that fully matches the remote key. A second theme is more reassuring in character. The two are treated to a full development that is largely happy, though there are moments of poignancy.

The *second movement* opens with the piano playing solo again. The graceful and placid lyric receives repeated statements in a quasi-rondo form with constant variation in ornamentation and harmony. The spirit is an immaculate and pastoral calm.

The *third movement* opens with the solo piano again, this time playing a flowing and symmetrical melody that is promptly repeated by the violin. A contrasting motif appears, three descending octaves in forte with a following running figure. The melodic material is treated in rondo form with extensive running triplet passages. The spirit is cool, delicate and transparent for the most part but passages of virtuosic figuration in the piano and in the violin provide brilliant episodes.

Commentary. Written in the same summer as the monumental last three symphonies, this trio reflects the level of Mozart's genius at the time. Its balanced treatment of the three voices makes it easier to play casually than K. 502, but its transparency makes it more difficult. It is not necessarily a better work than K. 502, but it is much different. The two represent the apex in the form for Mozart. Pleasure—4; Effort—3.

Piano Trio in C major, K. 548 | (1788)

I *Allegro.* II *Andante cantabile.* III *Allegro.*

The *first movement* opens with an abrupt and martial motif, a comic-opera march stated in unison. It is developed in fragments before a second lyrical motif appears. The development section, in the minor mode, introduces a new melody, a wistful and harmonically ambiguous line that returns in the coda. This movement is remarkable for its variety of moods, its freshness and its vigor.

The *second movement* themes, both introduced by the piano, are long, lyrical and calm. The materials are developed with rich invention, the movement retaining a warm, romantic and religious quality throughout. The cello has lush solo passages to play.

The *third movement* rondo uses a lively hopping tune introduced by the solo piano. This theme rarely disappears from view in the astounding manipulations of this movement. The ending is a triumphant and diatonic expression of the leaping rondo motif in unison.

Commentary. Einstein and other experts downplay this trio a bit. But many who play it consider it to be every bit as good as its predecessors. It possesses wonderful variety and color and it offers fewer problems of ensemble than its immediate forerunners. It is the best trio for an experienced group to start with in undertaking to study the Mozart piano trios. Pleasure—4; Effort—3.

Piano Trio in G major, K. 564 | (1788)

I *Allegro.* II *Andante.* III *Allegretto.*

The *first movement* themes are simple and graceful. Their development is brief and unimaginative. The spirit is a uniform placidity.

The *second movement* treats a smooth and rather staid melody to six variations, one in the minor mode. The variations are charming. The spirit remains a cheerful placidity.

The *third movement* is a rondo. The sprightly but rather square melody, introduced by the solo piano, is never far from the surface. The mood is cheerful except for one episode in the minor mode.

Commentary. The explanation for the comparative inferiority of this work is that it was first conceived as a piano sonata for beginning students. It is a cheerful, good-humored, and well-mannered work with little more to recommend it. Beginners might want to play it but it offers little that is inspiring or challenging to more experienced players. Pleasure—2; Effort—1.

Piano Quartet in G minor, K. 478 | (1785)

I *Allegro*. II *Andante*. III *Rondo: Allegro*.

The *first movement* opens directly with an unusual principal theme that has two highly contrasting components. The first is dramatic and the second is sparkling. This complex melody, containing such a contrast in itself, requires no second theme. Derived thematic material dominates a complex and contrapuntal development section. The overall tragic and dramatic character of the movement reaches a climax in the brief coda.

The *second movement* treats a wandering and asymmetric melody with great tenderness. A mood of quiet sadness persists throughout this lovely andante.

The *third movement* rondo uses a gavotte as the principal theme and this dancing character persists throughout the movement. The mood of vigorous gaiety is maintained, though there are episodes of turbulence. The movement ends in a brilliant flourish.

Commentary. This work, overall, remains in the memory as a tragic work, the gaiety of the rondo failing to dispel fully the splendid tragedy of the *first movement* and the tender sadness of the second. This work is one of the monuments of the literature. It is deeply felt and highly personal in character, devoid of any effects that seem calculated or contrived. The antiphonal treatments give it a remarkable transparency. It is not a particularly difficult work in technique. Good amateurs can easily read it, but it is a very difficult work to get exactly right. All amateurs should play this quartet over and over. At any level of playing or polish, it is an unfailing source of joy for players. Pleasure—4; effort—2.

Piano Quartet in E-flat major, K. 493 | (1786)

I *Allegro*. II *Larghetto*. III *Allegretto*.

The *first movement* opens directly with a first theme that is lyrical, pensive, and subdued. The second theme, which has the same character, dominates the development and the coda. The whole movement possesses a gentle and dreamy spirit, full of warmth and optimism.

The *second movement* continues the mood of the first. The rather sensuous melodies are treated freely to produce a lovely cantilena with a sustained spirit of tender dreaminess.

The *third movement* is a cheerful and rousing rondo. A long episode in the minor mode provides some contrast of mood and it gives the piano an opportunity for a display of virtuosity. The closing passages contain some especially innovative treatments of the melodic subjects.

Commentary. Although this work resembles its companion in overall structure, it differs considerably in its character. The piano quartet in G minor was not well received when it was first heard, probably because of its tragic and personal character. This may have prompted Mozart to produce this one with such a different mood. If that was the case, Mozart's effort shows, for this one seems a little more formal, a little more studied, a little less spontaneous. Despite that, this is also a splendid work. Like its predecessor, good amateurs can readily play it at sight. That is, it is just as readily accessible, but it is also just as difficult to get exactly right, for it is just as transparent and full of pitfalls in ensemble playing. Pleasure—4; Effort—2.

RAVEL (1875–1937)

Ravel first established his reputation with a piece of chamber music, the string quartet written in 1902, when he was twenty-seven. Despite this early success, he did not write much more chamber music in the traditional mold. His only work for piano with strings is the much later piano trio from 1915, written just before he entered military service in World War I. Like some other composers who were virtuosic pianists, Ravel seems to have avoided confronting the problem of combining the piano sound with strings alone.

Some authorities have called the piano trio Ravel's most important piece of chamber music. It possesses the characteristic sensitivity, color, rhythmicity and transparent scoring of his idiom. The movements conform to classical structure and the work exhibits Ravel's characteristic cyclic treatment of melodic materials.

Piano Trio in A-minor | (1915)

I *Modéré*. II *Pantoum*. III *Passacaille (Tres large)*. IV *Finale*.

The *first movement* presents a broad and sweeping melody in uninterrupted 8/8 (3/8-2/8-3/8) meter, one that the composer called Basque in nature. The principal theme is delicate and mysterious, while the second is somewhat slower and more relaxed. The mood later becomes highly impassioned and dramatic but the sense of dark mystery is maintained throughout.

The *second movement* is a scherzo substitute. The irregularly accented and skipping theme is derived from the principal theme of the *first movement*. Pizzicato harmonics and exotic bowing techniques exploit a broad range of possibilities for color in the string parts. A middle section presents a broad cantabile theme that is warm and romantic. The breathless and skipping scherzo then returns.

The *third movement* passacaglia presents a noble, long and broad theme that is derived from the first theme of the *first movement*. It is played first in the bass register of the piano and then passed to the cello and the violin. Each repetition is more complex so that the theme builds to a climax. A gradual reduction in the tension follows so that the movement ends quietly. The overall mood, a dignified and noble melancholy, is sustained by the simple structure of the melody, by its constant repetition and by the simple structure of the movement.

The *fourth movement* again makes use of a theme that is derived from the first theme of the *first movement*. There are three main motifs, all with similar rhythms. These materials are treated extensively in an elaborate and contrapuntal manner to create a sustained sense of excitement and agitation.

Commentary. This masterpiece seems, at first glance, to be beyond the playing capacity of all but the most accomplished amateurs. But curious amateurs must not be put off by that first glance. The problems are both identifiable and soluble, though they require much effort to solve. The rewards of study and practice are great, however, and they are well worth the work required. Pleasure—4; Effort—4.

SCHUBERT (1797–1828)

Although Schubert was playing the keyboard and composing from childhood, his interest in writing music for piano with strings developed fully only after about 1815 when technical improvements occurred in the evolution of the piano. The major works for piano with grouped strings are the piano quintet in A major (The *Trout Quintet*) from 1819 and the two piano trios from 1827.

The *Trout Quintet* was written as a result of a vacation trip that Schubert made to Hungary and Upper Austria in 1818 and 1819. An amateur cellist and patron named Paumgartner had admired Schubert's famous song, 'The Trout', and he requested a quintet using the theme of that song with the same construction and instrumentation that characterized a recently-published quintet (Op. 87) by Hummel (1778–1837). Schubert immediately complied. The *Trout Quintet* is the earliest of Schubert's great chamber works. The first of the great string quartets, the *Quartet Movement*, came the next year, in 1820, the later string quartets date from 1824 and 1826, and the cello quintet was written just before Schubert's death in 1828.

The *Trout Quintet* was written for amateurs who wanted something new to play rather than for public display. This probably accounts for its technical ease, its simplicity of structure, and its frank openhearted charm. It consists of a standard four-movement work with the variations on the song inserted as an added movement to create a sort of divertimento. The unusual scoring with a string bass shifts the registry toward the bass, a shift that Schubert countered by placing the piano part in the upper registers. The unusual texture produced in this way has much appeal to us today, but it may not always have been so, for no later composers imitated the form. The antecedent work by Hummel in this instrumentation, Op. 87, is virtually unknown today.

The two piano trios from 1827 were written at the apex of Schubert's career, only one year before his death. He had become associated with the Bocklet-Schuppanzigh-Linke Trio, and the virtuosity of those musicians may have prompted him to undertake these works. Schuppanzigh was the virtuoso violinist so closely associated with Beethoven. Schuppanzigh is also said to have influenced Schubert in the composition of his later string quartets.

The two piano trios were probably written nearly simultaneously. The second, D. 929 (Op. 100) is known to have been performed in public at that time and it was actually published only a little later, in 1828. D. 898 (Op. 99) was not published until 1836, eight years after Schubert's death. The two works, though closely linked, have quite different characters. Schumann described Op. 99 as "passive, feminine and lyrical" while he characterized Op. 100 as "active, masculine and dramatic."

The trios are structural twins. Both have four movements and the four movements in both have similar structures. The famous slow movement of Op. 99 was added at the last after Schubert had briefly considered another lyrical movement that was later published separately as a Nocturne.

Piano Trio in B-flat major, D. 898, Op. 99 | (1827)

I *Allegro moderato*. II *Andante un poco mosso*. III *Scherzo: Allegro*. IV *Rondo: Allegro vivace; Presto*.

The *first movement* is happy and peaceful throughout. The long exposition is straightforward and simple, using only two themes and two keys. The development is relatively compact, the recapitulation is normal and the coda is rather brief. This simple structure enhances the simplicity of spirit of this lovely movement.

The *second movement* is a long and relaxed andante in three parts, ABCAB. The A theme is a *Lied* while the C section is quite decorated. The mood is quiet and pensive throughout this famous movement.

The *third movement* is a cheerful, light-hearted, and crystalline waltz. This joyful dance is most memorable.

The *fourth movement* is a long rondo with elements of the sonata form. An enormous exposition is followed by a return of the sprightly theme, a rather perfunctory development, a full recapitulation and a presto coda. The bulk of the movement is expository, but monotony is avoided by the variety of keys that appear. The gay and frisky theme tends to lose a little of its freshness in the magnitude of the movement.

Commentary. This popular work is especially memorable for its lovely inner movements, for the marvelous texture, for the splendid balance achieved among the voices and for the seemingly interminable finale. The parts are quite difficult, the cello part especially so because it lies in an uncomfortable register. The string parts are mercilessly exposed. With practice, this trio can be a delight to play, but when it does not go well, it is a misery. All amateurs should keep trying! Pleasure—4; Effort—4.

Piano Trio in E-flat major, D. 929, Op. 100 | (1827)

I *Allegro.* II *Andante con moto.* III *Scherzo: Allegro moderato.*
IV *Allegro moderato.*

The *first movement* opens with a tranquil declamatory theme. It soon gives way to a cryptic and rather imperative staccato motif that dominates the long exposition. Near the end of the exposition, a second tranquil theme appears that comes to dominate the long development section. The development is repeated three times. The declamatory theme of the opening recurs in the recapitulation. Despite the length and complexity of the structure, a sense of forward motion is retained in this pensive and tranquil movement.

The *second movement* opens directly with a lyrical minor-mode theme in the cello, said to be taken from a lost Swedish folk-song, 'See, the Sun Is Sinking', played over a funereal march in the piano. The long and stormy development makes almost exclusive use of small fragments of this theme, which are expanded into a new motif. The movement has a rondo element in that the original theme is repeated in the middle and again at the end in a major-mode brief coda.

The *third movement* scherzo is a relatively small movement, a light and transparent canon. The trio is a bucolic folk-dance.

The *fourth movement* opens with a simple and straightforward theme. This soon evolves, however, into an enormous and rather loosely constructed exposition. After some time, the Swedish folk-song of the *second movement* appears, and it appears again later. Such a long and seemingly formless structure might become tedious but a sense of variety is maintained by the progression through many keys. An operatic finish provides a triumphant conclusion.

Commentary. This trio is as brilliant, lucid, and delicate as Op. 99, but it is also longer and more redundant. It is considerably easier to play because the keys place it in a better register for the strings. The finale can seem interminable if care is not taken to make it as varied as possible. This work is less popular than its companion. Amateur players who wish to undertake the Schubert piano trios should try this one first because it is easier to make it work. Pleasure—4; Effort—3.

Piano Quintet in A major, D. 667, Op. 114 | (1819),
The Trout Quintet

I *Allegro vivace.* II *Andante.* III *Scherzo: Presto.* IV *Theme and variations: Andante; Allegretto.* V *Finale: Allegro giusto.*

The *first movement* opens with the statement of two introductory elements, one a triplet arpeggio figure and the other a simple legato motif. The following principal theme is neutral and benign. A countermelody appears and the development carries these melodic elements cheerfully through many keys. A joyful optimism pervades the whole movement.

The *second movement* opens with a noble and rather tranquil air. Decorative elements appear almost immediately, and a complex and expansive development follows with some melancholy passages. This gives way to a conclusion that is strongly rhythmic yet pastoral.

The *third movement* is a powerful and rhythmic scherzo in which the string and piano parts have strongly contrasting characters.

The *fourth movement* is the set of variations on the theme of Schubert's song, The Trout. After its initial exposition, the theme is treated in five variations. In the first three, the theme appears with florid ornamentation in the treble, alto, and bass registers, in succession. The fourth variation is stormy, in D minor. The highly ornamented fifth variation returns to the major mode. A final cheerful allegretto ends the movement in high spirits.

The slightly Hungarian *fifth movement* provides a cheerful and inconsequential march. The movement is entirely symmetrical with two sections that are identical except in key. The march moves briskly and maintains a superficial gaiety to a flourishing conclusion.

Commentary. This wonderful work was written for amateurs to play and it shows. There is little profundity and the results of a reading are always pleasing. There are no major problems in ensemble or interpretation but it certainly requires technically expert players. It displays all the qualities one associates with Schubert in his happy youth. Pleasure—4; Effort—2.

SCHUMANN (1810–1856)

Schumann's principal year to write chamber music was 1842. As early as 1838, he had written that he found the solo piano to be too limiting and he began then to explore chamber music. He wrote the three string quartets in the first half of 1842, and the piano quintet and the piano quartet followed before the end of the year.

The three piano trios are later works. Op. 63 and Op. 80 were written essentially at the same time in June-October 1847, and the third, Op. 110 was composed in 1851, the year of the two sonatas for violin and piano. The three piano trios are considered by some experts to be inferior works as compared to the masterpieces of 1842, a difference attributed by them to the inroads of the chronic mental disorder that culminated in Schumann's tragic collapse in 1854. Inferior works or not, these piano trios are relatively opaque and difficult works to play.

The piano quartet was held back a little after its composition in 1842 and it was probably modified before it was published. It is dedicated to a fine amateur cellist, Count Mattieu Wilhorsky, whom the Schumanns had met on a visit to St. Petersburg soon after the work was first written. The splendid cello part in the slow movement is thought to be a tribute to him. The work was first publicly performed at Leipzig in 1844 with Clara Schumann at the piano, Ferdinand David as the violinist and the Danish composer, Neils Gade, as the violist.

The piano quintet, written just after the string quartets and just before the piano quartet, was a novel venture. There was no substantial precedent for a work with this instrumentation though Schumann may have had Schubert's Trout Quintet in mind, for he knew and admired that work. Mendelssohn played the piano part in the first private performance where Mendelssohn suggested that Schumann should insert the agitato section that is so prominent in the *second movement*. Schumann dedicated the piano quintet to Clara who later became an aggressive proponent of the work, advancing it in many public performances. It quickly became a popular favorite.

Piano Trio in D minor, Op. 63 | (1847)

I *Mit Energie und Leidenschaft.* II *Lebhaft, doch nicht zu rasch.*
III *Langsam, mit inniger Empfindung.* IV *Mit Feuer.*

The *first movement* opens directly with a long and rambling first theme
that is sullen and undirected in character. A second theme appears,
more syncopated and chromatic but no more directed. A third theme
(Tempo I, nur ruhiger) that is more focussed, soaring and romantic
occurs in the cello and a long development takes place. The long
movement ends full of vitality but it still remains in a somber mood.

The *second movement* scherzo is a quite characteristic Schumann
scherzo. The dotted rhythm of the opening theme has great energy
and agitation that is contrasted with a legato trio. The trio is based on
a rising semitonal theme set in a canonic imitation. After a reprise of
the agitated scherzo, a brief coda ends the movement. This movement
must not be played too fast lest the sense of the 3/4 meter be lost.

The *third movement* theme is a vague, syncopated, and seemingly aimless melody. After a first section in which this melody is explored, a middle section (bewegter) presents the melody again, now slightly altered
in character, after which the first section is repeated. The mood throughout is one of uneasy repose, metrical and romantic but never achieving
a sense of rest or finality. The next movement follows attacca.

The *fourth movement* firmly dispels the unrest of the antecedent
movement with a jubilant and expansive theme, first played by the
piano and then by the violin. A second theme, in the cello, is contrasting in its whispered but still confident spirit. This section is a musette,
a kind of dance. The development is long and brilliant. After a recapitulation, a long coda (nach und nach schneller) builds to a brilliant
close. The mood throughout is one of triumph.

Commentary. This is an energetic yet gloomy work, only the last
movement being free of a troubled mood. The first and last movements are long and so the work overall seems very large. The texture
is thick and orchestral, quite lacking the transparency of the piano
quintet and the piano quartet of five years before. The string parts are
not really easy and the piano part is reasonably difficult. For all these
reasons, this trio is not wholly grateful to play. It will, however, appeal
to Schumann enthusiasts. The principal danger in this work is to play
it too fast. It is much more comprehensible at moderate tempos.
Pleasure—2; Effort—4.

Piano Trio in F major, Op. 80 | (1847)

I *Sehr lebhaft*. II *Mit innigem Ausdruck*. III *In massiger Bewegung*. IV *Nicht zu rasch*.

The *first movement* begins with a theme that loses some of its intrinsic liveliness by being played in octaves in the strings so that it has a rather peremptory quality. A broader second theme gives some contrast, and a legato piano third theme, derived from Schumann's song, 'Dein Bildniss Wunderselig', appears before an extensive development. The tempo throughout must be gentle and easy so that the work is lively without being frantic.

The *second movement* is a moving, lyric and poetical work. The violin plays the opening theme with a countermelody in the cello over triplet figures in the piano. The melody is then repeated in fragments or short phrases, leading to a section (lebhaft) where a new lighter theme appears. The poetic first theme returns to end the movement. Care must be taken not to make this movement too sentimental.

The *third movement* presents its fragmented theme in imitations among the three voices. The effect is one of poise or suspended energy with a touch of humor. A second section briefly presents a flowing melody, after which the first theme returns with a little coda. This movement is a scherzo equivalent.

The *fourth movement* theme, introduced by the cello, is a staccato running figure lending itself to contrapuntal treatment. This figure is further treated in an ingenious combination with a cantabile melody. The movement has a somewhat pedantic quality, being devoid of much that is heroic, deeply felt or dramatic.

Commentary. Schumann said of this trio, written at the same time as the first, that it makes a quicker and more ingratiating appeal. In fact, it seems no more appealing than the first. It is just as long, almost as thick in texture and perhaps a little less interesting in content. It, too, benefits from restraint in tempo and enthusiasm. It will appeal to those who love the Schumann idiom. It is quite difficult in all respects. Pleasure—2; Effort—4.

Piano Trio in G minor, Op. 110 | (1851)

I *Bewegt, doch nicht zu rasch.* II *Ziemlich langsam.* III *Rasch.*
IV *Kraftig, mit Humor.*

The *first movement* opens with a romantic, anguished and soaring melody. A similarly romantic second theme offers little contrast. In the development, a strange pizzicato passage in the cello part, then repeated in the violin part, conveys a sense of the ominous. After a short recapitulation, a brief coda (rascher) brings the movement to a shadowy end. The mood overall is one of unrest and foreboding.

The *second movement* begins as a lyrical duet for the strings, a broad, mournful and unstructured cantilena. In the central section, a 9/8 meter replaces the 12/8 meter of the first section. Here, a restless motif in the cello provides a sense of quickening, drama and foreboding. The first section returns with its somber mood to end this lovely movement in a hush.

The *third movement* is shadowy, flickering and ominous in the first section. Its long running motif lies principally in the piano part. A second section presents a syncopated legato melody of considerable passion. After the first section is repeated, a third section provides a restless and excited dotted-rhythm motif. The ominous first section is repeated, and a brief coda ends the movement in an angry outburst.

The *fourth movement* opens with a theme that is full of rollicking good humor. Its exuberant leaps are witty and even comical. A second section, in D major, returns to a lyrical theme from the preceding movement. A pompous march in G minor appears and this is cut off abruptly for the return of the exuberant comical theme of the opening. The lyrical theme from the *third movement* makes another brief appearance, now expressing jubilation, and the movement ends in this spirit.

Commentary. Some critics have disparaged this work as inferior to the other two trios. Though it may appear to experts as relatively deficient in invention and workmanship, it is easier to understand in musical terms, more transparent in texture and a more pleasing work for amateur performance overall. There is an interesting variety of moods. It is, however, not an easy work by any means. Those who wish to explore the Schumann piano trios should probably start with this one. One can get considerable satisfaction from this one at a first reading, more so than with the earlier two. Pleasure—3; Effort—4.

Piano Quartet in E-flat major, Op. 47 | (1842)

I *Sostenuto assai; Allegro ma non troppo.* II *Scherzo: Molto vivace.*
III *Andante cantabile.* IV *Finale: Vivace.*

The *first movement* opens with an eleven-bar introduction that is made up of questioning phrases in the piano to be answered in the strings. The principal theme then appears as a spirited affirmative response to the questioning introduction. A second theme is even more imperative. The introductory material is recalled before a long, eloquent and ingenious development. After a recapitulation, a più agitato introduces a new subsidiary theme before the ending. The spirit is one of joyful exhilaration throughout.

The *second movement* scherzo uses an agitated running theme, full of suppressed excitement. The first trio provides a naïve folk melody in the minor mode. After a reprise of the scherzo, a second trio appears having a theme of syncopated chords. The scherzo returns to end the movement.

The *third movement* opens with a three-bar introduction after which the cello plays a long, sentimental and sensuous melody. This melody is then repeated in the other voices. A second theme, syncopated and less sentimental, is heard after which the sentimental theme is treated with ornamentation. The finish features hints of new melodic material, a series of falling fifths, anticipating the melody of the finale to follow.

The *fourth movement* opens with three chords that sound the fifth. An agitated fugato theme follows and comes to a speedy close, leading to a second theme, a broad cantabile. The fugato and cantabile are treated contrapuntally. Other themes then arise, the whole building to a great climax on a dominant seventh chord, after which the fugato reappears as a coda that builds to a brilliant ending.

Commentary. This work resembles the piano quintet in spirit and form and it is nearly as innovative and skillfully written. It has a less brilliant texture, however, because the strings are placed in a lower register. The resultant difficulty with balance among the parts is the only important problem, for the work otherwise presents no major obstacle to accomplished players. This is a fine work, not quite so splendid as the piano quintet but well worth learning as another product of Schumann's genius when he was in his prime. Pleasure—3; Effort—3.

Piano Quintet in E-flat major, Op. 44 | (1842)

I *Allegro brillante*. II *In modo d'una Marcia: Un poco largamente*.
III *Scherzo: Molto vivace*. IV *Allegro ma non troppo*.

The *first movement* opens abruptly with an immensely vigorous and heroic theme played by the piano. The second theme is a warm, strong and yearning melody that is first played by the cello and the viola. These two themes are then explored and developed with great ingenuity. A full recapitulation and a brilliant coda end this exhilarating movement.

The *second movement* opens with a dark and whispered funeral march. This is succeeded by a warm, legato and yearning melody played over a rhythmically complex accompaniment. A violent agitato section intervenes suddenly and storms darkly after which the funeral march returns, now full of agitation. Then the warm second theme return in consolation and the funeral march, now subdued, brings the melancholy movement to a quiet close.

The *third movement* scherzo is built on a simple ascending scale whose presentation is agitated and vigorous. This strong section is followed by a lyrical trio after which the rushing scale of the scherzo returns. A second lyrical trio features a running figure, and further developments of the melodic ideas lead to a strong and spirited ending.

The *fourth movement* opens with a strong and rather square theme that is contrasted immediately by a fervent second melody, soon to be treated in canon. The two themes recur to be elaborated with increasing ornamentation and variation in a development that climaxes dramatically in a sustained diminished seventh chord. The following coda begins as a double fugue that is built upon the first themes of the first and last movements, and the work ends in triumph.

Commentary. This is a justly celebrated work, a great favorite of listeners and players alike. To the great benefit of amateurs, it is fully accessible in all respects. The brilliant piano part is technically difficult, however, and when it is played with too much enthusiasm it can easily swamp the strings in places. All amateurs must get to know this work. Pleasure—4; Effort—3.

SHOSTAKOVICH (1906–1975)

Of the principal piano-string works of Shostakovich, only the piano quintet seems to be played much by amateurs. The emotional content of this work reflects the circumstances of its composition in the period of uncertainty before the German army invaded Russia. It was quickly acclaimed, winning the Stalin Prize in 1940.

Piano Quintet in G minor, Op. 57 | (1940)

I *Prelude: Lento.* II *Fugue: Adagio.* III *Scherzo: Allegretto.*
IV *Intermezzo: Lento.* V *Finale: Allegretto.*

The *first movement* opens with a long recitativo passage in the solo piano that sets a mood of mystery and anticipation. The strings then enter without the piano with the cello leading another recitative, but this one is dramatic and declamatory. After this, the laconic tune that appears in the viola to introduce the main body of the movement seems a letdown. The viola and violin present this simple melody over a two-part linear accompaniment in the piano. The materials soon build from this spare beginning to a powerful climax, full of tension and drama.

The *second movement* follows attacca. A slow legato melody, played by the strings con sordino as a fugue, creates a mood of quiet melancholy. The piano joins after a time to play barren octaves. The fugue builds slowly to a climax, and then it falls back to the bleak atmosphere of its beginning. Though it gains some warmth thereafter, the fugue ends in the quiet gloom with which it began.

The *third movement* opens with a catchy tune, an ebullient dancing theme. A second theme, a spiky Russian melody, appears in the violin, and the mood of a boisterous dance continues. The texture remains light throughout, despite the forceful nature of the thematic materials.

The *fourth movement* opens with a linear and melancholy melody in the violin played over a pizzicato accompaniment in the cello. Later, the other strings take up the melody, giving it a warmer and more romantic character. The mood begins as a sweet and poignant melancholy, builds to a brief passionate climax, and then falls again to quiet sadness.

The *fifth movement* follows attacca. A bright, peaceful, and optimistic melody is treated very freely. It is carried through a wandering course to a climax characterized by a sense of triumph, after which the intensity of mood subsides. Material from the dramatic part of the first (prelude) movement is briefly recalled in a recitativo before the quiet and optimistic coda.

Commentary. The prelude seems to promise a work of great drama. What follows are two magnificent but melancholy slow movements framing a boisterous folk dance, with a finale that is bland and optimistic. Thus, the work seems to lack a sense of unity, coherence or direction. It is a wonderful work for amateur performance. The string parts are not really difficult, and the piano part is slender enough that balance between the piano and strings is never a problem. This is a better work for amateurs who wish to begin to play the works of Shostakovich than are the string quartets or the piano trio. It is an immensely satisfying work to play either in a reading session or in a more detailed study. All amateurs should get to know it. Pleasure—3; Effort—2.

SMETANA (1824–1884)

Smetana established a new style prominently rooted in Czech folk music. Unlike Dvořák, Smetana found it difficult to express this idiom in the forms of absolute music, favoring programmatic structures such as opera. His important chamber works, the string quartets and the piano trio, are flagrantly programmatic.

The piano trio was inscribed in memory of Smetana's eldest child, Frederica, a musical girl who died at the age of four in 1865. The trio was written in that same year. It was received poorly at its first hearing but Liszt greatly admired and actively promoted the work.

Although this piano trio is now established in the standard repertory, it is not so popular as other piano trios of the period, probably because of its melancholy character, its programmatic content and its lack of subtlety.

Piano Trio in G minor, Op. 15 | (1865)

I *Moderato assai*. II *Allegro ma non agitato; Andante: Maestoso*.
III *Finale: Presto; Moderato assai*.

The *first movement* opens abruptly with a lament, a soaring, melancholy and declamatory theme in the violin that is repeated with a countermelody in the cello part. Later themes express tenderness. The mood shifts between expressions of grief, consolation and melancholy and the movement ends with a vigorous passage of profound gloom.

The *second movement* is considered to portray the child who had died. The opening scherzo theme is bustling and vigorous though in the minor mode. The first trio (alternativo) is sweet and tender. The second trio (alternativo) is a strong lament, solemn, grieving, poignant and full of wonderful suspensions. The half-playful opening scherzo returns to end this memorable movement.

The *third movement* opens energetically with a strongly rhythmic figure that is full of melancholy. A hymn-like tune takes the foreground and it is developed in a mood of tenderness. A funeral march follows and the agitated melancholy of the beginning returns to end the movement.

Commentary. Amateurs avoid this work because its almost unrelieved melancholy and drama make it seem to be unsuitable for an evening of playing for fun. This is unfortunate, for this is a pleasing work to play for those who do not disdain sentimentality. The writing is skillful and the work presents no important problems in technique or understanding. In playing it, the amateur can see what Smetana was capable of. Knowing that makes one wish that the composer had given more attention to chamber music. Pleasure—4; Effort—3.

TCHAIKOVSKY (1840–1893)

Tchaikovsky wrote no chamber music from 1875, the year of the last string quartet, until 1881, confining himself to orchestral and operatic writing. His friend, Nikolay Rubenstein (chief of the Moscow Conservatory) died in 1881 and Tchaikovsky wrote the piano trio in A minor as a memorial to his friend.

Piano Trio in A minor, Op. 50 | (1892)

I *Pezzo elegiaco: Moderato assai; Allegro giusto.* II *A. Tema con Variazione: Andante con moto. B. Variazione Finale e Coda: Allegro risoluto e con fuoco; Andante con moto.*

The *first movement* opens with a mournful subject that is first heard from the cello and then from the violin, with a countermelody in the cello. After a full exposition of this melody, a bridge passage (ben sostenuto il tempo) leads to the second subject (allegro giusto), a heroic and triumphant theme. This leads to a third subject (in tempo molto sostenuto) that is passionate in character. After a long development, the exposition is repeated (adagio con duolo e ben sostenuto), all subjects returning in the original sequence. The brief coda is built on the first subject played in augmentation. This movement is long and varied in character, but it has, overall, a solemn and melancholy tone.

The *second movement* opens with a beautiful andante theme in 4/4 meter. The tune gains a striking Russian character from its irregularity. It is first presented in the piano alone and then eleven variations follow before the Variazione Finale e Coda. Variation I presents the theme unaltered over a running figure in the piano with a counterpoint in the cello. Variation II puts the theme into 3/4 meter with the rhythm of a mazurka. In Variation III, the piano plays the tune as a brilliant scherzando, the violin and cello accompanying it with pizzicato chords. Variation IV returns the theme to the strings who play it as a dignified slow dance in dialogue over chords in the piano. In Variation V, the theme returns to the piano as a music-box variation. Variation VI is a waltz variation played mainly by the strings. Variation VII, in 3/2 meter presents the theme as a chorale in the piano. In Variation VIII, the theme receives a long and detailed fugal treatment. Variation IX is a wistful and ghostly fantasia. Variation X is a brilliant mazurka. Variation XI presents the theme again in its original form, more or less, to be followed by the Variazione Finale e Coda. This begins with yet another variation of the theme treated to a brilliant polyphonic development. An elegiac rhapsody on the first theme of the *first movement* (andante con moto) intervenes and leads to the coda (lugubre), a presentation of the first subject of the *first movement* over a funeral march in the piano.

Commentary. This work was intended as a memorial to Nikolay Rubenstein, the Director of the Moscow Conservatory and a virtuoso pianist. The result is a massive work in all respects, a masterpiece. Its major defect is its awesome length, for which reason the composer himself authorized the omission of Variation VIII (the fugue) and a cut of 136 bars in the finale. This work requires a really skillful pianist, but the string parts are not quite so difficult. Balance is a problem. It is easy to overdo the drama so as to make this work seem tawdry or maudlin. Still, it is always fun to play at any stage of practice, at least for those who can tolerate Tchaikovsky's brand of sentimentality. Those who can't should pass this trio by. Pleasure—3; Effort—4.

Your Chamber Group: Practical Advice

Like athletes, bridge players and Sunday painters, amateur chamber musicians often pursue their hobby with considerable intensity. The following set of rules comes from a lifetime of observation of many such players.

1. Establish a stable group. Define a circle of friends with whom to play regularly. Do not exclude casual performances with outsiders and strangers, of course, but stay with a core of colleagues. Chamber music is an intimate conversation; even one stranger in the group challenges the intimacy.

2. Play with those who share your abilities, tastes and temperament. A stable group of players resembles a family that must face and reconcile inescapable disagreements with mutual respect. The sharing of abilities, tastes and temperaments minimizes misunderstandings and conflicts.

3. Meet regularly. Ideally, set one evening each week to devote to the group. It then becomes a fixed part of the weekly routine. When you have more than one group in action, do not let one group compete with another.

4. Plan your sessions ahead. Evenings of playing for fun, arranged on short notice, will not necessarily advance your skill much. A stable group, interested in progressing together, should plan a course of action three to six months or more ahead. For example, the group could determine to study the six quartets in Op. 18 of Beethoven over a six-month period and allocate the sessions appropriately. For variety or contrast, however, any single session may include another work. If it is a familiar one, it works better to play it first, as a warm-up. If it is unfamiliar, play it last because it will sap the energies of the players to play it before the study work.

5. Have each player stay with his position. When it is possible, players often wish to interchange parts. This practice can benefit players by giving different perspectives on a work. However, only by staying with a part can you learn it thoroughly. Also, because different players may have somewhat different styles, switching parts can disorient the other players to some degree. Trading parts should become a special event for a special purpose.

6. Vary the seating arrangement. The current common seating arrangement of the string quartet (violins at stage right, viola and cello, front to back, at stage left) may be a convention meant to help the audience hear best, but it has varied at different times and places. When a group observes the same seating in all rehearsals, the members become accustomed to hearing the same voices in the same slots. A change in the seating commands the players' attention and reveals relationships in a different way.

7. Tune by a prescribed method. Tuning seems best accomplished by using the cello as the reference point. That instrument has the longest strings so that it changes pitch less rapidly than the others do. Also, it usually lies at the bottom of the harmony so that its intonation tends to cue the intonation of the other players. The cello should tune first in the usual way, making the D-G-C fifths 'tight'. That is, the G and C strings should be tuned very slightly sharp. Next, each instrument should tune its A, D and G strings separately with those of the cello. Then, the viola should adjust its C string to that of the cello. Finally, the violins should tune their E strings against the A string of the cello. All this seems a bit fussy, but it can make a great difference in the sound of the group.

8. Have good chairs and good lights. Serious players need to be comfortable. The best chair to use has a vertical back and a horizontal seat 17 0r 18 inches from the floor. Some players like to use adjustable piano benches. Each player should have a separate light, if possible.

9. Learn to communicate by eye as well as by ear. Togetherness or 'ensemble', uniformity of style and mood, requires the utmost communication among the players. As well as listening, players must watch one another out of the corner of the eye seeking cues and clues in body language and arm motions. Cellists find this easier than violinists because of their upright posture without a fiddle in the line of vision.

10. Practice the basics regularly. Good playing requires good technique. Those who play for pleasure may forget the necessity for practice. To most enjoy the hobby, the player must practice the basics through etudes and exercises.

11. Study your part independently. Facile players may tend to neglect part study when they learn that they can "wing it". Mastery of a part and optimal use of rehearsals requires separate part study. Thoughtful players pencil in fingerings, bowings, phrasings and cues in advance of rehearsals.

12. Use your own copy of your part. When you buy a full set of parts, set aside your own part to use whenever you play, even when you move from one group to another. That way, you will continuously update your part.

13. In building a library, comparison-shop and buy the best editions. The works you buy now will remain with you for life. Some possess the heavy editing of the last century. Some may contain errors. Many new editions are newly set, edited lightly (or not at all) and seemingly free of error. Know what you are buying!

14. Learn the work as a whole. Full satisfaction in playing comes from knowing the work as a whole, in all its parts and all its movements, not just from knowledge of your own part. Lots of practice can give such an understanding but you will reach it faster by studying scores and recordings. Also, the study of recordings reveals how the great artists vary in their own interpretations.

15. When you take up a new work, play it straight through at first. Very few musicians can tell how a work sounds by reading the score. You can discover textures and moods only by playing. A first run through the whole work is the best way for a group to decide whether or not to take it up for serious study.

16. Work toward public performance. Those who play only for their own amusement run the risk of never achieving the best that they can. Performance for anyone else, even if only family or friends, provides a point and focus in avocational playing that cannot be found in any other way. Plan to perform once or twice yearly.

17. Keep a musical diary. A diary of your chamber music sessions helps you to recall special experiences and special people and to document your own progress. You can also use it to make notes about the works that you study.

18. Study chamber music as a discipline, not only as a craft. Your joy in music will increase if you broaden your scope to encompass the whole world of chamber music. You can do this in many ways. Read the authoritative books. Read periodicals like *Strings* magazine and *The Strad.* Join Amateur Chamber Music Players, Inc. (545 Eighth Avenue, New York, NY 10018). Join the Cobbett Association (601 Timber Trail, Riverwoods, IL 60015), or contact them on the internet at www,neiu.edu/voodo/Cobbett/join.html. Attend some of the many annual conferences, courses, camps and other get-togethers for amateur players of chamber music that now occur all over this continent and in Europe. Lists and descriptions of such events can be found in the directory published annually by Amateur Chamber Music Players, Inc., and in *Strings* magazine.

Suggested Reading

Aulich, Bruno, and Ernst Heimeran. *The Well-Tempered String Quartet*. London: Novello, 1938.

Barrett-Ayres, Reginald. *Joseph Haydn and the String Quartet*. London: Barrie and Jenkins, 1974.

Berger, Melvin. *Guide to Chamber Music*. New York: Dodd Mead, 1985.

Blum, David. *The Art of Quartet Playing*. New York: Knopf, 1986.

Cobbett, Walter Willson, and Colin Mason, eds. *Cobbett's Cyclopedic Survey of Chamber Music*. London: Oxford University Press, 1963.

Cohn, Arthur. *The Literature of Chamber Music*. Chapel Hill: Hinshaw, 1997.

Delbanco, Nicholas. *The Beaux Arts Trio*. New York: Morrow, 1985.

Einstein, Alfred. *Mozart: His Character, His Work*. New York, Oxford University Press, 1945.

Farish, Margaret K. *String Music in Print*. New York, Bowker, 1965.

Fink, Irving, and C. Merriell. String Quartet Playing. Neptune City: Paganiniana, 1985.

Forsyth, Ella Marie. *Building a Chamber Music Collection: A Descriptive Guide to Published Scores*. Metuchen: Scarecrow, 1979.

Geiringer, Karl. *Brahms: His Life and Work*. New York: Doubleday, 1961.

Geiringer, Karl, and Irene Geiringer. *Haydn: A Creative Life in Music*. New York: Norton, 1946.

Griffiths, Paul. *The String Quartet: A History*. New York: Thames and Hudson, 1983.

Headington, Christopher. *A Listener's Guide to Chamber Music*. New York, Quarto, 1982.

Horton, John. *Mendelssohn Chamber Music*. London: BBC, 1972, and Seattle: University of Washington Press, 1972.

Hughes, Rosemary. *Haydn String Quartets*. London: BBC, 1966.

Keller, Hans. *The Great Haydn Quartets: Their Interpretation*. London: Dent, 1986.

Keys, Ivor. *Brahms Chamber Music.* London: BBC, 1974.

Lam, Basil. *Beethoven String Quartets.* London: BBC, 1975, and Seattle: University of Washington Press, 1975.

Ostwald, Peter. *Schumann: The Inner Voices of a Musical Genius.* Boston: Northeastern University Press, 1985.

Page, Athol. *Playing String Quartets.* New York: Longmans, Green (David McKay), 1964.

Reich, Nancy B. *Clara Schumann: The Artist and the Woman.* Ithaca: Cornell University Press, 1985.

Robertson, Alec. *Dvorák.* The Master Musicians Series. London: Dent, 1964.

Volkov, Solomon. *Testimony: The Memoirs of Dmitri Shostakovich.* New York, Harper and Row, 1979.

Westrup, Sir Jack Allan. *Schubert Chamber Music.* London: BBC, 1969, and Seattle: University of Washington Press, 1969.